Dear Penny,
Happy
Enjoy th
glad we
passion of re
As always thanks,
your friendship!
Love,
Veronica

dropped threads

WHAT WE AREN'T TOLD

EDITED BY

Carol Shields

AND

Marjorie Anderson

VINTAGE CANADA
A Division of Random House of Canada Limited

VINTAGE CANADA EDITION, 2001

The essay by Margaret Atwood was originally published in *Language in Her Eye: Writing and Gender*, eds. Libby Scheier, Sarah Sheard and Eleanor Wachtel, Coach House Press, Toronto, 1990; and the essay by Miriam Toews originally appeared in *Saturday Night* magazine in March 1999.

Canadian Cataloguing in Publication Data

Main entry under title:

Dropped threads : what we aren't told

ISBN 0-679-31071-1

1. Canadian literature (English) — Women authors. * 2. Canadian literature (English) — 20th century.*
3. Women — Literary collections. I. Shields, Carol, 1935– .
II. Anderson, Marjorie May, 1944– .

PS8235.W7D76 2000 C810.8'09287 C00-931158-0
PR9194.5.W6D76 2000

Cover design: CS Richardson
Cover illustration: Katrina Koven

Printed and bound in Canada

Visit Random House of Canada Limited's Web site: www.randomhouse.ca

10 9 8 7

for our daughters,
Anne, Audrey, Catherine, Cheryl, Dena
Heidi, Meg, Renata and Sara

and for
Andrea MacLennan Hauen
1966–1999
whose life was a gift of joy

CONTENTS

Marjorie Anderson is a professor in the Faculty of Management at the University of Manitoba.

Carol Shields is a novelist who lives in Victoria.

Bella Pomer, of the Bella Pomer Agency, offered her services pro bono for this project.

Special thanks to Ruth Partridge.

FOREWORD

The focus for this anthology floated out one day amid soup and salad at one of those gatherings where Carol and I take the emotional pulse of our worlds — or The World, it seems to us.

"The woman's network let me down. Nothing I've ever heard or read prepared me for this!" This particular yelp resulted from the plummet of energy and purpose I experienced with menopause and quickly led us to wider, more lively musings on what else had caught us unprepared, where else we had experienced gaps between female experience and expression. We were surprised by the number of topics and by the ease with which they came to mind. The image of dropped threads from the fabric of women's talk occurred to us and the familiar, satisfying assumption that women could talk about *anything* unravelled as we spoke.

We included other women in our speculations: friends, colleagues and family members took up the conversation with enthusiasm and immediate revelations as though, for some, the topic was one they had wanted to discuss for years. They identified gaps in their communal talk and named life-altering surprises in their individual lives. Most spoke of serious issues, of surprise bruisings or blessings, private moments of intense connection or bewilderment. Other women reported insights that bordered on the hilarious: one friend mentioned that her greatest surprise was "sagging earlobes" and another claimed it was "a husband who flosses his teeth in front of you and then expects passion in bed."

The idea for an anthology of writings on the topic blossomed naturally. We had obviously tapped into a rich vein of stories that touched on defining moments in women's lives. We invited a number of acquaintances and friends to write these stories, the ones they wanted and needed to tell, recognizing, of course, there would be private spaces that everyone needs to keep beyond the claim of words. We thought women writers would have interesting observations: what subjects hadn't they written about that needed communal airing? We also asked women of other backgrounds, academics, ranchers, politicians, homemakers, journalists, lawyers, to identify the areas of surprise and silence in their lives.

The responses were immediate and the topics wide-ranging: everything from the joys of belly dancing to the shock of gender inequities in politics. There seemed to be a general embracing of the license implicit in our invitation, but also some reticence: more than one respondant commented on the courage it would take to write on personal issues that had long been beyond the limits of acceptable expression. A few women identified experiences which they *could not* write on because the pain was too new or the fear of judgment still too strong. What was particularly satisfying to us was that we were contacted by women who had heard of our venture and wanted their stories included. One of these surprise offerings is among the most powerful of the anthology.

The collection of thirty-four reflective pieces is the end

result of those conversations and connections started back in the spring of 1999. Many of the voices will be familiar to readers; others will be new. Some are forthright and take the reader to the heart of intense experience. Others approach distinctly personal moments with caution and then veer away, as though the walls around the silences they've been keeping are impenetrable. What unites all these writings is the uncommon honesty, courage and acuity of emotion these women bring to their topics — and to us.

They tell us that once life slows down enough for reflection, women uncover truths several beats away from the expected and the promised: female friendships are often more central in our lives than those we have with men and children; what we are told can be as limiting as what is never spoken; and vanity, dominance and blasts of lust that break through marriage and age barriers can be good things. From those who document the private contours of grief and shame, we learn about survival instincts and minute-by-minute coping strategies that rise up and guide people to new spaces of accommodation. Other women point to the individual colourings of common human happenings: spiritual stirrings, aging and the discovery of fundamental gender inequities continue to catch women unprepared because these experiences can never be the same for any two people.

What the stories and the essays indicate about the variety and uniqueness in women's lives is visually reinforced by the Vinarterta Lady sketch on the cover. This stylized woman speaks to the rich rhythms and shadings of our moods and approaches to life. As well, there is a mystery about this sketch that reminds us of the impossibility of capturing in any medium of expression all of what we are and what we experience. There are still blank spaces before us, and women are still asking, as one of our young contributors does, "What shall I tell my daughter?" When we scan through the topics that even this collection has skipped over — mother-daughter relationships, lesbian experiences, life without partners or children, to mention some, we realize that women's conversational weaving will forever be a work in progress.

In the meantime we're reminded not to forget the joys and potential growth from the uncharted. In the afterword Carol Shields writes a characteristically wise, gentle unfolding of the central theme as it relates to her personally. She tells of meeting the "surprises of self-discovery" with "gratitude" and then nudges the reader into embracing the unexpected: "Who isn't renewed by startling scenery or refreshed by undreamed-of freedoms? Surprise keeps us alive, liberates our senses."

Our wish is that this anthology will be liberating for readers. It offers a community of voices that are relevant to everyone, not just women, because the experiences recounted are ultimately those that give us our jagged human dimensions of joy and sorrow. We hope readers of all ages and backgrounds will be inspired by how the contributors answered the initial question we posed and will be drawn to examine their own crevices of surprise and silence.

Marjorie Anderson
July 2000

Starch, Salt, Chocolate, Wine

Joan Barfoot

The first man I ever slept with was a cop named Clancy. He had a blue uniform with white and gold trim, a wonderfully soft, bulky, embraceable body and a hard, unyielding head. When I was lonely or scared, he was my comfort. Night after night, falling asleep, he was unfailingly in my arms.

We were brought together by my Aunt Geneva, a large woman who lived in Detroit and seemed to me to combine a certain bright, foreign glamour with an excellent, down-home alertness to youthful desires. I hadn't known I needed a Clancy, but my aunt evidently recognized him for what he could be.

Clancy and I were inseparable for three, maybe four years. But life moves on, changes, and finally our interests diverged, my attention lapsed, we drifted apart. For years we lived in different cities, and I didn't give him a thought. Still, we must have retained a kind of connection. If nothing else, a person doesn't quite forget she once had such a purely dependable, safe, solid presence to hold on to.

A decade or so ago, many years after our initial attachment, we reunited. Clancy's uniform is a bit grimy these days and his head — well, his hard unyielding head hasn't worn well; but then again, I'm not what I once was myself.

One difference is that I now realize I was mistaken to assume the universality of his virtues: I appear to have reckoned that other men, too, would tend to have hard, dependable heads and warm, soft, embraceable bodies and hearts.

Whoops.

Before this gets too desperately whimsical, let me just point out, at the risk of explaining the obvious, that Clancy is a doll, albeit an extraordinary one who entirely ruined any affections I might otherwise have developed for Barbies or bride dolls; and that our deepest attachment occurred before I was five.

These facts don't, however, diminish Clancy's effect on my first impressions about the essential comforts of men and, by silent implication and inference about, the essential irrelevance of women. Whoops again.

It wasn't all Clancy, of course. It was the whole 1950s world I could see. It looked, then, as if men were free, at least in the sense that they got out of the house, and women were not. Men got to explore, have adventures, tell stories and misbehave in interesting ways. Women got to vacuum, cook and make what sounded like small talk. There were, in both sexes, exceptions. I saw no pleasing alternative to becoming an exception. I also wanted to have as little as possible to do with the unexceptional. By which I meant, in general, women.

I can't imagine too many things more embarrassing to admit. On the other hand, I don't believe I'm uncommonly dim or unusual. I think I just inhaled a lot of information from the world that I didn't know how to reconcile properly with experience. Which may only (only!) demonstrate the power of impression over reality.

Because of course the truth is, my closest and most-knowing friends have always been female; it just took me ages to notice that the girls and women whose company I enjoyed and relied on were not free, clever exceptions at all. They were the rule. Boys and men could be lovely and interesting in a number of ways, but as friends — a dab of graffiti here — women rule.

The social information girls absorbed in my youth, and for all I know still absorb, was sometimes subtle, sometimes blunt — but always pervasive. Mainly it distilled to the notion that women's prime interest should be in obtaining the support and protection, preferably along with the love, of men. Because other females were our competitors in this, we would be wise to be wary and sly with each other. In this version of life's guerrilla warfare, other girls and women were our untrustworthy, smiling, camouflaged enemies.

We learned, too, that keeping watch in this way would have to be a permanent condition, even once we'd snared one of those wily, elusive creatures, a man. Because men, like crows or squirrels, we were told, were apt to wander off if they spotted more tempting objects lying about glittering in the grass, and then where would we be?

Alone in the world, that's where. Helpless, solitary, in despair, humiliated by the failure to gain and sustain our chief purpose in life.

Redbook magazine, to which my mother subscribed, was a monthly, most reliable, cover-to-cover source of advice on getting a man and then keeping him from the clutches of other, predatory women. After a time, the thought had to occur: didn't the alternative, being predatory, sound seductive?

Only a tickle, a hint of subversion — but seduction surely sounded more entertaining and various than the *Redbook*-recommended round of preparing sturdy-yet-flaky meals; creating an unobtrusive, calming domestic atmosphere for the head of the household, who might be weary and potentially cranky at the end of the day; and submerging in recommended and, finally, chillingly automatic ways personal interests and passions in favour of the well-being and comfort of home.

There was almost no mention in *Redbook* of friends. If there were like-minded women to talk to, they were mainly discussing their troubles with husbands, and one was advised not to do likewise.

Not to treasonously let guards down, not to treacherously confide. Psychic walls far sturdier than the aluminum siding of bulk-built, postwar houses.

And yet.

And yet, beyond and outside those powerful, discouraging messages were girls giggling, competing, feuding, running, playing, holding hands, making up dramas together, acting them out. Whispering secrets, betraying them, keeping them. Shifting alliances, as sinuous as amoebas, taking on new shapes together, trying on new sizes.

Where were the boys in all this?

Elsewhere on the playground. Doing whatever boys did.

Boys become men, who do not stay in their part of the playground; nor, for the most part, do we want them to. Between women and men there are generally chemistries, appeals, and, for most grown-ups of whatever age, also occasionally love. Sometimes respect. Even, if so rarely it could make a person weep, the sort of friendship that manages to enter something close to communion.

The sort of friendship, in fact, that as it turns out is not especially rare among women. The sort that endures, periodically dented and scratched but sturdy as an old kitchen table, through upheavals and changes, differences of opinion and distances, through circumstances that merge and diverge, with shared sorrows and laughter and thousands and millions of words.

It's unwise, of course, to romanticize. Real friendship is

as tough as real love. It requires flexibility, determination, care, attention and empathy. Food, water and fuel. It has its vicissitudes and can, just like love, slip away. Or slam away.

And it can, nearly inexplicably, almost chemically, endure.

Gail was my best friend in high school. This was so even though we had strangely separate lives, with distinctly different sets of other friends, different interests, different gifts and desires.

I always thought (still think) of Gail as a pink sort of person: slight, wispy-voiced, gentle-gestured, mysteriously able to lure large boys into doing whatever she wanted. Except it all went awry in the last year of high school, when she got pregnant and her family, her mother, began furiously, literally furiously, planning a wedding.

I wept my way through the ceremony. (One benefit of writing is finding a purpose for moments like that. Years later I took that memory and translated it for a wedding-weep scene in a novel about, mainly, enduring friendship.)

What that marriage meant to me was not a beginning for Gail but, at the age of eighteen, an ending. It seemed it meant much the same thing to her. We were in and out of touch. She had two excellent children and lived in apartments; I went to university, began a career, lived in houses with people she didn't know. Eventually she, too, started university. Her marriage ended. She raised her kids. I began writing novels. She began a dissertation.

In the same week the novel *Charlotte and Claudia Keeping in Touch* was published, the one that included the tiny allusion to Gail's first wedding years before, she asked me to stand up with her at her second wedding. For this occasion, she was in charge and in love. There were tears again, but this time they were for pleasure at her happiness, and also for pride — well, love — for our long, in-and-out-of-touch, middle-aged, well-aged friendship.

Romantic love, sexual love, partnership love — whatever we call it — takes many forms, but for most of us it involves one other person at a time, and sometimes just one person, period.

Which gives it a grave and particular focus, a unique quality of attention, its own set of measures and weights. If we're fortunate, a partnership includes friendship, but it is not solely friendship. Our expectations, desires and responsibilities are not necessarily higher, but they are decidedly different.

"Why," an aggrieved man once asked (asked uncomprehendingly several times, actually), "do your friends get more leeway with you than I do?"

"Well, because," I replied, just as uncomprehending as he, and amazed such a question needed asking. How odd, I thought, not to know.

If partnership love is singular, friendship is expansive. It embraces, if not multitudes, at least a big canvas, muu-muu-sized, tent-sized, of humans. It's a marketplace of interests, temperaments, experiences; a potluck dinner in which we all bring something different, our choice, to the table. (Speaking of potluck — does the role of food even need mentioning? We eat and drink together a lot; the major female friendship food groups, we like to think, are starch, salt, chocolate and wine.)

Little girls and adolescents tend to have best friends — bosom friends, kindred spirits, as Anne of Green Gables phrased it — although the chosen person may not be the same one from one day to the next. Youthful friendships are volatile, explosive. They involve girls trying on new roles, different moods, rapidly altering demands, perceptions and plots — like playing with dolls.

By the time we're adults, friendships have begun to accumulate and there's often no particular need to label them, "best" or otherwise.

My sister is my dear friend. So is my niece. So is a union leader with a rigorous passion for justice. So are some ex-colleagues from various newspaper jobs over the years, with whom far more profound bonds were formed than are accounted for by mere work or worldly events. So are a few writers who know things about this sort of existence, and about life, that are otherwise hard to explain. So, still, for that matter, is Gail.

I am perfectly capable of understanding that I may be the person a friend thinks of first for solace or laughter in one aspect of her life, but not necessarily in another. That not all information is shared, and when it is, it can take different forms with different people. That two friends together may speak of certain matters with one another, but not be happy discussing them in a group.

That some friends are embraceable and others are not. That some like each other, some should not be put in each other's company and some, from different settings and circumstances and times, have never met.

Our similarities and differences should make old age, should we achieve it with any rough simultaneity, pretty interesting. One truth women gradually become aware of is that, quite apart from divorce and life's various other gender wreckages, the odds are they'll outlive any male partners they have. This is one reason middle-aged and old women are free to travel in packs, as funny and formidable as the umbrella-wielding, sidewalk-hogging granny gangs of the Monty Python skit.

And it's one reason that the subject of what some of us call "the feminary" crops up now and then. This place would be, in our envisionings, an enormous old house with individual bedrooms and offices, many bathrooms, and common living room, dining room, kitchen, library, media room and garden.

In this feminary, we old women friends would entertain and amuse each other, confide in, console and look after each other. The halt would be leading the blind, or vice versa. We would hire whatever medical and housekeeping care would come in most handy, and beautiful men to weed the gardens, mow the lawns. We (rude old women) would observe them from our cushioned wicker chairs on the white-painted, wrap-around porch.

Our conversation, give or take fresh infirmities and the odd vanished brain cell, wouldn't likely be radically different from what it is now. Much of it would probably be what, as a girl, I mocked as "small talk" or "gossip," a maligned word it is now one of my projects to redeem and redefine — as, say, "the close analysis of interpersonal relationships."

So we'd be sitting around talking about the usual stuff: "How did today go, what did you do, how are you feeling? Let me show you the new pictures of the kids I just got. My back is killing me. You'd love this book, I'll trade you for that one. Want to watch the election tonight, or should we rent a video? What's the biggest secret you've ever kept? Here, have another chocolate. I wish I could get through just one night without having to get up for a pee, and one day without having to rummage my mind for a missing noun, or a verb. Look at that young man, isn't he lovely, no, I don't think you can have him. Would you prefer heaven or reincarnation, and what do you think you'd come back as? How many people do you reckon you've actually loved, romantically, in your life? So far, that is. How was the sex? How was the talk? Try this one. I think it's got a cream centre. That one over there has a cherry inside. Now, whose turn is it to get drinks, my glass is empty again."

A little girl clutching a Clancy doesn't dream of such endings. On the other hand, she doesn't dream of any endings at all, or of the hours, days, months, years she will spend laughing, feuding, weeping, playing, arguing, embracing, telling secrets, sharing dreams, and giving and receiving that most important gift: loyalty. She has no vision yet of all the wonderful, terrible things she will learn, and unlearn, while growing up, growing older, growing sick, well, and old with her friends. But with great good fortune she will; because that's how the real story goes.

What Stays in
the Family

Lorna Crozier

"It's too late," my mother said when my father wanted her by his side when he fell ill. For the first time in forty years, he stayed home in the evenings. They ate their supper together, and then he sat in the La-Z-Boy beside her smaller chair to watch TV. Sometimes he was well enough to sip a beer, sometimes not. Even before he was hospitalized in the palliative ward, the tumours in his throat from lymphatic cancer made swallowing a chore. Often what he tried to drink dribbled from his nose.

It was difficult to watch him try to satiate his hunger or walk the few steps from the kitchen to the bathroom; difficult to watch him sit so small behind the wheel of his car and drive around the block just for the sake of getting out. But my mother's distress went beyond these things. His sudden need of her company, his new-found domesticity, didn't sit well with her. At seventy, she had spent the best part of their marriage making a life of her own, one that didn't depend on him for companionship or money. In the past, he'd spent his nights at the Legion or in the Imperial and Healy hotels, drinking beer and playing shuffleboard or pool. He'd had no problem paying for his games, his gambling and his drinks, but when Mom would ask for grocery money, he'd hand her a one-dollar bill with the attitude of a patron bestowing great gifts — and for that, she'd almost have to beg.

When I was eight Mom found a job at the outdoor swimming pool, lifting heavy baskets stuffed with shoes and clothing to their numbered places on the four-tiered shelves, lifting them down again when the swimmers plunked their metal tags on the counter and claimed their belongings to get dressed. It was hard and menial work, but it was a paying job, and she finally had money of her own. She also did "day work," the name then given to cleaning other people's houses, and in the winter she sold tickets at the Bronco hockey games. After her first paycheque, I don't think she ever asked my father for grocery money again.

In her social life, she developed the same independence. I can't remember her getting together with women friends for a night on the town, but she curled and bowled in afternoon ladies' leagues, and she met her neighbours for coffee once a week. If she wasn't working, she'd be home with me, keeping Dad's supper warm on the back of the stove, knitting, reading, watching television. After my older brother left home when I was eleven, she and I spent Christmas Eves alone, Dad finding somewhere else to go after the bars shut down. Who can blame her for not welcoming him with open arms when he wanted to cling to her the last months of his life? It was too damn late.

My father was a drunk. It brings me great relief to say that now because his drinking was the biggest secret of my childhood. My mother never spoke about it to anyone but me, and I was warned not to tell my friends. His drinking was our skeleton in the closet, our mad child hidden in the attic. The bones rattled, the feet banged on the floor above our heads, but if someone else was around, we pretended not to hear.

Mom's attitude was small-town and pragmatic. What went on in the family stayed in the family and was no one else's business. It wasn't that she was hiding any kind of physical or sexual violence — no matter how much my father drank, he never hit her or me or my brother. He never abused us. She was simply covering up embarrassing behaviour, like the time he woke up in the middle of the night and peed in his shoe. Why tell anyone about that? Or the time he tripped on an imaginary branch on the sidewalk and came home with his nose scraped and bleeding and his glasses broken. Or the nights he spent in jail. Or the summer evening we caught the train to Winnipeg for my brother's wedding and he kept everyone in the car awake with his shouting and singing, my mother and I hunched mortified in our seats as the porter threatened to throw him off. Her insistence on privacy had something to do with pride. She was honest and hardworking and she wanted, in spite of our family's poverty and her husband's bad behaviour, to hold her head up high. Although I respect and love her and understand her need to conceal our family troubles, I suffered terribly from our silence.

What our secret meant in small and practical terms was that I couldn't ask a girlfriend to sleep over if Mom thought Dad was on a toot. I couldn't tell anyone the real reason that Mom and I walked everywhere — Dad was too inebriated to drive, or he'd already lost his licence and then his job operating heavy machinery in the oil patch. I couldn't tell my high-school boyfriend why I didn't ask him to spend Christmas with my family when he was left alone, his parents responding to a distant relative's emergency. When Dad didn't come home the night before my grade twelve graduation, Mom sent me to tell the teacher advisor that he'd been called out of town for work. I had to let the teacher know of Dad's absence because I was the valedictorian, and my parents were to sit at the head table beside the principal. As the gymnasium doors at the school banged shut behind me, I walked towards the teacher who stood at the far end by the stage, the distance I had to cross seemingly endless, the crepe-paper graduation streamers and balloons swaying above me. A few steps away, I stammered the excuse I had been rehearsing. I'll never forget the look of pity in his eyes. I turned around and walked back across that long shining floor, the soles of my runners squeaking with every step, the back of my neck burning. Later, when I was dressed in my first long gown and Mom and I were about to leave the house, Dad showed up. He couldn't even tie his shoes. I walked ahead of my parents to the gym, told the same teacher that the job had ended early, my father would sit at the head table after all. Beside the principal he took his place. Soon his head was nodding over the jellied salad and slices of ham, his mouth drooping open as I stood up to speak.

Perhaps the worst effect of our secret was that it forced me to hide my sadness. I buried it beneath an exterior that had little to do with what was going on at home and with how I saw myself. My cheerful, outgoing double sang in the operettas, captained the cheerleading team, served on the executive of Teen Town, taught swimming lessons, acted in drama nights, went steady with boys, worried about how far a good girl should go, delivered the valedictorian address and never spoke of anything that mattered. On the surface I was well-adjusted, popular, optimistic. Inside I burned with shame. My father's drinking was such a disgraceful thing that it couldn't be talked about. It had to be carried invisibly like a terrible disease that had no name.

By the time I went to university, the only one in my extended family to do so, the shame over my father's drinking went hand in hand with the fear that I, as well as he, would be found out. It would be discovered that I was the daughter of the town drunk, and that I came from the kind of working-class poverty where not one good book, not one piece of art graced the shelves or walls of our run-down rented house. The fear that I have been tricking people has been with me almost all my life.

One day someone will rise from an audience and say, "You're not good enough to read, publish, teach, write, pass those exams, get those promotions, win those awards. I'm going to tell everyone how dumb and bad you really are. I'm going to tell everyone where you come from."

When I went back to my home town at twenty-four to teach in the high school, I returned with my husband's name, not my father's, which had felt like such a burden. Most of my colleagues didn't know who my father was. One Friday night I joined a group of fellow teachers at the Legion for a beer. An older man came to our table and asked me to dance. I rose to his outstretched hand and he whirled me around to a country tune. A few songs later he returned and I danced with him again. He slurred his words, but he moved with grace across the floor, his arm around my waist guiding me through a two-step. The teacher beside me when I sat down the second time said, "That old drunk really likes you." I paused. I was tempted to say "Yes" and laugh it off, but instead I replied, "That old drunk is my father." As I hesitated before replying, I had to muster some courage. It would have been so easy to deny him. That moment of honesty loosened something inside as if my breath had been held in a fist that was slowly beginning to open.

It took ten years before I dropped my married name and reclaimed my father's. In 1983, "Crozier" appeared for the first time on a book of my poetry. Not until 1990, when I was over forty, did I write about my father's drinking in a poem. My mother still hadn't spoken of this area of her life with any of her friends. Since my poems would be the first public acknowledgement of it, I warned her they were coming and excused myself by insisting I had the right to my own version of my childhood. She wasn't pleased, but she didn't pressure me to stop. Some days I think I should be more concerned with privacy, or at least with my mother's sense of what should remain confidential in the past we shared. But the harm our silence caused continues to compel me to speak as openly as possible about those old family wounds.

At the same time I feel almost driven, now that my father has died, to put him on the page, to give him life in the music of my lines, not out of anger or shame but out of love, for the censorship of my childhood damaged him as well as me and my mother. It made him smaller because we let his drinking loom above everything else he brought to our lives. The shame I felt made me deny the other things he was — the young man who lost the farm, the hard worker, the one who believed things would always work out okay, the curler who won all the local bonspiels, the old-time fiddler who loved to dance, the man my mother loved and married. It's too late now for me to make amends to him, but it's not too late to tell our family secrets, to find words for what could not be spoken. My father was a drunk. What a relief to say that! And what a delight to know there is so much more I need to say.

Notes on a Piece for Carol

Isabel Huggan

I laugh right out loud when I read on the screen what I've written — quickly, without thinking — as a file heading. Doesn't that just tell the whole story? Still doing whatever I do "for" someone else, still the little girl seeking approval from some higher authority even with my mother and father long dead and no chance of a parental "good for you, dear." Still needing the focus of someone outside myself to whom I offer whatever it is I have to give — in this case, my thoughts about aging, the odd surprises for which I have been unprepared. Who could have told me that at this age I would still be — at heart — the plump child wanting to please?

I do not mean to sound as if I am speaking about some "inner child." Not that, God forbid. So, what, then?

I thought that when I was old I would be confident, that somehow there would be within me an accumulation of experience, an accretion of knowledge that would form such a solid, dense core that my being an adult woman would flow from that source in some, I don't know, molecular or electromagnetic way.

Instead, it feels much more as if I have made a grown-up-looking shell around a space in which the same *me* as I've ever been dwells, hidden from view. The outer surface is sagging, pouching, and creaking; it knows exactly how to appear as if the years have passed and are passing still. The body is doing its part — and from inside it, I am acting my role superbly. The long-married middle-aged mother: responsible, sensible, sane.

"All virtue is a form of acting." That's Yeats, and when I read this quote in Annie Dillard's essay "The Stunt Pilot" years ago, I felt the notion resonate in my own life and wrote it down in the little daybook I keep, which is full of thoughts that would otherwise flitter off into the dark of forgetfulness. I know how to act like a grown-up but it is only acting.

Why should I be surprised? In fact, my mother told me this truth, in her way, but I was a mere twenty-seven at the time and did not listen with ears tuned to the deep meaning of what she said. I was leaning against the door frame of the bathroom in the house where I spent my childhood, and she was bending towards the mirror over the sink, tweezers in hand, looking for that one last offending whiskery hair (there is always one). She was sixty then, frail because of her heart condition but — I see this only now in photographs, did not see it then — very pretty. She looked intently at herself in the mirror and turned to me, laughing.

"It's such a shock," she said, "to see this face. It doesn't look like me. *I'm* still a girl, and *this* person is so old." We both laughed, and I took the tweezers from her and said, "there's one just there on your chin," and plucked it in comradely fashion.

"If I ever have a stroke," she said, "you make sure you come to the hospital and keep my chin smooth." Again we laughed, little knowing that within a year it would come to that, and that, indeed, I would sit by her bedside with the tweezers, and that both of us would feel tears slipping down our cheeks.

That was my mother, and I did not hear what she said, not then, maybe not ever. I did not know she meant it would be like that for me. She told me, but I did not understand. Maybe it is always impossible for daughters to hear their mothers' voices until later, much later.

Seven years earlier, I'd read the same piece of news with the same disregard for truth even when it was slamming right in at me, fastball over the plate.

Studying English at university, I read a lot of Virginia Woolf, finding some of her novels tedious and others, such as *The Waves*, thrilling. Of course *Mrs. Dalloway* had to be read, but it fell into the tedious camp — so exasperatingly small in scope, I thought, so shallow. Giving a party, indeed! And that old friend of Clarissa's who turns up, Sally Seton: "fifty-five in body, she said, but her heart was like a young girl's of twenty. . . ." Well, it was clear that the reader was meant to regard her as silly, even pathetic. What was the point, I wondered, of reading about such unworthy women? Imagine, I thought, bending over my books and making notes on character development, what a failed woman was poor immature Sally. How sad. How ridiculous.

This year, rereading *Mrs. Dalloway* in preparation for reading Michael Cunningham's splendid novel *The Hours*, I came across the passage again, and thought, Twenty! Imagine feeling as old as twenty! I am still seventeen. . . .

So you see, I was told, and told again, but I could not know until I got here what it would feel like, how it would be. I think there have been many places and many times when the information has been imparted, but you cannot know the path through the forest until your feet are making their own footsteps in the ground. What possibility is there of being yourself if you place your feet in another's imprint? Perhaps that was the way for the generations before ours, when duty shaped the substance of what a woman must be — but not now, and not for our daughters. Not only will they not follow in our footsteps, they will make new paths. What can we tell them, then, of where we've been and what we are? Better to say nothing, and only listen. Better not to say what confusion and pain may lie ahead, what ambiguities and ambivalences.

The holes we leave for our daughters are for them to darn with the yarn of their own lives. Just as we did. Just as we are doing.

This image comes to me as I sit tanning myself, naked in the Haliburton summer sunlight, while talking with the woman friend with whom I have shared forty years of growing old and with whom I can dare to say anything. We expose our aging bodies to the sky and the lake without a shred of shame over droopy breasts or sparse pubic hair — we are still seventeen for all the world, whooping with laughter at each new turn of phrase as we chew together the tough rind of this problem I tell her I must deal with before the end of August, my deadline for this piece.

What is there that we haven't been told or that we don't tell? With each other, we can think of nothing, although we have not always told at the moment, sometimes disclosing our faults and fears and falls from grace long after. But always telling, in the long run, always able to share our failures, to confide the secrets of our hearts, trusting enough to ask: Is it this way for you? With each other, we are transparent.

With our daughters, we know we keep something back — the fact, for example, that our lives are not all they seem — but only because, we decide, it's for their own good. We must not deprive them of their own disillusionments. That's part of being a woman, like zits and menstrual cramps, like labour pain and heartbreak. This must be nature's way of keeping the species going. We laugh at this until we weep at our teenage wit. Serves them right, we say, for all those times they wouldn't listen.

Nights when I can't sleep — estrogen depletion, says the doctor — I lie in the dark feeling old and sad and tired. My feet ache, or sometimes my hip, or sometimes my heart, worrying about my family, or a friend whose husband recently left her after thirty years, or my own future without a pension. But the voice in my head, the voice that will not be stilled until the dawn, is a young voice, and sounds exactly like me when I was in high school. This is who I am.

Another friend of mine met and fell in love with a man who'd been recently divorced, and who brought with him into her life several pairs of synthetic socks meticulously mended by his first wife. My friend was appalled — these were cheap socks to throw out, not worth the effort of mending. She and I spent a long afternoon at her dining-room table, holding the socks in our hands, looking at the careful stitches back and forth, under and over, that held these nasty old things together at toe and heel. What good had it done her in the long run, we wondered. All that loving energy put into darning, and where did it get her? Why hadn't someone told her that was no way to keep a man happy?

Maybe someone did. But she had to find out for herself.

Maybe she wasn't happy, either.

What did my mother tell me about her life as a married woman? "I think I have been a good partner to your father," she said, implying by her tone that this would be my role with my eventual husband as well. Only that. Is there anything she might have told me? What might I have asked? We had no vocabulary for such a discussion.

Alone now in France at the end of the summer and pondering what I have written here, I realize I have already addressed this issue in fiction. In a story called "Fine Tuning," two sisters talk on the telephone as the younger asks the elder to explain what has kept her long marriage going, and what she has meant by the phrase "acting her way through the years." The elder, narrating the story, thinks about how she learned — from movies, from Broadway songs — how women were meant to square their shoulders and get on with it — to put on a happy face. Acting is not hypocrisy, she assures herself, it's just a method of coping. Pretending is what women *do*.

When finally she reaches deep into her memory and finds one moment that explains everything, she decides that it won't make sense to her sister, and she abandons the attempt. "I don't think I have any wisdom to pass along anyway."

Why do I keep returning to marriage as a central motif defining women, I wonder? Perhaps that has to do with my generation's intake of values in the '40s and '50s, the way our mothers' expectations — even unsaid — coloured our lives.

Searching for who my mother might have been, I go to the Archives in Ottawa and ramble through microfiche pages of the *Kitchener-Waterloo Record*. This is what she read every evening after the supper dishes were done and her apron was hung in the pantry. I start with 1943, the year of my birth, both repelled and fascinated by the Women's Pages, a churning froth of social and personal items, weddings and church events, recipes and dress patterns. There is a hectoring tone on these pages, exhorting women (or "wives") to do their best for the war effort. In its broadest sense, this involves feeding their husbands (or "the men") as well as possible within the constraints of rationing.

More telling, however, are the daily columns of Dorothy Dix, whose advice is stern and cranky and frankly misogynist. The worst female fault in marriage, Dix tells readers, is nagging, followed closely by bad cooking, slumping (in looks, love and manners), whining and laziness.

> Practically all girls are capable of pulling off the Lady Love stunt before marriage but alas, only too many of them think a wedding ring gives them the right to flop down on the do-nothing stool, get fat and eat onions . . . When a man sees his beauteous bride slouching around the house in a soiled house-coat with cold cream on her face, he feels he got cheated at the altar.
>
> Too often after the first baby, [women] cease being wives and are only mothers . . . giving all their tenderness to Junior and letting poor husband go heart-hungry.

Heart-hungry. Swell phrase. But my heart is chilled when I contemplate the world in which my mother formed her ideas of who she was meant to be — and, thus, of who she would want me to be.

In Toronto I visit a friend who is the age my mother would have been had she lived. She is one of my favourite people in the world, a great reader and conversationalist who likes to discuss matters at length. I explain what I am writing and she listens attentively. "What *are* the things women don't say?" I ask.

"Well, in my day, we didn't tell each other a *thing*," she says, her lovely wrinkled face shining with humour, "but I can't think of much women don't talk about now. There's *nothing* you could tell me that would shock me, I've read it all!" Or did she say, "I've heard it all"? I can't remember but it doesn't matter. The fact is, I am at ease with her in a way I never was with my mother. Is that because times have changed or because she is not my mother?

In Ottawa at the end of August I am one of the three women spending time with a fourth who is undergoing chemotherapy for cancer and who, as a consequence, is feeling dreadful and in need of cheering up. The four of us have been a tight little group for many years, with a running gag (since 1967 when we saw the film *Two for the Road*) that each of us looks like Audrey Hepburn. A few summers ago, the woman who is now sick staged an Audrey Night in my honour to celebrate a successful operation in which my ovaries and cancerous appendix were removed — an elegant dinner for the four of us complete with tiaras, white gloves and champagne. Since then, we have continued to work variations on this utterly ridiculous theme, going as far as adding "aud" to our names (so that I, for example, am Isaud) in our e-mail correspondence to each other. Somehow, the joke never goes stale; we feed it with new material year after year. And now that one of us is in real peril, we've even made an illustrated programme for this year's reunion, as a diversion from the mortal danger in which she dwells. We do not speak of it, but it does not escape our attention that Audrey Hepburn died of cancer.

Individually, we are mature, responsible women who've worked in government, radio, newspapers, schools and universities — we are all writers of one sort or another. Collectively, we act like kids. We *are* still kids when we're together. Apart we suffer greatly, but *ensemble* we defeat despair.

The woman who is ill spends her waning life in bed at her mother's house. Her mother is eighty-five years old, a widow watching her only child fade before her eyes, bewildered by the bad hand life has dealt her but somehow still at the table and still in the game. A trooper. We make her an Honorary Audrey; it is the least we can do. One morning, while we Auds are visiting, another woman comes to the door and announces on entry that she must dash for a pee. "Too much coffee this morning," she gasps on her way down the hall, leaving us all in gales of laughter and a round of stories about our own weaknesses in that particular area.

Our friend's mother laughs with us, shaking her head. "You girls are terrible!" she says. "My generation *never* talked like this." She is so amused by our anecdotes about bodily functions that she says she'll pass them on to her friends later that day when she goes out to play bridge. She acts as if she is learning something new from us — whereas we, in fact, are learning from her and her daughter. How to be brave. How to fight and forgive. How to hang on and how to let go.

And so here we are, aging women coming up against illness and pain and the eventual ends of our lives, and what might anyone have told us to prepare us for this? Nothing. We are making it up as we go along, we are filling in the blank spaces with companionable laughter and love, and the deep certainty that our youthful play in the face of disaster gives us strength and some way of staring down the terrifying dark. Who we are at this point has less to do with the men and children in our lives than we ever would have imagined. We recognize this and are amazed. We are girls dressed up in ladies' clothing, pretending.

We are strangely like Woolf's sweet Sally Seton, that middle-aged woman with a twenty-year-old heart who felt, she said, "more deeply, more passionately, every year."

Lettuce Turnip and Pea

Anne Hart

No one would have called my grandmother a witty woman, but she managed her life with panache. I only knew her towards the end of it, when she was very old and I was very young and each of us living an awkward life — my grandmother's because, at ninety-one, she was bowed over in a half-hoop, could move with but the tiniest of shuffling steps and was nearly blind, and mine because, at seven, if asked where my parents were, I had to admit they weren't. They were dead.

Looking back on that summer, I think it's fair to say that my grandmother and I were each dealing with her particular sad circumstance with commendable fortitude, my grandmother because she had what Victorians called "backbone" (even though her real one was in such a shocking state), and I because of my good fortune in having been taken into the household of a very fine aunt, my grandmother's youngest daughter.

In the hot Ontario summer I'm remembering, my aunt and I had come by train from Nova Scotia to stay with my grandmother, while the eldest aunt, the caretaker, the unmarried daughter, enjoyed her annual consolation prize: three weeks in a hotel on Lake Huron.

My grandmother's house stood in an overgrown garden of fading paths and beds, of hedges, rose arbours and raspberries out of control. Inside, it was as good as a fairy tale: windows shuttered against the sun, clocks ticking upstairs and down, locked trunks, sealed envelopes in pigeonholes, curios under glass — and, of course, my grandmother, the spellbinder herself.

Years later I found a newspaper clipping, an essay that my aunt had composed for Mother's Day, 1931, in her mother's honour:

> . . . Suddenly I come upon a garden and there, tucked away in one corner, peeps out an old, quaint, rambling white house with its gables and green-shuttered windows beckoning a welcome. At one side, in the midst of a cloud of riotous, golden, nodding daffodils, I find the "Heart" of the garden. It is she who mothered the whole neighbourhood of children, as well as her own. Ah, sweet little Mother, how far does the influence of that spirit go? From sea to sea and to the uttermost parts of the earth . . .

Even back then, it's clear, my grandmother was the family's ritual object. But if I, in the eventual summer of our brief overlap, had read that clipping I'd have been astonished. Ancient and tottering she had become, in her long black dresses and shawls, and a prideful and fascinating force she still was — a repository of stories well-honed to illustrate gritty accomplishments of family notables (mostly dead) or cautionary tales about those who hadn't measured up. But: *sweet, mothered the whole neighbourhood of children, from sea to sea and to the uttermost parts of the earth,* I would have sworn this wasn't the grandmother of my acquaintance.

It was in fact on the matter of *the whole neighbourhood of children* that our confrontation occurred. Time had moved on since my aunt had composed her lyric tribute. The *old, quaint, rambling white house* stood pretty well unchanged, but not the others on a street overtaken by a new wave whose ancestors had never seen a highland or a loch, or done their share of chopping down the virgin forest. This was a recurring theme between my grandmother and my aunt: "*Not* the MacLauglins' house turned into apartments!" or, "Who *are* those people in the stone cottage? What if the Guthries could see it now?" or, "Those noisy children are still on the street and it's *after dark!*"

Oh, those noisy children — how, after dark and stifling in bed, I envied them, and how, by day, I lurked toward the front of the garden hoping they might notice me.

One day a girl about my age sidled up to the hedge. "Wanna come over and play?" she asked. Her name was Nancy Bodiuk, and she lived across the street.

There followed an exciting afternoon. Nancy turned out to be a lot of fun, and the focus of it was the backyard of the house she lived in, a backyard shared by the children of three floors of families. That afternoon it was in the possession of girls, and a great deal of noise was coming from a shed attached to the back porch. Inside were cartons of cast-off clothes — lacy old nightgowns, tattered slips, grubby crepe dresses with sequined straps, wrinkled polka-dot dresses, floppy flowered hats, pillbox hats with spotted veils, waist cinchers and brassieres, scarves, stoles, an old feather boa, a moth-eaten fur muff, slingback shoes with peep-toes, platform shoes with stiletto heels, blouses with broad, padded shoulders, long skirts, enormous handbags, gloves, a beaded clutch purse, necklaces, chokers, bangles, a broken rhinestone tiara, old lipsticks and compacts, a wedding dress.

"My mother's wedding dress!" cried Nancy, parading around the backyard in it, while the rest of us, cobbled out in lesser finery, played giddy bridesmaids with the train. What would my grandmother think of that? *Children allowed to play with a wedding dress?*

We were well into a gypsy phase when we heard a scramble at the back fence and over it came a young man, jacket slung over one shoulder, tie loosened at his neck. I can see him now, thin and endearing, his face alight.

The gypsies surrounded him. "Jerry! Jerry!" they squealed. He bowed and beamed. "Hide and seek, ladies," he said, heading towards the back porch. "I'm going behind the shed door." This was clearly a game, but what came next?

What came next was Nancy's mother. She came through the back porch and behind her, on tiptoe, finger to his lips, emerged the young man from the shed. As soon as I saw this mother, I knew exactly where those wonderful clothes came from. With her arched eyebrows and her rolled-back hair, she looked like a movie star, a somewhat businesslike movie star in a close-fitting black dress with big white leaves on it, a full, swinging skirt, high-heeled pumps. On that hot afternoon she also looked cranky and preoccupied. What I was seeing for the first time, I now realize, was a mother home from a long day at work with a lot on her mind.

"Nancy!" she began impatiently, and then: "Boo!" cried Jerry from behind her and clamped his hands down on her shoulders.

Nancy's mother gave a little scream and dropped her parcels. "Jerry!" she cried, "Where did you come from? Why didn't they tell me you were here?" But it wasn't real scolding, I knew that at once. For perhaps the first time in my life I was seeing a look of pure joy.

"Yes! It's Jerry! It's Jerry!" screamed the gypsies. He smiled benevolently. "Well, girls, it's time I treated you to popsicles," he said, and he reached into a trouser pocket and pulled out a handful of change which he gave to Nancy without even counting.

"Wow!" cried Nancy. "Let's go!" and we bolted after her

in our gypsy clothes, squealing through the cool hall of the house and out into the heat of the sidewalk.

At the corner store (where I'd never been before) Nancy bought us all double popsicles. We sat on the curb outside, and we licked them and ate them and waved at passing cars. Though I wouldn't have admitted it, this was the first popsicle I'd ever eaten.

"I know a dirty joke," said Nancy.

A dirty joke? What was that?

"Tell us!" demanded the gypsies.

With great solemnity Nancy stood up and faced us, a teacher in front of her class.

"Name the three best vegetables!"

"What are they?" we chorused.

"LETTUCE . . . TURNIP . . . AND . . . PEA!" Nancy screamed.

There was a moment of silence, and then we all got the joke. We doubled up, we laughed till we cried, we made a lot of noise. The man who owned the store came out and wondered if it might be our suppertimes by now?

Nancy walked back with me to my grandmother's house. At the gate, I divested myself of gypsy clothes and gave her the bundle.

"There's an old woman in that house, isn't there?" she asked. "Is she your grandmother?"

I said she was.

"I've always wanted to see her," said Nancy. "Can I come in?"

"Sure," I said, in the reckless spirit of the afternoon. Up the steps we went, through the front door and into the gloom of the hall in which gleamed darkly the brass nails that formed the initials on my long-dead grandfather's goatskin-covered trunk, the hanging mahogany-hued shell, head and flippers of a long-dead turtle an aunt had brought back years before from the Bahamas, and a comparatively lively engraving of John

Knox thundering from his pulpit at Mary Queen of Scots. We went past these and into my grandmother's sitting room.

There she sat, ancient and archetypal in her black silk dress, a light shawl of white wool around her shoulders, her nearly transparent hands poised alertly on knitting she could hardly see.

"Where have you been and who is that with you?" she asked suspiciously.

"It's my new friend Nancy. She lives across the street."

"You've been playing with one of those children from the street? Tell her to go away at once!"

Nancy disappeared The front door banged behind her.

My aunt appeared from the kitchen. "What on earth's happening?" she asked.

A terrible anger came over me, tears to my eyes, a painful lump to my throat. At the same time I suddenly discovered within myself a euphoric and useful certainty: that in certain exchanges *I* could be in the right.

"Grannie!" I shouted at her, "How could you be so rude to my friend? She's just as good as I am!"

My grandmother stared at me. For the first time, I think (I was by far her youngest grandchild, an afterthought, really), she took my measure.

"What a temper you have!" she exclaimed, and then, accusingly, to my aunt: "But I thought she was such a quiet child!"

"I've had a lovely afternoon!" I cried, and the pain of its ruin gave me a heady courage:

"Name the three best vegetables!"

"What?" exclaimed my grandmother (thereby breaking her own rule: never say "what?")

"LETTUCE . . . TURNIP . . . AND . . . PEA!"

There was a moment of silence. Then: "Good gracious!" cried my grandmother, putting her hands over her ears.

"Why don't you run upstairs, dear?" suggested my tactful aunt.

Shaking, I went upstairs, but I stopped on the landing to listen.

". . . seemed like such a quiet child," my grandmother was saying again.

"But very highly strung," my aunt replied. "We must take that into account." The sitting-room door closed.

After a while my aunt came upstairs and sat beside me on the bed. It was important to know, she explained at length, that a country's moral well-being depended on its women. If women let their standards slip, the whole country would be doomed.

Finally: "And now we should go downstairs."

In the sitting room I approached my grandmother. She held something out to me.

"Your father's christening mug."

I took the silver mug. We regarded each other warily.

"And this."

It was a small envelope. I opened it. Inside was a little white card. On it, in large shaky printing, my grandmother had written: *Grannie loves her dear little Anne and hopes she will always be a good girl.*

Every few years I polish the christening mug. I rub it with considerable relish, conjuring up a Bacchanalian afternoon. Upstairs and downstairs the clocks are ticking in my grandmother's house, and I've just confronted a dragon. No one has ever told me how to do that. I've figured it out, all by myself.

Casseroles

Bonnie Burnard

I

When she was sixteen and finally responsible enough and skilled enough to drive her father's big white boat of an Oldsmobile, one of her jobs was to wrap her mother's freshly baked casseroles in newspaper, set them carefully into small cardboard boxes and deliver them to a house a street or two away, or on the other side of town, or somewhere out in the country. If it wasn't a casserole, then it was a berry pie or dinner rolls or pecan tarts or a layer cake, all of it made from scratch, from recipes her mother knew by heart and had long since mastered.

There was never a note tucked into the box. Her mother did not tell her what she might say when she handed it over.

The deliveries were made to families grieving a death, sometimes a hard death, or celebrating a big occasion, a wedding or an eightieth birthday party or a child confirmed, something anyone, even a slight acquaintance watching from a distance, would want to acknowledge with a bit of baking.

The driveways were usually filled with cars. A few of the cars would have strange but quickly recognized license plates, from Manitoba or Michigan or Quebec, but once in a while there were plates and state platitudes that signified a long drive from a more interesting world, Illinois or Delaware or Florida.

In the winter months she saw only the person who opened the kitchen door to accept the box of food, the person who had noticed her walking up the sometimes slushy, sometimes icy driveway, but in the moist heat of Ontario summer the shaded front porches were crowded with thin-haired, rugged old men and with elderly women in sturdy, laced shoes who sat without complaint on straight-backed dining-room chairs, the chairs carried out just for the afternoon, for the air. On the lawn, middle-aged women in dark muted suits or bright floral skirts stretched their legs in a row of Muskoka chairs, or they lay on quilts spread over the grass, guarding the babies and toddlers who were held like prisoners in the circle their bodies made. Little girls in good dresses brushed against the old women on the porch, hoping for praise, or they ran in all directions across the grass, holding hands and squealing, making the only noise. The young women, no longer girls but not yet mothers, huddled together on the porch steps like mannequins, careful with their posture and proud of their shining, page-boy hair, their bare, brown shoulders, their high-heeled sandals, their tanned feet.

Sometimes the extra cars had to be parked at odd angles on the grass beside the driveway and more than once she saw through a car window boys too young to know what to do with themselves fighting, climbing over the seats, rocking the heavy, big-fendered chassis with their bursts of mindless energy. Men leaned against the hoods of the cars with folded arms, talking and smoking cigarettes, watching the women, all the women, watching her as she came up the driveway hugging her mother's food.

Occasionally, perhaps to make her feel less awkward,

more known, one of these men would call out to her: Hello, Janey Brock. And once, just before she left for university, for good, one of them offered her a drink, a rye and ginger in a tall yellow picnic tumbler. This will put hair on your chest, he promised, lifting the tumbler to tempt her, acknowledging with a wide grin the laughter of the men who watched him do it, his admirers.

There was no pattern to her mother's gestures, no particular recipe offered to grief, no one cake to mark achievement or celebration. But the dishes were always the same; the sturdy casserole with the green tint and the handles and the heavy lid, the big deep pie plate or the just-polished silver tray or the heavy, lead crystal bowl with the pattern of daffodils cut so deep into the glass, the smooth-ringed rim an inch-wide circle of gold.

II

Late every Sunday afternoon, year in, year out, her elderly father calls with bad news. Someone (surely you remember Ed McLaughlin, he cut hair for years in the shop that used to be beside the new muffler place) has lost a grandson, the terrible fight with lymphoma now over. (Mercy can be found in death, he tells her. Believe it.) Someone, the piano teacher (you took from Eva didn't you, for a few years?), the plumber's wife (not from this area, not originally), your aunt Jane (your bullheaded namesake) has broken her hip, her other hip. Five of this year's crop of high-school grads took that curve out of town too hard, just before dawn, likely still drunk from the dance. (Fools with everything to live for. And three of them too smart for seat belts, thrown beneath the rolling wreck. Gone.)

When she was a fool with everything to live for, one of her fellow high-school graduates had left town briefly for mortuary school. She remembers being told soon after she moved away that he'd failed a practical examination because he had neglected to apply his flesh-tinted makeup to a pair of pale folded hands. This was a joke he told on himself. (The people she knew then liked a self-deprecating joke, it's one of the very few things she misses, and sometimes terribly.) But by now this high-school friend will be a very prosperous man. She'd guess that he is very accomplished. By now he will know precisely what he should do.

She has not lived there for thirty-five years, although she hasn't gone far, not as the actual world is measured. Sometimes she drives up to attend a funeral with her father, or to offer her condolences at a visitation, guiding him along the line of mourners quite a bit faster than he'd like because he can slow things to a crawl. He is a very good talker and many of the dead have been his friends. His mind is his best friend now and while it is, like any friend, not absolutely trustworthy, it is faithful in its way. He says he is often entertained by his mind.

Years before she could drive the big white Oldsmobile she had been trained to attend funerals and visitations, taught by example how to conduct herself. Once, just before high school, when for month after mysterious, adolescent month she had cried copious, reflex tears, when some of those tears gathered and spilled at the loss of a miserly, cranky neighbour she hadn't even really known, she had been advised in the car, by her mother, "This is not about you." She had been hurt and then steadied by those helpful words. Hurt and then steadied, made calm.

So why, when for all the intervening years she could glance at a body calmly, do her eyes now wander? Why is it that she can look only up, or down, at the strained but living faces, at the men's haircuts, the backs of their necks above their shirt collars so recently, so precisely clipped, at polished shoes and the several possible lengths of dark dresses, at the baskets of flowers, the inevitable, bursting, ceremonial glads?

Thirty years ago she lost a son. In infancy, as people liked to say then, in true innocence, the formality of the language like a wreath around the loss. She had looked at him, she couldn't stop looking, the face so small and round, so rosy, as if he had been perfectly prepared to live.

More recently she has lost a sister, in a car, against a truck skidding broadside on a slick winter road, the face in death not anything remotely like a sister's face but, thank God, an older, truer-to-life photograph placed on the casket (the first fleshy promise of a double chin, the small eyes squinting behind the windshield of the new boat, the loud raucous laugh you could hear again if you turned your head slightly, toward the memory).

And she has lost a friend, Sally, we could call her, lost to depression, or perhaps not depression but rather a long-lasting, low-grade sadness, a retreat from a world where a grown son is hooked on something wretched, his own family gone, his money, his house, his very good job. Sally never calls, although she will answer her phone and once or twice a month she will respond with good cheer to an invitation to share a spinach salad on the deck or a bowl of chili at the kitchen table. This friend used to know how to open a door and shout Hello, I'm here, but now she rings the bell and waits on the step as if she believes there might have been a misunderstanding, as if she believes the invitation wasn't truly meant for her. Each time she comes she is properly dressed, very well dressed, but always, soon after she is comfortably settled into a chair, she will begin to fidget with a collar or a sleeve or the pulled-out pocket of her shorts, apparently annoyed to discover that she is wearing a collar or a sleeve or a pair of shorts, and then she will stand up in the middle of someone's sentence, it could be her own, to say, Thanks, I liked that, I'll call you in a day or two, and quickly let herself out the door. Almost pulling it off.

III

Every Friday night, soon after the dishes are cleared, she calls her father with good news. Without warning, the girls are pregnant, both of them, her daughter, married in the middle of her degree but ploughing on, and her son's wife too, a puzzling but undeniably lovely red-haired young woman who once proclaimed with a practised pseudo-sophisticated lilt that she didn't like children much at all. "I am going to be a grandmother," she tells him. "Twice. And you a great-grandfather."

She couldn't begin to knit a pair of booties but she has ordered two handsome copies of the English edition of Winnie the Pooh, turning her back firmly on the Disney interpretation, the oversized eyes, the cloying sweetness of the illustrations, hoping with this gesture to set the tone for some small part of the world these babies will occupy, her guidance now almost always oblique, considered, sly. "Best not to get excited until they're safely born," her father tells her, and then corrects himself. "But that's good news."

After a dozen years of unsung dedication, she has been promoted, and from now on she will be travelling quite a bit, sometimes, perhaps twice a year, to Europe. "You don't have to tell me anything about Europe," he says, then stops himself in his tracks. (Who wants to hear about it now? It's all just documentaries now, that beach, the wretched waves pouring in over the stones, the bloodless, black-and-white gore.) "But I'd say," he tries, "that you are just the kind of woman who will enjoy travel. That's been your strength. Turning corners."

Her husband's brother's kidney, transplanted eight months earlier to another brother in Edmonton, is evidently thriving, happy to be alive anywhere, in any body. They are all meeting in July, at a place on Lake Simcoe, to celebrate. "Seems a long way to go," he says. "Certainly long in my day. But bless that bloody kidney."

Her neighbour's sister, I think you met her, Dad, the young woman with the green buzzed hair who came over to the car when you were leaving last time, has written a play that is going to be produced somewhere. It's a story about an immigrant family, Dutch, in the fifties, in Southern Ontario. The girl has allowed her to read the script and although she's no drama critic, she thinks it's quite fine. It could almost be about us, she tells him, if we were Dutch, and it's not nostalgic but kind of, well, actual. (And rich. This is precisely the word she'd use. Rich.) Several of them are planning to see the play in the fall, they are going to make a week-end of it, blow some hard-earned money on a posh hotel. "Imagine that," he says. "A spindly legged, green-haired girl writing a play."

She could go on. The trees planted last fall, the white pines with the long, soft needles, are filling out very nicely, better than expected. They are already soaking up some of the noise from the increased traffic at the corner, already earning their keep. She has finally learned to play chess, to wage pretend war with little carved, pretend warriors from Mexico, and not badly for a novice, for someone who believes it to be a useless skill, who has agreed to learn only for the companionship.

She has had the dining room painted the colour of beach sand, and it is much more inviting now with the teal blue chandelier and her mother's cut-work ivory cloth spread on the table below it, and on the cloth the bowl of intricately carved vegetables, a recent unnecessary gift from their son's friend Jackson, who stayed with them for a while last winter when he was broke.

Her husband has bought her a short peach nightie, which she isn't supposed to know about but does know about because she dusts under that bed too. Why would she stop? Dropping the dust mop, stripping to her middle-of-the-morning, middle-of-her-life flesh and gently lowering the nightie down over her head, she has just today stood at a bedroom mirror appreciating the way the diaphanous folds suggest the possibility of the body they used to know, and both remember, at least some nights. This isn't the first offering. There have been several other gifts.

The man who wants her in this kind of nightie insists that he feels not a bit of remorse about his own middle-aged body, the thinner, weaker legs, the chest just beginning to sink, the beefy thickness on his back like something you could cook and carve to a platter, and he continues to believe that gifts like this will release her soft, nighttime laughter, that such extravagant gifts might make her feel young again, highly sexed again, eager to do the things she has almost always, almost without cease, done to him, and for him, and with him.

I am happy about many things, she almost tells her father. I stand here with the phone in my hand, eating a leftover spring roll, happy as can be. (I'm so happy I could bake a cake, she thinks, convinced for just this quick, lifted moment that she has held her ground, has held some limited but nonetheless sufficient part of her ground.)

And did my mother know, she wants to ask, when she sent me off in your big white Olds, did she realize in that generous, hard-working heart that everything I saw those afternoons, every common measure of grief and jubilation, would come, in time, to me? And did you, in collusion, throwing the keys to me across the kitchen, throwing them high and watching me reach to grab them as they began to fall, did you comprehend? Did you believe that I too would be able to withstand it?

Tonight, or tomorrow night, after her husband gives her the box, which she has skillfully taped and pushed back under the bed, he will wait with his strong arms folded. Waiting, he might offer up the further gift of a word, *love*, perhaps, or *pretend*, and then he will watch her pull back the tissue, hoping for — what? What? A come-hither smile? A wink? A look of wild surprise?

Hope for the Best (Expect the Worst)

Susan Lightstone

I spent my childhood waiting for the other shoe to drop. No surprise, really. In my family, the other shoe had fallen frequently — and tragically.

I grew up on stories of death and loss. Businesses failed, babies were born deformed, trees fell killing those in their path. My favourite was a cautionary tale of my grandmother's. While helping in the fields, her sister Sarah had had three fingers ripped from her hand by the threshing machine. The fingers were carefully preserved by her mother, pickled in a jam jar, stored in a cupboard, brought out occasionally for inspection. I relished the story but I was secretly happy the pickled fingers had been lost years before I was born.

Every family has its own cycle of tales, its history, its pattern. In our clan, the pattern is to walk with our heads down, looking for obstacles in our paths, knowing they will be there — lots of them. Looking back, I see generations afraid to hope and plan for happiness, afraid to enjoy the present for fear of jinxing the future. Looking back, I see a young girl who planned to leave that dreary pattern in the dust, shucking it off as easily and cleanly as a snake sheds its skin.

"Whoever said life was fair?" My mother said that to us — still does, in fact — whenever things didn't work out just so. That sense of foreboding was bred in her bone. Her father died of a stomach tumour when she was four, leaving her mother scrambling to raise a family of six. They were poor; life was a struggle. Her early life fit the pattern, reinforcing it for eventual transfer to the next generation — her children. But it all seemed crazy to me as a child. Life *did* seem to be eminently fair in our house. We shared a warm home. We were healthy and loved, treasured even. There were books, toys, food and pets. My mother and father had left the poverty of Toronto's Junction neighbourhood behind but still we couldn't escape the pattern. "Don't get your hopes up." That was another of her favourites. Still is.

Talk of childhood begins many conversations I have with friends. Our stories serve as a point of comparison when we try to figure out whether we're doing right by our own kids. By now, in our mid-forties, we've isolated the overriding patterns that define our families. The stories are rooted deep in our histories, handed down as religiously and carefully as were the silver Shabbos candlesticks sitting on my sideboard. For the most part, the stories are ordinary. You'd recognize them immediately: the devotion to authority, "friendly" competition among family members, the constant search for praise from others — to name but three. They seem innocuous enough.

When I told my friend Janet about my family's pattern and how it affected us, she shook her head. Life isn't always fair and kids need to hear that sometimes — hard knocks and injustice are part of the whole experience, she told me, emphatic and sure. She's right, I know. But in Janet's family, the acceptance of life's injustices is only a *part* of their experience, not the main event, not the defining pattern. When they become entrenched in families, patterns function as a well-trod path that is familiar, even comforting. But inevitably they offer a recourse that limits rather than enlarges.

My friends and I are intimate with our patterns. We can examine them, standing back to look them over as we might inspect artifacts in a museum case. But we can't leave them. We can't turn our backs on them. They keep returning, repeating and resurfacing when we least expect. For better or worse, they define us.

My friend Beth struggles with a pattern opposite to mine. Her mother tells stories of an idyllic childhood. Beth's grandparents were loving and attentive parents. Yes, they were dirt poor, but the family was close, loving, happy. The problems the family encountered were never their fault, never their responsibility. Landlords were thieves, bosses were knuckleheads, business partners were greedy. The reality, Beth has learned, was quite different. Her grandparents were both alcoholics, abusive to their children. But her family sticks to the pattern, every lousy trait gilded for the family history books, eyes closed tight to the reality around them. Beth's mother talks about her two alcoholic sons in glowing terms, the golden-haired boys who still like to have so much fun. So much fun, in fact, that they've both abandoned their families, lost jobs, refused to grow up.

I listen to Beth tell the stories of her family. Though she struggles to see the truth around her, she's programmed to believe in the "happily ever after" pattern she grew up with. Beth fights the pattern but she's regularly yanked back into her family's surreal world, where illness is overlooked, violence obscured, and abuse left unnamed and unexamined. She is fearful of lapsing into the "idealized world" pattern with her own children. She strives to be honest with herself and her family. She wants out of the pattern. But it's not that easy. It has a way of sneaking back in — no matter how hard she works.

I remember summer afternoons spent in the cool of my grandmother's basement, watching her piece quilts, threading needles for her as she stitched warmth for her family, listening to her stories. "Whoever said life was fair?" That was one of her expressions too. I see this pattern now for what it is: a coping strategy. By assuming that nothing good will ever come, you will never be disappointed, never have your hopes dashed. You can live your life in a steady, controlled state, avoiding risk. Why bother taking a chance? If any good comes from your throw of the dice, it will surely be erased two times over by ill fortune. So keep the dice clutched tight. My grandmother spent her summers in her basement, piecing her quilts according to the patterns that had been passed down to her. She handed them on to me, her favourite. But these were crazy quilts and I knew it. I was different. I could be the heroine of my own life, lived my own way. I wanted to try new things, take risks.

Every Saturday morning, my mother drove us to the Sarnia Public Library. "Be quiet, people are trying to read," insisted Miss Knowles, the ancient librarian, who would ask what we wanted to read that week and then make her own selections for us. She introduced me to Heidi, Anne of Green Gables and the Fossil sisters of *Ballet Shoes* fame.

My heroines were consistently perky, "the sky's the limit" girls. Anne with her carrot braids and unsinkable optimism, the Fossil sisters with their undeniable talent, Heidi with her determined kindness. They took charge, changing their lives for the better with the force of their talents and personalities. They took risks, they hoped for the best, they knew everything would turn out. I could do that too. As soon as I could get out of Sarnia, I *would* do that.

I look at these books differently now. They're still in my life, courtesy of my young daughter. I read them to her, the two of us curled up in her bed. Now I understand what attracted me to these storybook girls. My heroines were free agents, orphans all. Without a family and its patterns, they moulded their lives to suit themselves. The future was theirs to create because of their loosened ties to the past. But there's nothing unusual about these stories. Everything, everywhere told me I could shed my pattern, my history. No one, nothing told me otherwise.

We grow up learning details of the wars that birthed our country, the names of heroes, the battles they fought. All our high-school teachers told us the same thing: "If you don't learn the past you're doomed to repeat it." But what of the history of our families? The popular culture that raises us — our books, television, movies — tells us we can all be Anne, we can all find our own Green Gables. It's easy. Forget the past, seize the future you want. Yet generations repeat their patterns. Why didn't they warn me? In the answer to that question lies the true power of the pattern. I know now they couldn't give voice to a warning. The pattern had swallowed them whole, leaving them incapable of either recognizing or questioning their behaviour. This is just the way we are — simple as that.

I started saying it when my husband was in the hospital with a broken leg smashed in a skiing accident. "Whoever said life was fair?" I'd say it to the kids when they complained about yet another dinner of scrambled eggs and toast, to my husband when he moaned with pain, to myself as I fruitlessly chased sleep. This is our lot in life, this is what we deserve. It became my coping strategy, my mantra. I had reverted to type — effortlessly. Repeating my unanswerable question kept a bit of my out-of-control life in check. It was so easy to give myself over to the old pattern.

A few months after I started, my son asked me to stop. He'd just returned from summer camp, where the phrase, he told me, had been banned. Too easy, his counsellors had told their charges, to say it and then do nothing. Too easy to keep your head down. "It's not easy to stop," I told him.

"I'll keep reminding you," he replied. And he has.

Tuck Me In:
Redefining Attachment Between Mothers and Sons

Marni Jackson

When my son was four years old, I began writing a book called *The Mother Zone*, which is essentially the story of my own family, and of the hidden emotional terrain of motherhood. The parenting books I read — it was 1987 — told me far too much about nipple care and not enough about this mysterious new relationship I had embarked upon. Before I gave birth, I became fixated on buying the proper baby furniture, especially that fetish item, the "change table." My obsession with this little padded altar turned out to be metaphorically apt. Our main activity from the moment my son arrived would be changing — and not just him, but me.

As the psychoanalyst D.W. Winnicott has famously said, "There is no such thing as a baby — there is only a baby and someone else." We are always relational, he wrote, and from the beginning "the baby holds the mother as much as the mother holds the baby." I like his description of motherhood: "A mother's love is a pretty crude affair. There's possessiveness in it, appetite, even a 'drat the kid' element, there's generosity in it, and power, as well as humility. But sentimentality is outside it altogether and is repugnant to mothers." Child-care books tell you how to "manage" infancy, but the truth is that babies are powerful partners. My own book tried to describe the growth of this reciprocal twosome, from the moment of conception forward.

Now my son is sixteen. When I look back on what I wrote about motherhood then, I see that it was mostly about attachment and separation — that flicker between the oneness you try to have as mother and infant, and the two you must eventually become. But special inhibitors come into play when you are a mother with a son, and every day, it seems, this distance between you must be renegotiated. Oedipal fears still lurk. Touch in this culture is so eroticized that teachers must not ruffle heads. We don't know exactly how close we ought to be.

For instance, when should we stop tucking in our sons? At seven? Ten? Twelve? When does affection turn into that terrible, anti-male toxin, "overmothering"? When boys hit adolescence, mothers are expected to back off, because we need to let boys turn into men — a mysterious process, which, like bread rising, must happen undisturbed, in a dark warm place. (Personally, I think tucking in should have no age cut-off; in fact, if hotels were smart, they wouldn't offer a turn-down service but a tuck-in policy. I am cheered by a new ad for an airline that shows the flight attendant tucking in a tired, horizontal businessman.)

As with most crucial transitions, I cannot remember the exact night when tucking in faded in our house. One night I was probably watching Noah Wyle insert a breathing tube into someone on *ER* when I noticed that my son's bedroom light was already off. No call to come up and tuck him in. Fine. Noah Wyle needed me now.

Between the ages of twelve and fifteen, my son went about carving out his independence, but he never closed the door on us, for which I'm grateful. Twelve was the tough year.

I never worried about him getting into the usual sorts of trouble, because by nature he is cautious and responsible. I just worried about his heart. That year he disappeared into an intense friendship that ended sadly. His friend ran away from home, for good. Independent to begin with, my son responded to this loss by making sure that he controlled as much of his world as possible. He went about becoming as self-sufficient and self-defined as he could: out of sincere poultry-pity he became a vegan, which made for long bouts of label-reading in the supermarket. When cooking two-tier dinners made me cranky, he began to help out with the cooking. He hemmed his own pants, did his own laundry, built his own bike, and rode it to school all winter long. He took up dancing on stilts, and got good marks in school. He volunteered at a community store and a native school, and showed up at city hall when the government tried to cut education funds. He borrowed my old Pentax and went about the city taking pictures of lost corners and discarded furniture. He would come home on his bike happily announcing that he had found a "great piece of wood," then disappear into the basement to turn it into a sculpture. Art was his pal. He liked to climb trees and play guitar, sometimes both at the same time. There were days when I would come home and find him cleaning the fridge, digging the vegetal gunk out of the crisper (or, as the CBC's Bill Richardson calls it, the slimer). I take no credit for his domestic skills, by the way. Since I work at home I treat housework as a form of procrastination, and I dislike the idea of "making good men" in any case. Anybody with more than one child knows just how much temperament determines the way a child goes about tackling life. No, I was mostly in awe of his new creativity and connectedness to the world and I tried not to mess with it too much.

Through most of this, he talked. He talked with his father too. But when you are morphing into an adult, being able to talk to your parents will only take you so far.

Our conflicts were mostly over minor things — for

instance, at fourteen he considered shampoo a culturally imposed artifact. We had a lot of discussions about how, in an ideal society, the human head really ought to smell. We talked about the differences between beaver pelts and human hair, and the fact that sebaceous oil goes rancid. He let me smell his head before he left the house, and explained to me the clothes system of his room: things in piles are clean, items on the floor are dirty.

But the year he turned fifteen, we went through an interesting patch.

That summer he spent a month at a new camp — a vegetarian camp, his choice, where the main activity was not winning merit badges but functioning as a community. The owners lived on the property year-round and had dreams of starting an alternative school. When we visited, it looked exactly like a friendly, slightly ramshackle hippie farm, but the kids who went there thrived under the warmth and attention of the couple who ran the camp.

Our son ended up on staff for the last two weeks of summer, in a tough job that involved building a straw-bale house (this decade's version of the recycled yurt). He was earning his own room and board for the first time, and — within the safe, idyllic confines of the camp — he was free. His own man. That's when our communication began to fall apart.

Our phone calls were wary and went off the rails quickly. I was curious about this alternative family and asked lots of questions, which he read as suspicion. When the summer ended and I met him at the bus, he got off with cool eyes. He let me hug him. I had stocked the pantry with soy products. I was light-hearted and non-impinging. Still, we had problems.

Within a week, he had laid various plans to keep his new independence alive. His first plan was to ride his bicycle to Burlington, 50 kilometres away, to see a girl named Fennel, whom he had met, needless to say, at the vegetarian camp. This was not a girlfriend, he informed me, but a good friend, and he felt like an expedition. The trip involved highways with traffic, and even though he rode his bike everywhere, summer and winter, I thought it was too dangerous. I was also a little hurt that he was trying to put miles between us so soon. I said no.

But my son was now a veteran of conflict resolution workshops. "Well," he said, "we need to keep talking about this." And in the end, after research into bike trails and much map consultation, I let him go. It took him four hours to make the trip, and he got "a little lost" along the way. He had a great day hanging around with Fennel, which I was relieved to learn was a nickname, and he took the train back the next day.

Then, several days later, another issue of autonomy arose. He went off to visit another camp friend, a girl who was also a schoolmate. He called home that evening to say he'd like to sleep over, because more camp friends were coming to visit the following day and it would save him biking home at night. It all sounded reasonable, but I didn't even know the last name of this friend, or her parents, and his nomadic ways were getting on my nerves. I told him no. "I think you should sleep at home," I said.

"But it's fine with her mother," he said. "I'll sleep on the rec room floor."

"This is your home," I said rather lamely. "This is where you sleep."

He biked home several hours later and stalked in, very upset with me. "I probably would have come home anyway," he said, "but you didn't give me the chance to decide."

"You weren't saying, I want you here at home, you were just trying to have a hold on me," he said, with his usual alarming insight. "I haven't done anything to make you not trust me, and it makes me feel bad when you don't."

I was shocked. He was right. What he wanted was to stay close to me, but to have more freedom — he didn't automatically see our closeness and his autonomy as incompatible. My response had been to withdraw emotionally a bit — to give him space, I thought — and at the same time to exert control over him, to rattle his leash. He was asking me to treat him more like a person, and in response to my fears and worries I was pulling rank as traditional mom — which, come to think of it, I've never been.

"So, what should I have said on the phone?" I eventually asked him.

"You should have said, 'I'd like you to come home, but use your own judgement,'" he said, adding glumly, "Then I probably would have come home."

Now I still think I had a point. It's not so terribly clinging to say no to a sleepover under mysterious circumstances. But right or wrong was not the point; it was how we negotiated that caused problems. And I realized then that my worries over being the mother of a son have always been about whether I'm in too close — "enmeshment" in the analytical phrase — or whether, in response to those worries, I withdraw too far.

"It's bound to happen," friends say, meaning that boys inevitably leave their mothers. "A boy's a son till he gets a wife, a daughter's a daughter for the rest of your life." But perhaps the idea that mothers should brace ourselves for separation and for surly, remote boys is as much a figment of our culture as the notion that we shouldn't be too close to our sons in the first place. Our attachment to our sons as babies is tinged with the fear that overmothering will somehow weaken and undermine their growth as men. We may think we've outgrown Freud, but the spell of the Oedipal complex lingers on — the belief that only through renunciation of the loving mother and identification with the aggressor father can a boy become a man. This has set up a wrenching paradox: If we are truly loving mothers to our sons, we must work at withholding our love.

My theory about mothers and sons is simple. The closer and more physical the bond between a mother and son is from the beginning, the greater the independence both can enjoy later on. If a mother withholds her warmth and love from her son out of a fear of "spoiling him" or ruining him with her mother-love, the son can only feel what that means — that she fears the power of the feminine in herself, and in him as well. He ends up losing more of her than he needs to, and perhaps shutting down that mother side in himself. In fact, the classic male teenager's rejection of Mom may not be his initiative at all. Maybe it is a response to a more subtle, pre-emptive withdrawal on his mother's part. (This idea has been explored in several recent books, specifically *The Courage to Raise Good Men* by Olga Silverstein and Beth Rashbaum, and *Real Boys: Rescuing Boys from the Myths of Manhood*, by William Pollack. Both describe how the culture encourages the withdrawal of the mother in a number of ways.)

Then there is the business of physical affection as sons turn into People Who Shave. Tricky. Touch has primarily sexual overtones in our society. Incest, abuse, harassment — sex has become the bogeyman under every bed. Our suspicion of sexuality means that we associate physical intimacy first of all with sex between adults. As a result, the intensity of that first erotic bond with an infant sooner or later begins to feel "inappropriate" (the Clinton word), or dangerous.

This means that, as our sons grow up, there is a tremor of uncertainty in how we hold them, and in the messages that go between our bodies and theirs. We associate intense love with sexual urges, and the culture defines sex as potentially disruptive, uncontrollable, predatory and devouring. We think our job as parents is to keep the wolf of sex safely outside the circle of the family — rather than accepting that family relations are embedded in the physical too: Think of those nights when everybody piles on the couch together to watch TV. We forget that the more affectionate we are with our sons, the sturdier their sense of self will be — and that a strong sense of self is the best protection against sexual exploitation by others.

I see the modern family as both oversexualized in its fears and undererotic in its behavior. We fear that touch will lead to clinging and dependence, to a weakening of the self, when in fact it helps define and strengthen us, and lay the foundation for autonomy. "Holding is the basis for what gradually becomes a self-experiencing being," Winnicott believes. Holding leads to wholeness.

And as the mother shapes the baby, the baby is busy reshaping the mother. Instead of seeing touch as a kind of potential robbery — which incest and other forms of sexual exploitation truly are — we need to reimagine touch as the first language.

Ironically, if a mother is afraid of overmothering, her child receives an entirely different kind of message; the withholding of affection, rather than close contact, becomes sexualized instead. It is the self-censoring mother who is more likely to set up an erotic tension in the family, the sort that leads to a pattern of interdependency followed by rebellion. In other words, too much closeness is usually not the problem between mothers and sons — it is the anxieties around closeness, most of them culturally imposed, that can lead to a damaging distance between mother and son.

Ah, but don't let's blame the self-censoring mother, who is only reflecting the dominant ideas in our society about touch and intimacy. Freud's theory, after all, was that everybody in the family from infancy onwards is dying to sleep with each other. He saw this as the very infrastructure of family relations. Boys fall in love with their mothers, and they can only clear the path to manhood by rejecting the "relational" world of the mother and joining the "achieving" world of the father. Any mother of a doting four-year-old boy passing through the stage when he wants to "marry" her will recognize that there is some truth in this. But the paradox Freud set up was that mothers are both all-powerful and potentially destructive — so the good mother must erase herself in order to raise a sturdy man. This double bind continues to saddle women with guilt and ambivalence about their roles as mothers.

Ironically enough, trying to make a boy into a little man

does exactly that — creates a son who is forced to impersonate masculinity, as we narrowly define it, rather than a child allowed to discover who he is.

Winnicott takes a calmer view of things. He makes the mother's body into a kind of nautical marker — the reliable object that shows the child where he is on the map. In Freud's world, the mother-as-potential-Jezebel is not exactly a reassuring figure. But in Winnicott's, the mother's subconscious motives are not as important as her physical, animal, flawed, "good-enough" presence. In other words, what is crucial is not so much our teaching and controlling, but the setting we provide for a baby's active discovery of his mother. There is no need to limit love. Parents don't have to censor themselves in order to toughen up their kids. As my son put it, "That's what the world is for."

We have moved from the idea of children as miniature adults and property (the Victorian view) to the view of them of the embodiment of our subconscious desires (the Freudian view) and are now moving — fitfully — towards the Winnicottian notion of babies and mothers who exist in equilibrium.

In other words, growth is a co-operative venture. The mother with her new son is not a flustered CEO trying to keep her tiny new employee happy and in line. She is involved in a dance.

When I look back on my early years with Casey, I realize that I managed to successfully pull off what Winnicott would call a "failure to adapt." What I failed to adapt to was the prevailing wisdom of childrearing. In North America, we think good babies are babies who sleep through the night, alone in their own cribs. Our goal is to make them verbal, accomplished and independent. Only half of American mothers breastfeed their babies, and for an average of five months. By the age of two months, American babies spend 65 percent of their time alone.

Despite the recent debates over "co-sleeping," many parents still see sleeping with babies as a lax, almost shameful thing to prolong. Our goal as parents is to organize, control and teach.

A recent book by anthropologist Meredith Small called *Our Babies, Ourselves* has some fascinating things to say about the way different cultures raise their infants. In 67 percent of cultures around the world, children sleep in the company of others. The !Kung San people of Botswana sleep with their infants, carry them into the fields in slings on their hips, and let the babies seek the breast whenever they want. Their infants spend more than half their time in passive physical contact with adults. They do not grow up in special cribs and four-wheel-drive strollers, like tiny real-estate moguls, but upright, in the adult world, where their needs are met as soon as they express them. It's both a softer and a harder world than the one in which our babies grow up. It sometimes seems as if our culture would rather teach babies than touch them.

I found that the best way to muddle through motherhood was to stay as close as I could to the physical fact of my son, who seemed to know how to lead me through this dance. One factor that influenced the level of intimacy I had with my son was arbitrary, yet in a way fortuitous: he had asthma, including a long bout of illness, one winter when he was six. This meant that we spent many nights sitting on the bathroom floor with the hot shower on, the pages of his books wrinkling up, as we whiled away hours of coughing and throwing up.

I felt quite different as a mother during these sick times. I had licence to just be there with him, in an animal way, doing nothing. During the day there were all those mother things to do — overseeing his nutrition, encouraging him to like books, taking him to playgroups. But when he was ill, I would lie down with him to help him get to sleep, and I could swear that my breathing helped him breathe. My calmness could calm him. I felt that my proximity alone was crucial — not organizing, not disciplining, just vaguely bored, loving proximity. There was a comradely atmosphere between us as he coughed and I whacked his back or read him books. I never felt he was clinging, and he never felt I was being oppressive. I have good memories of those peaceful times in the lee of illness. And I think they freed me from the sometimes phony agenda of being a Good Mother.

"So much depends on the way the mother holds the baby, and let it be emphasized that this is not something that can be taught," Winnicott said. (Lest we elevate poor Winnicott too much, rest assured that you don't want to know about his own marriage, or even his views of feminism.) What *is* taught is a lingering anxiety. "The fear of alienating a male child from 'his' culture seems to go deep," wrote the poet and esssayist Adrienne Rich, "even among women who reject that culture for themselves every day of their lives." (Considering that there are, at last count, seventy-two different kinds of psychopathology attributed to mothers, this is no wonder.)

The message of our culture to the mothers of boys is not to hold, but to withhold. In overcoming this, we're just beginning to discover the true contours of the relationship between mothers and sons.

When I was vetting this piece with my son, I asked him what his concept of masculinity was. "Frankly, Mom, gender's really more your issue than mine," he said airily. Next, I asked him if he wanted to give me some of his thoughts on this detachment business. "Do you really think that's a good idea, when we're right in the thick of it?" was his reply. Then he went off to his stilt-walking class.

How Do
I Look?

Joan Clark

When I was seventeen I began smearing cherry jelly bean on my lips in lieu of the lipstick my father had forbidden me to wear because, he said, he did not want me looking like a hussy. I had come across the word "hussy" in my reading and knew it to be a woman with loose morals, a scarlet lady, a trollop. I did not know why my father got it into his head that my wearing lisptick was immoral; my mother and older sister wore lipstick and their morals were far from slack. I did know that the notion came from my father's Cape Breton Presbyterianism and from a wish to protect me from overweening vanity. As my mother put it, he did not want to turn my head.

There was little danger of that. My parents rarely commented on my appearance except to caution me to stand up straight. Occasionally my mother would pass on a received compliment. The one I remember most clearly came from Mrs. Roper, the chinless, dumpy woman who worked in the stationery store that in our town passed as a bookstore. Mrs. Roper told my mother that I was better looking than I used to be.

Backhanded though this compliment was, I was grateful for it and did not stop to wonder what I used to look like before Mrs. Roper's comment. I did not dwell on the thought that my mother had not passed on a compliment so much as a sober observation of fact. Mrs. Roper's comment gave me hope. Tall and skinny — at five foot eight I weighed one hundred pounds — like many teenaged girls I nourished the secret hope that one day I could be beautiful.

This did happen once, on my high school graduation night. On that occasion my grandfather looked at the strapless dress of layered net my sister had sewn for me and called me a princess. Later the same night my sister's friend, Charlotte, said I looked beautiful. I put these words inside the fortune teller's ball where I stored my erratic and ambivalent stirrings for romance.

My father could not protect me from physical vanity. As soon as I set foot on the university campus I became rampantly vain. The presence, at last, of all those real men (older and, I thought, more experienced) set me to brushing my hair one hundred strokes a night, camouflaging pimples with beige acne cream, arranging my banlon sweater so that my breasts looked just so. All this fussing was time consuming, some of the sessions lasting up to half an hour. I was trying to achieve a look I hoped my father would approve of — a soft, natural beauty, nothing tartish or cheap. This was the Breck look of the shampoo ads, which aimed for an understated, virginal beauty.

Given the fact that I had little money, it would have been simpler to have abandoned lipstick, powder and blonde hair rinse and go on dates just as I was. Such a thought never occurred to me. This was, after all, the mating game, a game I enthusiastically embraced. I relished the complications of attaining beauty. And I believed that my looks could be improved by way of self-attention. Wasn't it logical that all those hours spent in front of the mirror would result in the enhancement of my appearance? These attentions were undertaken even if my date was a stroll alongside a brook or a ramble through an orchard. On those occasions I went for the casual, country look — the scarf or sweater contrived to look thrown on, ditto the artfully tousled hair. Fortunately I had "big" hair that lent itself to looking windblown. The women at my college continued this casual look throughout the winter; no matter how fierce the wind, wearing hats was verboten, coats were left unbuttoned, and even in the bitter cold our legs were bare (and blue). Not for us those ugly beige nylons.

There were of course lapses in these prostrations to vanity, if only because I needed time to catch my breath and renew my resolve. These plateaus of doubt usually came to me in the basement of the library where, every morning by nine o'clock, I would be huddled against the radiator in the theology reading room, beneath a small window through which I watched the intermittent passage of feet — an occupation consistent with reading Plato's *Allegory of the Cave.* I remember these interludes of reading and study as hours of bliss: the smell of drying wool and dry books, the gulping of hot water pipes, the luminous rectangle of light falling on my page.

Though I was not interested in reading the theology books on the shelves and was unacquainted with anyone who did, in the solitude of that room I would sometimes imagine myself as the wife of a theologue or, even better, a missionary. There I stood in an ill-fitting dress, my hair cropped short, my face scrubbed and beaming as I strove to be of service to others and to God. At other times I would imagine myself as a pure-hearted nun who had given herself over to a life of contemplation and prayer. These imaginings fed my appetite for melodrama. They were the Presbyterian version of sackcloth and ashes, a reminder that my attentions to vanity, not to mention men, were misguided and shallow. If I continued this folly, not only would my grades suffer but, as my father feared, I would become a fallen woman or — and this was far worse to my way of thinking — a dim-witted blonde. Should I not reform before it was too late? Perhaps I ought to stop wearing lipstick and powder altogether. Perhaps I ought to model myself after those dowdy girls in residence who did not give their appearance a second thought — girls who had so little vanity or self-preservation that they did not often wash their hair. But these false aspirations and feckless doubts vanished the moment I was called to the telephone and asked for a date.

I continued to follow the slavish rituals of surface grooming until I married and took myself out of the mating game. It came as a relief to slough them off to make room for my new preoccupations. Except for a pass with lipstick and comb, I was unwilling to give time to looking any better than I did. In any case, within a few years of marrying I had children to look after; there was no time for self-ministrations. Even a daytime bath was out of the question. I barely had time to wash my hair, let alone use a blonde rinse. Once I fell into writing, which I did after the birth of my eldest son, I was unwilling to give leftover time to anything that did not feed the Word.

Which is not to suggest that my nods to vanity entirely disappeared. When the doorbell rang I tied a kerchief over my unwashed hair, hooked my bra and made a swipe with the lipstick. When I put on nylons, earrings and dress before going out for the occasional evening, I would say to my husband, "How do I look?" My husband obligingly would tell me that I looked fine or lovely or ravishing, whatever it took to get us out of the house on time.

After my children left home I had time — if I wanted to use it — to improve my appearance. Now my efforts to improve were attempts to look not better but younger, or at least not to look my age. I was not unhappy with my age, but I began noticing that if I disclosed it I was treated differently, too often as a matron or as somebody's mother. I was addressed as ma'am. I did not take kindly to this, not wanting to mother anyone except my children. I did not like the assumptions made about aging, especially the one articulated by writers and seized upon by critics that by age sixty a writer's best working years were over. It was not until I was confronted with ageism that I thought of attention to physical vanity as a strategy for survival.

By now, of course, I had met dozens of people who carried physical vanity further than I had ever been prepared to go: the glam who wouldn't dash to the superette without a forty-minute fine-tuning job; the woman who waited until after her lover fell asleep before removing eyelashes and wig; the man with gold medallions who had a chest-plate implant beneath his unbuttoned shirt. I had seen countless magazine makeovers and marvelled at the sacrifices that women especially were prepared to make at the altar of beauty: tooth filing and straightening, chin and eye tucks, silicone breasts and liposuctions, diet and exercise regimes intended to achieve twigginess. All of this made my father's old-fashioned attempts not to turn my head quaint and even touching, almost — though not entirely — beside the point.

The hole in my father's discourse is obvious. Contrary to leading to my downfall, physical vanity has probably done me more good than harm. My early efforts to improve my looks may not have been commendable but they were strategically sound. If I had known that at seventeen, I would have defied my father, bought a tube of Cherry Ripe and eaten the jelly beans. To a point, physical vanity is not only a pragmatic response to the realities with which we live and work, but is an incentive to take better care of our health. I suspect that being vain helps us live longer.

Nevertheless, when I apply lip liner and pluck chin hair, there is someone with me in the mirror, standing slightly behind me. She is wearing a baggy shirt to cover the bulge. Her grey hair is cropped short. She wears no eyeshadow or mascara. Her gaze is as clear and guileless as a nun's. She is waiting, though not with impatience. She knows that I am travelling steadily toward a room where the only objects on top of the dresser are a bar of soap, a toothbrush and a comb.

Victory

Claudia Casper

It was the year of go-go boots, white mid-calf boots that zipped up the side. It was Centennial Year, the one hundredth anniversary of Confederation, and my grade four classmates all returned from Expo '67 in Montreal with miniature red-and-gold Chinese lanterns. Goldie Hawn's giggle was new, miniskirts were in, the Beatles reigned, images of the Vietnam War were burned in people's minds. We knew nuclear bombs might end the world.

It was that year that Sharon Fink asked to see a bracelet I had stolen. The bracelet was made of neon pink and green plastic lozenges threaded with elastic to fit snugly on the wrist. I'd seen it attached to cardboard backing hanging from a chrome pin in Kresge's and recognized that it possessed qualities I wanted: it was cool, modern, grown up. If I took it and wore it, I could transfer those qualities to myself.

Sharon kept the bracelet all morning, through recess, then handed it back at lunchtime, broken.

"It's a stupid bracelet. Besides, you stole it anyway."

I sat. My hands and legs felt suddenly hot.

"You broke it on purpose, didn't you?"

"You want to make something of it?"

"Yes," I said, surprised.

Sharon had been one of the girls who'd dragged a slightly plump classmate, Debbie, to a lane off school grounds the week before. Two of the girls had held Debbie by the wrists and pulled her taut, while a third, Nancy, ran and kicked her in the stomach. They did this until Debbie had an asthma attack.

Our fight was set for the next day after school, just outside school grounds so the teachers couldn't break it up. I got my stepfather to give me a boxing lesson. I expected to lose.

At the appointed time kids gathered by the fence. Sharon and I faced each other awkwardly, then Sharon stepped back, rushed forward and pushed me by the shoulders. I reeled, regained my balance, pushed back. She grabbed my shirt and tried to throw a punch, but I twisted away and punched her in the stomach, and she fell down. She got up crying and said she was going home to get her big brother. I couldn't believe it was so easy.

The next day I wore my favourite outfit: go-go boots, a pink corduroy miniskirt with a wide shiny white belt, and a white turtleneck T-shirt. I went to school feeling victorious.

Another girl in our class, Cathy, claimed she was a model. She always had the latest fashions first, and she lived in a new apartment building with her mother, who was young and pretty. Cathy announced that she was going to be in the new Simpson Sears catalogue. Every season my friend Susan and I pored over this catalogue, deciding which outfits we were going to beg our mothers for.

When it arrived we couldn't find Cathy in it anywhere. Still basking in the glow of my victory, I challenged her: "You're lying. You're not in that catalogue."

"Yes, I am. I'm on pages 24 and 27."

Susan and I went home and looked. Those pages only had

pictures of skinny girls from the waist down modelling underwear. The next day I challenged Cathy to a fight.

After school Cathy came out the girl's entrance with her friend Debbie and they hovered at the top of the stairs. I was down in the schoolyard. I started walking toward her.

All the kids in the schoolyard spontaneously gathered behind me and began to chant, "Go Claudia go!" My eyes sparkled as I marched forward. I thought, this must be what war feels like. I walked up the stairs feeling powerful, dominant, confident. When I reached the top Debbie said, "Cathy doesn't want to fight. Anyway, you can't fight here. It's school grounds."

I thought about that, then gave Cathy a contemptuous shove and walked back down the stairs.

Recently the media have been focussing on the so-called new phenomenon of increasing violence among girls. Subtextual questions lurk in these pieces: Is this what feminism has brought us? Are girls today adopting male behaviour? Et cetera. Whenever the media begins discussing a behaviour as new, I suspect it's something old in a marginally new form. The same old thing doesn't sell papers.

Scientists are just beginning to study hierarchies and dominance displays among females. Jane Goodall is still one of the first scientists to systematically examine dominant behaviour among female chimpanzees. Among women writers there has been discourse about the experience of being dominated, and of evading domination, but rarely of being dominant. For good reason. Confessions in this area arouse hostility and make friends suspicious.

In the story of my schoolyard scraps, clothes are an important conveyor of dominance. The coveted object, the stomped-on object, the object that bestowed power on its owner, was a bracelet. The response to victory was display — not with the bracelet, which was beyond repair, but with a treasured pink corduroy miniskirt and go-go boots — display in the manner of a peacock, gorilla or seahorse, a silent, colourful, textile roar.

When I went to write this story I couldn't remember why I had picked a fight with Cathy. I didn't dislike her; she was never mean to me. I figured there must have been a precipitating incident I had forgotten. Now I understand why it was her I challenged. She had the best clothes in the class. I was challenging her for her crown. She was the princess.

I don't know if I actually gained ascendency through the confrontation, but I probably tarnished the sheen of her feathers. I remember her still looking great in a way I couldn't, but more nervously.

I was proud of beating Sharon, but not of diminishing Cathy, if I did. Yet a smile escapes as I write, unmasking too earnest a tone, because, although I'd censure behaviour like that in my own children, I still wouldn't trade that moment when, with the sea of classmates behind me, I marched up the girls' staircase.

What I wear is frequently a matter of indifference, but there are occasions when clothes express and augment my confidence, or lack thereof. There are the nights when I eviscerate my closet finding nothing to wear; the image reflected in the mirror too exposed or too dowdy, too flashy or drab. These are nights when I am not content to be meek but a failure of nerve prevents me from strutting. I retreat to the little black dress and medium-heeled pumps, or the dark pantsuit with low-heeled boots, coasting, waiting for the next sensation of mastery in anything — my work, governing my own impulses, playing squash or purchasing a new garment to give me that transforming little rush of power.

On those glory nights, a frisson reminiscent of the thrill of battle returns as I don clothes — suggestive of royalty, with expensive tailoring, saturated colours or luxurious textures: velvet, satin, silk, leather, fine wool. I put on high heels, red lipstick, scent; I polish and sharpen my nails, highlight the gleam in my eyes, deepen the flush in my cheeks and step out, dressed to kill.

As an adult one hopes to experience a more diffuse sense of dominance — not triumph over an individual but a sense of triumph vis-à-vis a collective benchmark. Furthermore, one hopes to remember that all measurement is illusion. Yet even in enlightened moments, when the base pleasures and pains of measurement have faded away, the thrill of dressing up and stepping out on the town remains primitive, fun and never entirely harmless.

Middle-Aged Musings on Retirement

Janet E. Bradley

I like my job. In fact, I really like my job. Twenty-five years in the work force and not a single boring day. How many people can say that? I am fifty years old, in great health, active, fit — a high-energy kind of person. I have no pension plan and only a little savings, and my kids are just starting university. I am, in a nutshell, not what you would consider a prime candidate for retirement. Yet, more and more, thoughts of retirement keep floating through my mind. I have these flashes (hot, some would say) regularly and not only when I have had such a bad day that I just want to pack the whole thing in. These thoughts are never about money, the getting and saving of it. They are more of the mid-life-crisis variety: What would retirement do to me? Would it change who I am?

My thoughts about retirement usually start something like this: I quit my job, cold turkey, and then I find joy in the simple pleasures of home. Someone who has rarely ironed a shirt or baked a pie, in her reveries, is convinced that there could be happiness in those very things women have considered as drudgeries since the beginning of time. I think if I could shop in the market, make wonderful meals, garden, paint the kitchen, I could be content. I would like to have the time to contemplate travel rather than rush at it in a frenzy as I do now. I want to spend time with my mom and dad, make meals for my friends, write thank-you notes, just read the newspaper.

I get this notion that I've missed out on a life that might have been mine. I deliberately rejected the path women had trod for years and headed — yes, eagerly plunged — into a world traditionally held by men. I so firmly believed that a meaningful life would be found where the men were, where the jobs were. But now, after twenty-five years in the workplace, I wonder — what did I lose? Can I still make up for missed experiences?

It's probably not surprising that I feel uneasy now and then about having devoted so much time to the office at the expense of my home. For my generation, the transition of women working outside the home actually happened quite quickly. Most of us growing up in the 1950s had mothers who made it their job to create a warm and nurturing environment. Housewives. We came home from school to a perfectly maintained home and sat down, as a family, to a well-balanced meal. Even the *Leave it to Beaver* scenes we watched on television taught us how to be. I was programmed — indoctrinated, some would say — into this role that, historically and even biologically, was supposed to be mine.

Of course, as a working woman I simply cannot pull the same kind of domestic idyll off. I tear home from the office around 7:00 p.m., wondering if there is any frozen meal I can microwave for dinner. Our house, always cluttered, needs paint and decoration, not to mention a good cleaning. I haven't had guests to dinner in years. I know the well-managed home is out of my grasp and yet I seem to have occasional twinges of something I know is not guilt, but just might be regret. It's at moments like these that thoughts of retirement nudge their way into the corners of my consciousness, and I see myself shopping for perfect vegetables, preparing wonderful meals, planting a perfect garden.

It may be simple burnout that leads to these ideas of retirement. Here I am, like so many women, trying to do the job it took both our parents to do in the past. When I walk through the office of my law firm, I rarely see women hanging around, just chatting. Every second counts. "Women lawyers," I hear the staff say, "driven, humourless, unfriendly." But we have so little time to get it all done. A break in the workday is used to buy toothpaste or take the kids to the doctor. There is no slowdown time at the end of the day. It's out the door to pick up the kids, make the meals and clean the kitchen counter. Feminist resolve notwithstanding, my friends and I puzzle at our failure to train the men in our lives to assume an equal share of the housework. Our husbands see taking out the garbage as a major contribution. They make a big deal about occasionally making dinner for the kids by ordering pizza. After twenty years of living with the same appliances, my friend's husband called her at the office last week to ask how to turn on the oven!

So it may be plain exhaustion prompting these retirement ideas — a need to simplify life. "Those retirement notions of yours," says my friend, "are yearnings for a state of grace after all those years of chaos."

But then I think, whoa — hold on. Could I really just quit my job and be content? What about the other influences from my past? It's true my mother was an accomplished homemaker. But I also remember her boredom. She, who had always wanted to go to university, was determined that my sister and I would get an education and get off the farm. Frustrated mothers may have been the real driving force behind the feminist movement.

And then there were all those formative years in university spent strategizing, finding ways to reject our mothers' roles and seek our "rightful" places in the world. My friends and I were so self-righteous in our belief that professions and careers would make our lives meaningful and worthwhile.

We were not wrong in this belief. It's much easier to feel worthy in the workplace than the home. A patient, a customer, a client, a boss, will let you know when you did a good job. It is rewarding to win a court case, complete a transaction, be sought out by a new client. Making money for the work that we do is psychologically gratifying. How, I wonder, do women with no jobs outside the home maintain their self-esteem? It's hard work to keep a house maintained; it takes hours to plan and prepare meals for a family. Yet kids cannot understand a parent's dismay at seeing knapsacks, books, soccer shoes, coats and other debris left in waves as they drift from room to room. And how many meals are left uneaten or gulped down on their way out the door? In the home, all of that work is so often taken for granted: expected. There's rarely an expression of gratitude for a job well done.

Could a woman like me, then, be content finding herself suddenly in the home, when so much of her energy has always been directed towards the office and its many rewards? Could I give my job up?

Women, it seems to me, are torn in all directions in terms of work and what it means to them. For men, it appears to be much more straightforward. They see it as their right to devote their lives to their jobs. Men define themselves in large part by the work they do. Their self-esteem is primarily generated by a job.

But we can't take our cues from men. For women, it's not so simple. Our jobs are not the predominant factors in how we identify who we are. Work is clearly important to our self-esteem. But, paradoxically, the workplace often generates the greatest feelings of uncertainty in women. Being "new" to most professions, many of us never really feel a job is rightfully ours. My friends freely admit to each other that they often feel as if only by the grace of God do they have their jobs. They believe that if they can do the job, anyone can. "Tomorrow the hoax may be up," is how one friend puts it. Women lack that male sense of entitlement. This paradox is what really separates men and women in the workplace. For women, work is both a positive and negative force in the development of confidence and self-esteem. It tugs at us from two different directions.

Women are not as consumed by their jobs as men are. Listen, for example, to the different ways in which men and women talk to each other. Men tend to talk to men about their jobs, their successes, their achievements, their conquests. Work draws them together. It is who they are.

Eavesdrop on women's conversations and you'll hear a different story. Women rarely talk about their work in social settings. Or, at least not the actual work they do. For example, every day at 6:00 a.m. I join five other women from my neighbourhood for a "power walk." This ritual is supposed to keep our bodies fit, but is probably more beneficial for our minds. (My husband is not too far off the mark when he claims that only our tongues are properly exercised.) We are all in the legal profession but we never talk about our cases. This is not for confidentiality reasons; work just never seems to come up. Our work may provide the experience that gives rise to some of the issues we discuss, but the nuts and bolts, the details about our jobs, are rarely the focus of discussion. Work enters the conversation only in an abstract way — how people handled themselves in a situation, the emotions generated, the feelings expressed.

Given this less strong identification with work, then, you would think that a woman could leave the work force more readily than a man. But I wonder if that is so.

Women may need their jobs as much as men do, although for different reasons. A job validates us — or is this only my impression, based on the male values I am surrounded with? Work certainly gives us power in our interactions and relationships with men, putting us on an equal footing that is difficult to achieve otherwise. It's not just that we get respect from men for doing the jobs they do, but that we have knowledge about these jobs and so cannot be readily intimidated or patronized. This validation is important in the workplace; but it is essential in the home. We may not get equal help with the housework but our jobs put us on some sort of equal footing. They also reduce the degree to which men rely on us to look after their needs — a reliance that casts us in a subservient role. Work gives us not only some financial independence but a sense of freedom, of empowerment, of being in charge of our own lives.

While I don't define myself in terms of my job, I wonder if, without my work, I would be somehow different. I might not be as strong, self-reliant, independent. If so, why? Would my relationship with my friends change? Two recent insights have got me wondering. Chatting on a ski lift with a long-time friend from my university days I bemoaned my daily chaos, suggesting that I might quit my job and "get a life." Many things would change, but, I asserted, I would still have what counts: my family, my friends. "Oh, I'm not sure that's true with respect to your friends," she replied. "Your job is a big part of the package that makes you who you are." I was stunned.

Consider the experience of a professional woman I know who decided to quit her job and stay home after the birth of her child. She still gets together with her friends, one-on-one, but says she doesn't feel comfortable with her former professional friends in a group, for she has little in common with them to discuss. That statement really bothered me. How could she feel that way? Couldn't she remember the usual chatter: stories about the weird dinner party, the impossible husband, the great ski trip? Nothing had changed in terms of her contribution to the topics that fill our social lives. Yet all of a sudden she thought her place had been lost.

There is, I suppose, some shame in occupying my mind with matters such as these, which are insignificant in the greater scheme of life. But surely such concerns about retirement cannot be uncommon among the first generation of women to have commonly worked outside the home.

My sister offers three comments about these ideas: First, such thoughts could only occupy the mind of the truly privileged. For most people, she points out, money would be the only consideration. If people had enough money, then they would leave the work force and go on to more worthwhile pursuits. Second, they reflect the thinking of someone completely caught up in her job. A job, she reminds me, is after all only one part of the puzzle of life. And finally, these are the views of someone still too young to reflect properly on the subject.

She's probably right; she usually is. But what can I say? They are, after all, just thoughts that clutter my brain, just middle-aged musings.

The Imaginary Woman

Betty Jane Wylie

I once knew a little boy who wouldn't drink his milk, a common situation. His mother made literal use of an imaginary solution, tinting the boy's milk with food colouring. Then she'd say casually, "The green cow was here this morning." Sure enough, the milk would be green, or pink or whatever colour the day's cow was, and the kid would drink the milk.

Such imaginary solutions don't last forever, of course, but women have always known that all solutions are temporary as well as imaginary. No matter what the reality is, they make do, conforming to a worldwide, centuries-old tacit agreement, a benign covenant that keeps the world from falling apart. Women wrap scarves and encouragement around the throats of their brave warriors and send them out to battle, praying for their safe return and making the beds and pudding while they are gone. Mind you, duvets and Jell-O have reduced their praying time, and often, now, the women are out doing battle, too. Still, comfort and order have been kept and dull routine maintained. Every woman is a skilled pataphysician.

Pataphysics is the science of the particular: relating each event to the singularity that makes it an exception. The hard part is that everything, every single day, is an exception.

I read a story about a man who was spreading honey on his toast when the phone rang. In answering he transferred a dab of honey to the phone. From the phone the honey spread to a light switch, then to a doorknob, until all the surfaces of the house were sticky with honey. His only solution was to move. I used to tell this cautionary tale to my children when they were eating pancakes with syrup. When they left the table I'd say, "Wash your hands so we won't have to move." Now I say it to my grandchildren. This is not progress, this is life, and a perfect example of a woman's practical use of applied pataphysics.

I first came across the word, and the profession, in a science-fiction story about a colony travelling through deep space to another galaxy. It was a major trip, endless and empty enough to drive anyone insane. The ship, therefore, was equipped with trained pataphysicians, people adept in projecting, for example, the dull, boring, graffiti-laden banality of a New York subway train for others to see. I realized as I read the story that women everywhere have this amazing pataphysical ability. We are all on Spaceship Earth hurtling through the blackness of eternity. Women keep the ship on course by acknowledging dull routine, providing succour and soup as required, protecting and defending families from the terrors outside with soothing bromides and instant solutions.

"Pataphysics is the ultimate defence," wrote Alfred Jarry, the nineteenth-century French playwright considered the father of the Theatre of the Absurd. He thought up pataphysics as a schoolboy joke, forming a Collège de Pataphysique and inviting his friends to join. He didn't ask any women, but it didn't matter. Without realizing it, Jarry had stumbled on some of the laws of womanhood, pataphysical rules, which are not after all the nonsense the foolish schoolboy thought they were.

Women have practiced pataphysics for centuries. Now, as we move into the twenty-first century, we are doing our best to dump pataphysics, fearing its long-term effects. The fear is justified. In the nineteenth century the "Woman Question" analyzed the position of literate Anglo-American Victorian females and its effect on society. Farm women, factory girls and prostitutes were excluded, being too poor and too busy to enjoy ill health, faulty uteruses or expensive diagnoses. The sixteenth-century English proverb was recalled, the one describing woman as "a shrew in the kitchen, a saint in the church, an angel at the board and an ape in the bed." She was transformed into the Angel in the House.

Novelist Henry James defined his mother this way. "She was our life, she was the house, she was the keystone of the arch . . . no more of an angel today than she had always been." What man wouldn't love a woman like that: loving, self-sacrificing, the perfect stay-at-home Angel?

Virginia Woolf described the Angel for a slightly later generation: "If there was chicken, she took the leg; if there was a draught she sat in it — in short she was so constituted that she never had a mind or a wish of her own, but preferred to sympathize always with the minds and wishes of others . . . every house had its Angel."

By the late nineteenth century, that poor Angel was trying to assert herself out of the house. The writings of American feminist Margaret Fuller (1810–1850, her father's only son) opened the argument, claiming a special-but-equal role for women. Gradually, the Angels won a short leash and began to perform distinctive but feminine tasks outside the home as nurses, teachers and social workers, all the while continuing to work as waitresses, prostitutes and indentured (read: married) servants. In other words, they were practising pataphysicans — patas, for short. Pataphysics is too selfless a science for anyone to practise without the risk of losing the self entirely.

"Pataphysics," wrote Jarry, "is an inner attitude, a discipline, a science and an art, which allows each [woman] to live [her] life as an exception, proving no law but [her] own."

This inner attitude enables a woman to tell her skinny, brace-toothed daughter that she looks lovely before she goes to a birthday party, and to believe it, thereby giving her daughter self-confidence. It empowers a mother to confront teachers and principals and school boards when she battles to keep her recalcitrant son in the classroom instead of in the principal's office, and to demand extra tutorial help for him. It energizes a housewife to shop for bargains, feed her four kids and a husband on a budget for two, dress them all in decent clothes and shoes, and still have enough left over to sew new curtains for the living room. The attitude sustains a wife's unswervable loyalty and pride in her husband, no matter how defeated he may feel. Some people call this love, but it's really pataphysics.

Pataphysical discipline is not so much the discipline of other people as the discipline of self: doing the Twenty-Minute Workout without a personal trainer; taking a university degree credit by credit, finishing as the first grandchild enters school; working a sixty-to-eighty-hour week at two jobs, one inside and one outside the home, and still taking time to deliver soup to a neighbour who's ill and to run the winter pageant at the local school, church, synagogue or community club. I look back on what the women of my generation did and wonder what we thought we were doing, and how we survived. We were responsible for the Big Generation. (All those children! I can't think what possessed us.)

A pataphysical mother can look at her son, the president, the chancellor, the head man, big gun, top banana, and see that he didn't wash behind his ears this morning. X-ray vision through his shoes spies an incipient hole in his correct black socks. When did he last have his hair cut? She doesn't attempt cures; she knows better. She envisages no progress. As a matter of fact, it was when my first son was ten that I made up Wylie's Hypothesis: "If there were another sex, women would marry it."

One of the toughest writing assignments in the world is to provide simple directions in a recipe. The prose of a Jell-O package, while clear enough, leaves out details. I used to make terrible Jell-O. I confessed this in my first public lecture about pataphysics and moved my audience to offer me advice about stirring.

"It helps if you count to sixty," I was told. Remember that. Directions should be specific and pataphysical.

As pataphysicians we gradually develop our own methods and systems and then carry on as if reality conformed to them. The famous ham-bone story (first mother, then daughter confirming to grandma's method of cutting the end off the ham before roasting it, to find out years later that grandma did so only because her pan was too short) is a perfect example of tailoring a system as if reality conformed to it instead of the other way round. It's like running trains to fit a train schedule, or running kids to fit a sports program. The solution lies in pataphysics.

Occasionally a male will stumble on pataphysics, as young Jarry did, but his interpretation of it is too literal to do him any good. Each day is a voyage of discovery into what Jarry called "ethernity," which brings us right back to my science-fiction story; outer space used to be called ether. Here we are, rocketing through space as if we know what we're doing.

Up until now, we had no choice. Because women have always been there, perforce, minding the babies and stirring the soup, men have had the leisure to ponder the meaning of the universe instead of having to hold it at bay. Men have, in short, enjoyed the luxury of abstraction because women, the pataphysicians, have been sitting in the subway trains, keeping an eye on the schedules, watching for the next stop. Only women have the unhappy but necessary faculty of doing something — anything! — immediately, rather than doing the best thing a little while later. There is a fierce discipline to this, and a science, but it has never been what the world has identified or appreciated as art.

Outwardly, women have conformed to the demands of life while living an inner pataphysical life, watching themselves adapt to the demands of their external, observed lives. It can be quite funny. As Alfred Jarry said, "Only the comic is serious." But the pata must not laugh; she has to pay attention and stay calm, remain "imperturbable." Says Jarry: "[She] does not burst out laughing or curse when asked to fill out in quadruplicate a questionnaire on [her] political affiliations or sexual habits. No, [she] details a different and equally valid activity on each of the sheets." Of course.

Statisticians regularly make assessments of what a woman's unpaid work is worth today. Add to the roles already recognized (shrew, saint, angel, etc.) those of social secretary, accountant, shopper, chauffeur, babysitter, teacher, fashion arbiter, grammarian, mediator, seamstress and so on, plus mistress, lover and friend, and you have a woman of many parts, infinite in her variety. This endless diversity can be very tiring.

Women are fragmented, seldom having enough time to concentrate on any one thing. They are continually stymied by the perversity of husbands, children and inanimate objects. Nowhere is there a better example of the perversity of all three groups than in the disposal of a Band-Aid wrapper. Note this: No human being except the adult female is capable of getting all the parts of a Band-Aid wrapper into the wastepaper basket. A mother–wife can always tell when someone in the house has broken skin because of the telltale bits of orange thread and scraps of paper wrapping strewn on the floor around the wastebasket. Perhaps women have been so busy picking up Band-Aid wrappers that they haven't had time to tackle creation itself.

Permanent press and birth control have helped to blur the pataphysical lines, also antisepsis, literacy and desserts that don't need to be stirred to a count of sixty. Pataphysics doesn't die easily; women will never run short of pataphysical situations to deal with. So far the only defence has been a half-hearted attempt to ignore them. Unfortunately, women have a lower threshold of tolerance than men. They have greater difficulty ignoring the immediate, whether it's a child's runny nose, garbage that has to be taken out or a funny noise in the night. The question is, *should* these things be ignored? Like the good patas that they are, women will keep on doing what is necessary at the moment, dealing with what is uppermost, until they learn, finally, to neglect life for art.

Life's Curves

Rosalie Benoit Weaver

These hips are mighty hips.
These hips are magic hips.
I have known them
to put a spell on a man and
spin him like a top.

— Lucille Clifton, "Homage to My Hips"

In her tribute to women's hips, Lucille Clifton captures the key metaphor of womanhood. I was first aware of the promise of this powerful charge when I was a girl with no hips at all. I could hardly wait to trade in my skinny, unremarkable frame for womanly curves — magical hips that cast spells, made men mute, turned them dizzy.

Waiting was difficult. I knew hips would be my ticket to a life of endless possibilities. As Sandra Cisneros writes in "Hips," "One day you wake up and they are there. Ready and waiting like a new Buick with the keys in the ignition. Ready to take you where?" Like the narrator in this story, I knew that hips would change my life. I didn't know how or where they would take me, but I did know that I would get there fast, that it would be the most fun I'd ever had and that I would be in the driver's seat.

Waiting for our hips to turn up, my friends and I kept busy learning the best ways to advertise our soon-to-arrive adult sexuality. We wanted to be ready. We studied the movie images of Marilyn Monroe and Sophia Loren: tight-fitting skirts covering broad, curved, womanly hips, wide belts cinching in slim waists. I remember Marilyn and Sophia slowly walking away from the camera, high-heeled shoes accentuating their graceful, womanly swaying or sexy, agitated wriggling. Never looking back, they knew the tidal waves of energy that radiated from their undulating hips. They knew the damage they were doing, the men who were left reeling in their wake. The spellbinding motion of those movie-screen hips enchanted me and my girlfriends. Hipless, we tried to reproduce the sexy undulations as we tottered on our mothers' high heels. However, like today's supermodels who, with their exaggerated catwalk strides, try to presume hips they do not have, my friends and I could not replicate the serious, seductive sways of women with "real" hips. We could only pretend.

I could barely wait to wake up one day and slip my dresses down over hips that were as enchanting as Marilyn's or Sophia's or, heaven forbid, my mother's. My mother had hips, and she had babies, too! The babies were somehow connected with her hips. I witnessed the outward connection as she cradled my baby sister on one hip and stirred the pot on the stove or talked on the telephone; the inward connection was whispered about and dimly alluded to in grade five health-class films about menstruation and personal hygiene. I knew that between a woman's hips a baby could grow, but the miracle of procreation did not interest me. Hips but not babies — that's what I wanted. I wanted to feel the surge of sexual energy I saw in the mesmerizing sway of those movie screen hips. I wanted to project that kind of power; I wanted to spin a man like a top.

I did not know that the day I awoke to my womanly hips would mark a gradual turning of my attention towards the mystery of procreation. Slowly, the possibility of having a baby would become as mesmerizing and unrelenting as the promise of the sexual power of movie-star hips had been for me. The cultural image of secret riches hidden deep within an outer enclosure meant that a woman's hips guarded another sign of her womanhood: her womb. My high-school and university literature classes offered proof of this. The hip metaphor prevails in the Song of Songs as the Beloved prepares to open the gates of her garden to her lover. When he calls her a "garden locked up . . . a spring enclosed, a sealed fountain," she invites him to enter the gates of the garden and "taste its choice fruits." Using geography as the basis for metaphors of the female body is an ancient practice. In mythology books, I read about the sacred cave of Eleitheia hidden deep within the earth on the island of Crete, beneath a sheltering fig tree. In ancient times, women made pilgrimages to honour the goddess of childbirth who granted them fertility and blessed their pregnancies. Women today still journey to Eleitheia to partake of the mysteries of procreation at whose centre lies the womb.

Moving closer to full womanhood meant moving from my initial focus on the outward signs of my sexuality to its inner, central purpose: motherhood. Anthropology classes taught me that, according to tribal custom, a woman's fertility determined her value; replacing the population of her people gave her status and prestige among them. Power resided in her womb. As the public announcement of her hidden worth, a woman's hips, even today, are outward signs of her fertility and her ability to bear children. Hips are the cradle of women's life force; they surround the fragrant garden, the choicest fruits.

Now, at fifty, I am at a crossroads; I have enjoyed the headiness of my sexual power, and I have also come to value the miracle of the life force cradled between my hips. I watch my daughter rush towards the horizon of womanhood. This time, however, as she grabs the keys and drives off with abandonment, I am only a passenger. Through her, I can relive my own journey, one marked first by no hips, then by womanly hips, then by a swollen belly. As a young woman, I did not allow myself to consider the stages in my physical life, nor did I allow myself to fully register the strong connection between my physical and emotional lives. Now, as I watch my daughter's womanly powers wax, I am overwhelmed by the waning of my own and the prospect of my womanly life after them.

Acceptance of the crucial connection between my own physical and emotional lives has not come to me in a natural, conscious flow. It has arrived sporadically, sometimes wrenchingly. In fact, it took a serious accident to awaken me to the central connection of my physical state with my emotional life, and to make me examine my future womanhood.

One day, at age forty-eight, I went for my usual bicycle ride around the lake. A hot summer day. I pedalled uphill, hard. I don't remember the fall or the ambulance trip. When I awoke in the hosptial, my skull was cracked, and I had a severely fractured hip, which meant undergoing major surgery; the broken fragments had to be literally screwed together. The surgeon compared the shattered socket to a broken eggshell. I thought of myself as Humpty Dumpty. I underwent a lengthy hospital stay and a long recovery period. It has now been two years since my tumble. Over that time, my bone fragments have gradually mended, and I have worked hard to strengthen my hip. I still feel occasional stiffness and momentary "hitches" in the damaged joint, but overall, the bones have healed. Lately, people have commented that I no longer walk with a limp. Even so, I am only now realizing the extent of the emotional injury brought on by the break, and I am just starting to measure this healing process. While I could not avoid paying immediate attention to my weakened physical state, I could and did avoid my shattered emotional state, including the sudden loss of sexual power and its resonating effect on my marriage. My physical state is strong again; I am in the best physical shape ever. But now I have an emotional limp. The threat of limited physical movement, of damage to my womanly hips and the diminishment of my sexual power, haunt me.

Few pervasive cultural images exist to instruct women about the close connection between their physical selves and their emotional well-being. Moreover, because there are few positive images of the power that women can take into their time of waning sexual energy and the end of childbearing, they do not feel the urgent pull of the next phase of their lives as they did in the earlier stages. Perhaps it takes a sudden shock to make us consider our futures.

I was not prepared for the emotional damage that resulted from my physical injury. Wise friends told me that a traumatic physical injury often has a ripple effect in a person's life. I listened, but did not heed. I was aware, however, of the emotional pain my family suffered over my injury and limitations, and I was determined to regain my regular life with them as soon as I could. I did not want to be a burden. This, of course, was impossible. Little by little, I am understanding that. I am also understanding that I need to recognize and accept my emotional injuries. I am understanding that at my life's centre has been my sexuality, and that I cannot take it for granted. I am understanding that the aftermath of my trauma is akin, metaphorically, to having my car keys taken away.

In midlife, I realize how closely tied my sense of self is to the collage of cultural images surrounding female sexuality: the locked garden gate, the sealed fountain, the sacred cave, the keys to a new car, the undulating hips of movie stars. But I need new metaphors for where these hips will take me next. Breaking my hip shocked me into considering the future of my womanhood. I will have to do myself what the culture has not been able to do: create positive images of my physical self as I age.

When I was in hospital after my surgery, shuffling the halls with a walker, I was struck by the fact that almost all the patients on my floor were women. They were all considerably older than I, all with broken bones, several with broken hips — and I was one of them. They were not women in their physical prime with healthy bones who had fallen off their bicycles; they were elderly victims of the corrosive process of aging. At age fifty, I still feel my physical powers surging like a girl's. I do, however, have a hip joint held together with a metal plate and screws, and I carry with me the image of those aging women. Today, I hear a new resonance in Sandra Cisneros question about the arrival of a woman's hips: "Ready to take you where?"

Who knows? But I look forward to the ride. This time I won't rush headlong towards the horizon or worry about arriving in any particular place; instead, I hope for a gentler meander. This time I will stop to meet with the landscape. And if I do not wish to keep the car on the road, all the better to explore new paths, to map the detours. I will take life's curves and make them mine.

Cisneros, Sandra. "Hips." *The House on Mango Street.* New York: Vintage Contemporaries, 1991. pp. 49–52.

Clifton, Lucille. "Homage to My Hips." In *Women: Images and Realities,* edited by Amy Kesselman et al. Mountain View, CA: Mayfield, 1995. p. 130.

Old Age

June Callwood

I notice that I am beginning to look like my mother, who died at the age of seventy-four. I also bear an increasingly strong resemblance, especially around the mouth, to my father, who also died at the age of seventy-four. This year, 1999, which the United Nations coincidentally has designated as the International Year of Older Persons, *I* am seventy-four.

I always expected that I would die before I reached seventy-five, just as my parents did; it seemed a family trait. My pact with fate was that I would put in seventy-four years of muddling along in the general direction of good works rather than bad deeds — a common enough aspiration — and then I'd be outta here. Instead, I am the healthiest person I know and, unless there is a maverick Mack truck in my imminent future, I am going to make seventy-five. And far beyond.

I really don't know what to make of it. I agree with Santayana, who said, "Life is not a spectacle, or a feast; it is a predicament." I didn't develop a fall-back plan for the eventuality of being obliged to continue attending fruitless meetings. For instance, last year I joined a gang trying to prevent maiming cuts to the CBC, which proved a totally useless exercise. For a few years I've been part of a group trying to end child poverty, which continues to afflict one child in every five in Canada despite the dozens of pre-breakfast meetings I attend. You don't want to hear about my three-year endeavour to get publishers to pay freelancers for electronic rights (singularly futile), or about the Harmony Movement photography show I helped put together whose goal was to dispel racism across Canada. And it seems my inescapable destiny to go on writing books and articles that are not quite good enough.

I don't know what death is, but it can't be worse than the curse of an optimistic nature that learns nothing from discouragement.

Some, but by no means all, of my friends are also old. We talk about our amazement that we haven't learned a thing despite the march of decades. The faults of your youth are with us still. Those of us who were blunt and belligerent young women are blunt and belligerent old women. Those of us, notably me, born under the celestial sign of impetuosity are still reacting just a microsecond ahead of thought.

My two grandmothers, in contrast, enjoyed a placid, serene old age, time having worn down whatever edges they once possessed and suffused them with a golden glow. They wore aprons when they were at home, and hats when they went out. In summer the outlines of girdles were visible through their flowered dresses. They had endless amounts of available time, which they spent playing euchre or attending Mass (one each). They did not keep day books, knowing with perfect confidence what each gentle day would bring, and certainly they were not called upon to respond to faxes, answering machine messages or e-mail. Further, in the small towns in which they lived they were beloved. I always thought belovedness was something that came naturally, with age.

And then there is my appearance. I no longer have a

waistline, a development that was presaged about fifteen years ago when belts started to ride up on my torso. The face I see in a mirror is that of a very wrinkled, very spotted old woman with loose skin under her jaw and teeth shading to orange. This apparition never gives me a moment's pang because she clearly isn't me. This is not denial on my part: I simply feel no connection to that elderly person. In my mind's eye I look the way I did for most of my life, with a face and body neither so beautiful nor so ugly as to require upkeep.

One morning our granddaughter, age seven, was watching me dress. "Oh, I see," she said pensively. "When you're old your nipples point down."

I am a licensed glider pilot. I don't think I took up gliding a few years ago out of defiance of my septuagenarian status, because gliding seemed perfectly natural activity for someone seeking a spiritual space and lacking a hobby other than napping. Besides, I was licensed as a pilot of power planes when I was about twenty-two, so I know a rudder from an aileron. I quit flying a half century ago because I wasn't really very good at landing the plane, which is one of the requisites of successful flight, and I had small children who seemed attached to me. I'm not really very good at gliding, either. For that reason I don't take up passengers but I might make an exception for people I don't like.

What continues to perplex me is that all these years of existence have taught me so little. I had hoped for wisdom, but I don't even know what wisdom is. I hope it has something to do with putting the top of my car up when it rains hard, because I almost always do that. In *The Art of Growing Old*, written in 1944, John Cowper Powys noted that almost everyone approaching three score and ten is "struck by the oddity of the fact that inside their own skull they are aware of so little difference." Old people are perpetually astonished by the calendar. Where did all that time go? Only yesterday I sat in a cherry tree in the backyard of our house in Belle River,

Ontario, surrounded by blossoms that drifted into my lap. I was eight.

Maybe it was longer ago than yesterday. For sure, I no longer climb cherry trees. But I have retained that child's sense of wonder and ultimate aloneness. I am the best cloud-watcher I know. My inner life is full of the flotsam of messages about duty, deadlines and dusting, but also there are quiet pools of contemplation that I don't think I noticed before. People I loved deeply have died, which gives me perspective when I fall into a futile review of my errors, omissions and grudges.

Now that I am old I detect in others an absence of interest in my vast experience, which, if people paid attention, would enable them to avoid folly. This sad observation led me directly to one of the two pieces of wisdom I have accumulated so far, which is that I can't fix anyone. Having botched the lifelong task of fixing myself, I should have been suspicious of my former conviction that I was particularly good at solving the problems of others. But no. For most of my life I relentlessly brought cheer, instructions and wise counsel to loved ones and strangers alike. I still have occasional lapses of advice-giving, but mostly I stick to something that is a lot less trouble: vigorous, eye-contact listening. People then say, marvellously, "Thanks for your help."

The other truth I know concerns apathy, which I have on good authority (Hannah Arendt) is a workable definition of evil. This insight may only be true for me, but I seem to guilt myself a lot less if I interfere when something isn't fair — even if I screw up the intervention, even if it doesn't succeed — than if I decide injustice isn't my business and pass by. This is described, by people who haven't given it a try, as meddling. I prefer to think of it as character building.

I'm a work in progress. I always thought that when I got old I would have answers to the imponderable questions surrounding human existence. So far, that's not how it's turning out. Oh well.

Grace After Pressure

Jaqueline McLeod Rogers

When I was a graduate student in English, I used to exchange letters with a friend who, like me, was studying literature, but who, unlike me, was away at a prestigious school. Sometimes he wrote pop sayings or literary passages on the outside of the envelopes. While I can't remember much about the letters themselves, one of these quotations has stayed with me. It went something along the lines of our needing to choose our dreams wisely because we would have to be satisfied with their being fulfilled in our middle age.

Taken as useful advice, these cautionary words might simply encourage us to reflect on life's choices. Yet for me, underlying these words was an outrageous assumption of personal worth and deserving. I read the passage as a call to those who felt heroically cast for an inevitably bright future. It was galling to think that some people, believing we actually get what we want in life, were greedy enough to become hardened in their determination to want lots.

At that stage of my life, when accomplishing goals seemed

so far off and dreaming seemed like a dangerous diversion, part of me must have envied the self-assurance of those who could problematize the notion of dreams coming true. Now, when I think about the "room at the top," "every little boy can be president" quality inherent in the commitment to chasing big dreams, what interests me is not how this assertive optimism is linked to egoism, but how it likely works as a practical strategy for focusing personal ambition. Winners take control and work towards getting what they want. Winners dream so big that they can avoid the trap of learning to despise things they've admired. Only defeatists would keep in mind that the problem of being jaded by success is not nearly as common as the problem of trying to live with some condition of failure.

While I don't want to cast myself as an essentialist thinker who treats men and women as forever separate, I still think it's fair to observe that the determination and self-interested swagger of this approach corresponds to what many of us think of as a male attitude to life, based on some combination of attitudes we've known in real and fictional men. The idea of seizing control, of acting for the self, of worrying that someday you'll want even more — these attributes belong to the boys and men in stories about great expectations and poems about our reach exceeding our grasp.

Rather than hunting a once-and-for-all big dream, the "other way" that I have grown into slowly, and that I associate with female experience, is to respond to life with a kind of cultivated serendipity — with provisional plans that shape-shift over the course of being pursued. The dog that you always wanted is a grey tabby cat; the recognition you worked so hard for comes at its best from your kindergartener, who one day smiles and does what you ask without the usual debate and protest. Somehow, important things come to the fore as you make your way towards what you think you want, and eventually you find yourself in a different and richer place.

Perhaps I associate this approach with women because I

first learned to think about it in a course on women and literature. The centrepiece of the course was the myth of Psyche, which provided a frame of reference for evaluating female heroism. Psyche is a girl who is abandoned to a beast that comes to her in darkness at night, on the condition that she not see him. One night, out of curiosity, she lights a candle and discovers that he is in fact a Prince. But because she has broken the bonds of their arrangement by looking at him and learning his identity, he cannot stay with her.

To win him back, she performs a series of labours that seems as daunting as those undertaken by the male heroes of myth. What feminizes the story is that, rather than deciding and doing what needs to be done with rugged individualism, she solves each dilemma more indirectly, even intuitively, by being responsive to help at hand and by refusing to do all the work alone. Desire and open-mindedness more than wit and will help her accomplish her goals, although all of these personal qualities come into play. The question of whether a rule-bound and sulky prince is worth all of this attention and work falls away once he is understood as a metaphor for any object of desire.

As a student studying women's writing, I liked thinking about Psyche's progress as a way to understand the motivation and development of literary characters — like all the Laurence women, Hagar, Morag, Rachel and Stacey, who give up trying to control and direct lives and learn to begin liking change. On the other hand, I considered applying this indirect approach to my own life to solve problems or decide what to do out of the question. On a practical level, I just didn't think it would work. I couldn't imagine that direction would emerge from inattention or that conflicts could be resolved or accepted over time. If I were to ease into this sort of wait-and-see attitude, how would I ever do the painstaking work of writing and revising the chapters of my Ph.D. thesis? It seemed clear to me that I'd have to drive myself if I expected to finish as planned.

Some of my resistance stemmed from having been raised, like a Laurence character, to take living as a serious business requiring constant vigilance and concern. Good things, if they ever came, were hard won, and successful people were self-disciplined. And I think that at a deeper level still I was determined to resist recognizing or cultivating in myself anything associated with women's ways. It was one thing to allow that characters in books had a feminine side, and quite another to see myself as connected to a group whose very strengths seemed bound to vulnerability.

Because I admired the professor who taught the course about women's writing, I was skeptical when she claimed to take a "female orientation" toward life and wondered if she were teasing me with ghost stories about "women's intuition." I couldn't fathom a successful woman adopting an attitude suitable only to characters safe in the realm of story, where the plot is already sealed. How could she risk making a mistake by approaching a problem with flexibility rather than a firm plan? In real life, it seemed to me that to attempt to find and respond to the pattern in circumstances was to place yourself haphazardly at the mercy of outside forces.

Yet for her, the border between myth and life was open, full of compelling interactions. Once, she cut short my apology for saying the wrong thing by suggesting that sometimes when we think we've behaved badly or foolishly others have appreciated what they see as vulnerability or risk-taking. Another time, when she was reviewing a chapter of my work on female heroism, she pointed out that I was overlooking an important element of the Psyche myth by not discussing the labour required for her to sort through millions of mixed seed grains. She suggested that this task was a metaphor for our everyday efforts to find pattern in mayhem, to trust that order can come from chaos. "Really, it's just like the way we pause in life to sort things out when they get confusing and we need to see how they fit together."

Yet, rather than finding her bridge from myth to life immediately helpful, I remember feeling more stuck than ever. It was true that I had consigned the numbing demands of Psyche's repetitive seed-sorting task to a realm of mythic fantasy, well beyond realism. Unable to make sense of it, I had hoped to get away with saying nothing about it. My lack of interest in Psyche's efforts ran parallel to my real-life avoidance of dwelling on complexities that were hard to resolve. I had no experience with pausing from time to time for personal reflection, to sort things out. To reflect meant to worry or, on a decisive day, to decide how to change something. My image of getting through life was to see it as a series of small problems, each of which could only be picked off one at a time by setting a target and taking straight aim; pausing in this ongoing struggle would mean losing my place, flagging, failing. I was still trying to fight like a man despite being short on expectation and enthusiasm.

Over the past few years, finding myself more responsive to life and hopeful that the best course of action would come to light, I have gradually come to feel more closely connected to women figures who found in myth and stories what they needed, often in unexpected places. And from harder experiences I have recognized that there's little use in fighting to control life's events and outcomes. When I was thirty and my mother died suddenly, I had to struggle to accept that important things can't be controlled or changed. It felt like biting stone to learn that sometimes there's no healing.

As a mother, too, I have learned not to forget the limits of my control. These limits are brought home to me whenever I look at the perfect ease of my sleeping children and know that I cannot secure with permanence their safety and happiness. Recognizing the fragility of our hold on those we value must compel us either to build illusions of permanence or to figure out how to live with some form of trust.

Even shining moments can remind us that we have little

influence on events we want desperately to control. I remember feeling grateful and helpless together when my newborn daughter held onto life after episodes of struggling, barely clinging to it. She was born five weeks early yet so perfect that she was allowed to come home after spending only two days in hospital. But once we got home she caught a virus overnight and dehydrated so rapidly that when I looked at her legs all I could see was skin on bone. Calling for aggressive treatment, the Emergency Room staff performed a spinal tap, then sent us to spend the rest of the night in a deserted wing of the children's ward.

In the morning, a nurse came to tell me to go for coffee so that she could give the baby a bath. When I came back, the room was filled with emergency resuscitation equipment and the nurses tried to keep me out. I remember banging into walls so that I could feel something other than fear, telling nurses to listen more carefully to the noise of the instruments that were helping my daughter to keep breathing. She was lucky; we were lucky. Her long stay in the neonatal intensive care unit turned out to be the process of her recovery. For me, it became a process of learning about the depths of hope as well as about the need to link loving with letting go.

This habit of seeing what can happen with the passing of time and thought has made day-to-day choices more manageable and interesting. It is encouraging to find how often something puzzling or difficult resolves itself, so that what is right or best or necessary eventually emerges. Or how something undesirable or out of place can begin to make sense in retrospect, and can even be understood as a precondition to present circumstances.

As a teacher, I work best with a plan that can be set aside as soon as I see that something else needs to be done. Often, it is an off-the-cuff comment or story that students refer to later as having been especially helpful or warming. Or it's the embarrassing moment — misspelling a word, struggling to define a term, or losing a train of thought — that can rally students' interest in ways that a flawless performance cannot. From a student's perspective, my story about what I learned from my women's literature professor makes the case that the most valuable lessons may be subtextual or even non-curricular. The questions we were examining were about ways of reading, not about ways living; even if there had been questions in class about connecting women's literature to life, I might not have known what to say because the process of my understanding this link has been delayed and gradual.

Once intuition and intellect strike up a quiet partnership, a person's story can take an eerie turn. I recently experienced a bout of what I call "sleep thinking," which adds a fine dimension of mystery to life. I went to sleep not knowing how to organize a new course about narrative inquiry and woke up prepared to begin with Virginia Woolf's *A Room of One's Own* and Margaret Mead's *Coming of Age in Samoa* as examples of early autobiographical and ethnographic narratives. The library confirmed that both had been published in 1929, a historical coincidence that convinced me I had found a good starting place for the course.

I count substantive, sensible dreams as gifts, but of course they don't come out of the blue. I was able to come to an understanding of how to shape my new course, for example, because I was immersed in studying narrative texts and theory. I found what I needed by stepping back, by slowing down. As Psyche's story illustrates, a person needs to be prepared both to look for and to work with serendipitous events; this approach blends activity with indirection. It's not laziness but readiness.

I've used the phrase "grace after pressure" in my title as an alternate to Hemingway's notion of heroic struggle as "grace under pressure." His image of good writing as reflecting the tip of the iceberg comes to mind when I think about how we can sustain an attitude of hope and openness only with the support of inner strength and resources. To be responsive to life requires being educated and ready rather than blindly accepting.

Of course, once you start believing the world can work in mysterious ways, you are more prone to interpret events from this perspective. It is easy to slide into a helplessly accommodating attitude because you assume that most outcomes are both unpredictable and inevitable, and that it is therefore just as well to flatly accept things you can't change. Yet despite this pitfall of becoming passive rather than ready in the face of events, there are great advantages to an open agenda. It provides time for reflection, open-mindedness, and generosity — quickening attitudes that can get lost when we are driving ourselves and controlling others. There's pleasure in expecting to be guided rather than dogged.

If You Can't Say Something Nice, Don't Say Anything At All

Margaret Atwood

I

Long ago, in the land of small metal curlers, of respectable white cotton garter belts and panty girdles with rubbery-smelling snap crotches, of stockings with seams, where condoms could not legally be displayed on pharmacy shelves, where we read Kotex ads to learn how to behave at proms and always wore our gloves when we went out, where cars had fins like fish and there was only one brand of tampon, women were told many things.

We were told: A happy marriage is the wife's responsibility.

We were told: Learn to be a good listener.

We were told: Don't neck on the first date or the boy will not respect you. Home may be the man's castle but the fluffballs under the bed are the woman's fault. Real women are bad at math. To be fulfilled you have to have a baby. If you lead them on you'll get what you deserve.

We were told: If you can't say something nice, don't say anything at all.

Things that were not openly discussed: Abortion. Incest. Lesbians. Masturbation. Female orgasm. Menopause. Impotence. Anger.

Things we'd never heard of: Anorexia. Male-determined. Battered women. Metonymy. Housework is work. Bulimia. Herpes. Ecology. Equal pay. PMS. Surrogate motherhood. Faking it. Sisterhood is powerful. Dioxins. AIDS. The personal is political. A fish and a bicycle. Trashing.

Things we'd heard from men: Put a paper bag over their heads and they're all the same. She's just mad because she's a woman. Nothing wrong with her that a good screw won't fix. Bun in the oven. Up the stump. Frustrated old maid. Cockteaser. Raving bitch.

We were told that there were certain "right," "normal" ways to be women, and other ways that were wrong. The right ways were limited in number. The wrong ways were endless.

We spent a lot of time wondering if we were "normal." Some of us decided we weren't. Ready-to-wear did not quite fit us. Neither did language.

II

Technology changed first. Big rollers. Home hair dryers. Pantyhose. The Pill.

Some of us made it through the minefield of high school to the minefield of university.

We read things. We read many things. We read *Paradise Lost*, about Eve's Sin, which seemed to consist partly in having curly hair. We read the glorified rape scenes in *Peyton Place* and *The Fountainhead*, which proposed sexual assault as a kind of therapy. (For the woman. Leaves you with that radiant after-glow.) We read D.H. Lawrence and his nasty bloodsucking gold spiderwomen, and his young girls melting like gelatin at the sight, thought or touch of a good man's nicknamed appendage.

We read Norman Mailer, who detailed the orgasmic thrill of strangling a bitchy wife. We read Ernest Hemingway, who preferred fishing. We read *Playboy*, and its promises of eternal babyhood for boys, in the playpen with the bunnies — well away from the washer–dryer in the suburbs and the gold-digging wife and her (not his) screaming kids. We read Robert Graves, in which Man did and Woman was. Passivity was at an all-time high.

We read sex manuals that said a man should learn to play a woman like a violin. Nobody said a word about a woman learning to play a man like a flute.

We did some investigations of our own, and concluded that virgins were at a premium not because they were pure but because they were stupid. They made men feel smart by comparison. We realized we'd been well-groomed in the art of making men feel smart. We were disappointed that this was an art and not something inherent in nature; if men really were that smart, it shouldn't take so much work.

III

Some of us wanted to be writers. If we were in Academia we concealed this. Respectable academics did not "write," acceptable writers were safely dead. We did not want to be thought presumptuous. We were keeping our presumption for later.

We read writing by women. Our interest was not so much in technique or style or form or symbol or even content, although these were the things we wrote papers about. It was in something much more basic: we were curious about the *lives* of these women. How had they managed it? We knew about the problems; we wanted to know there were solutions. For instance, could you be a woman writer and happily married, with children, as well? It did not seem likely. (Emily Dickinson, recluse. George Eliot, childless. The Brontës, dead early. Jane Austen, spinster. Christina Rosetti, her wormholes, her shroud.)

It seemed likely that the husband's demands and those of the art would clash. As a woman writer you would have to be a sort of nun, with the vocation and dedication but without the chastity, because you would have to Experience Life. You would have to Suffer. We read Sylvia Plath and Anne Sexton, suicides both. Novel writing was safer. You could do that and live.

Even so, combining marriage and art was a risky business. You could not be an empty vessel for two. The instructions were clear: one genie per bottle.

Then there was the Canadian complication. Could you be a female, a writer, be good at it, get published, not commit suicide and be Canadian too? Here the news was a little better. Canadian writers were for the most part not at all well-known, but if you dug around you could find them, and many of the best ones were women. Of these, none had committed suicide.

Around this time, I was reading: P.K. Page, Margaret Avison, Dorothy Roberts, Jay Macpherson, Elizabeth Brewster, Gwen MacEwen, Anne Hébert, Marie-Claire Blais, Gabrielle Roy, Margaret Laurence, Ethel Wilson, Jane Rule, Miriam Waddington, Anne Wilkinson, Phyllis Webb, Colleen Thibideau, Sheila Watson, Dorothy Livesay and Phyllis Gottlieb. (Alice Munro, Marian Engel and Audrey Thomas had not yet published books, and Mavis Gallant was unknown — to me, and to most — as a Canadian.)

It was comforting as well as exciting to read the writers. I was not thinking, however, about a special, female *kind* of writing. It was more like a laying on of hands, a feeling that you too could do it because, look, it could be done.

Still, it was taken for granted then that you had to work harder and be better to be a woman anything, so why not a woman writer? I felt that I was writing in the teeth of the odds; as all writers do, to be sure, but for women there were extra handicaps. I was writing *anyway*, I was writing *nevertheless*, I was writing *despite*.

IV

Things that were said about writing by women:

- that it was weak, vapid and pastel, as in strong, "masculine" rhymes and weak "feminine" ones;
- that it was too subjective, solipsistic, narcissistic, autobiographical and confessional;
- that women lacked imagination and the power of invention and could only copy from their own (unimportant) lives and their own (limited, subjective) reality — they lacked the power to speak in other voices, or to make things up;
- that their writing was therefore limited in scope, petty, domestic and trivial;
- that good female writers transcended their gender; that bad ones embodied it;
- that writing was anyway a male preserve, and that women who invaded it felt guilty or wanted to be men;
- that men created because they couldn't have babies; that it was unfair of women to do both; that they should just have the babies, thus confining themselves to their proper sphere of creativity.

The double bind: if women said nice things, they were being female, therefore weak, and therefore bad writers. If they didn't say nice things they weren't proper women. Much better not to say anything at all.

Any woman who began writing when I did, and managed to continue, did so by ignoring, as a writer, all her socialization about pleasing other people by being nice, and every theory then available about how she wrote or ought to write. The alternative was silence.

V

It was the mid-sixties. We began to read subversive books. We knew they were subversive because we read them in the bathroom with the door closed and did not admit to it. There were two of them: Betty Friedan's *The Feminine Mystique* and Simone de Beauvoir's *The Second Sex.* They weren't about our generation, exactly, or about our country; still, some things fit. We didn't know quite why we wished to conceal our knowledge of them, except that the implications were very disturbing. If you thought too much about them you got angry. Something might blow up.

I first became aware of the constellation of attitudes or wave of energy loosely known as "The Women's Movement" in 1969, when I was living in Edmonton, Alberta. A friend of mine in New York sent me a copy of the now-famous "Housework Is Work" piece. There were no feminist groups in my immediate vicinity that I could see. Not there, not then. After that I went to England: similarly none.

I've said from time to time that I predated the women's movement, didn't create it, and didn't even participate in its early stages. I feel that this was a modest — and accurate — attempt not to take credit where credit wasn't due, but this has been interpreted by some as a kind of denial or repudiation. Why this pressure to lie about your real experience, squash it into the Procrustean bed of some sacrosanct party line? It seems, unfortunately, to be a characteristic of party lines.

Similarly, I've been under pressure to say I was discriminated against by sexist male publishers. But I wasn't. However sexist they may have been in their private lives, in their professional behaviour towards me no male Canadian publishers were ever anything but encouraging, even when they didn't publish my books. (I'm quite prepared to believe that the experience of others has been different. But your own personal experience is supposed to count for something, and that was mine.) It's true that my first collection of poems and my first novel were rejected, but, although this was hard on me at the time, it was in retrospect a good thing. These books were "promising," but that's all they were.

In general, the Canadian publishers then were so desperate for any book they thought they could publish successfully that they wouldn't have cared if the author were a newt. "Successfully" is the operative word. Success in publisher's terms can be critical or financial, preferably both, which means an audience of some kind. This state of affairs mitigates — at the moment — against poetry, and against new, experimental and minority-group writing — writing that cannot promise to deliver an audience — which is also the reason why a great deal of such writing first sees the light through small presses and literary magazines. Many of these have been controlled by men with a distinct penchant for the buddy system, which in turn has led to the *de facto* exclusion of non-buddies, a good number of whom have been women. Or that's my theory.

Finding that they were too new, offbeat or weird for what little "mainstream" publishing there was, many writers of my generation started their own presses and magazines. This is hard work and drinks your blood, but for writers who feel excluded, it may be the only way to develop an audience. Sometimes the audience is already there and waiting, and the problem is to locate it, or enable it to locate you. Sometimes audience and writer will each other into being. But many, even those belonging to the supposedly automatically privileged white male middle class, never make it all.

Being reviewed holds different perils. I'm quite happy to line up for a group spit on sexist reviewers, since over the years I've been on the receiving end of every bias in the book. *She writes like a man*, intended as a compliment. (I've always read it, "She writes. Like a man.") S*he writes like a housewife*. Witch, man-hater, man-freezing Medusa, man-devouring monster. The Ice Goddess, the Snow Queen. One (woman) critic even did an analysis of my work based on my jacket photos: not enough smiles, in her opinion. Girls, like the peasants in eighteenth-century genre paintings, are supposed to smile a lot.

And Lord help you if you step outside your "proper" sphere as a woman writer and comment on boy stuff like, say, politics. You want to see the heavy artillery come out? Try free trade.

VI

Looking back on the women's movement in the early and mid-seventies, I remember a grand fermentation of ideas, an exuberance in writing, a joy in uncovering taboos and in breaking them, a willingness to explore new channels of thought and feeling. I remember the setting up of practical facilities such as rape crisis centres and shelters for battered women. Doors were being opened. Language was being changed. Territory was being claimed. The unsaid was being said. Forms were fluid, genres were no longer locked boxes. There was a vitality, an urgency, in writing by women that surpassed anything men as a group were coming up with at the time. It was heady stuff.

Did all this affect my writing? How could it not? It affected everyone, in one way or another. It affected ways of looking, ways of feeling, ways of saying, the entire spectrum of assumption and perceived possibility.

But some people got hurt. Some men felt confused or excluded or despised, their roles questioned, their power base eroded. Some women felt excluded or despised or bullied or marginalized or trashed. When you've devoted much time and energy to bringing up your beloved children, frequently single-handedly, it didn't perk you up a lot to be called a dupe to men and a traitor to women. When you'd bucked the odds, worked your little fingers to the bone and achieved some form of success, it was not overjoying to be labelled a "token woman." It wasn't great to be told that your concern with race did not fit into the women's movement. It wasn't any more fun being told you weren't a real woman because you weren't a lesbian than it had been for lesbians, earlier, to be squashed for their own sexual preferences.

But you weren't supposed to complain. It seemed that

some emotions were okay to express — for instance, negative emotions about men. Others were not okay — for instance, negative emotions about Woman. Mothers were an exception. It was okay to trash your mother. That aside, if you couldn't say something nice *about Woman*, you weren't supposed to say anything at all. But even saying *that* is saying something *not nice*. Right? So sit down and shut up.

Women can domineer over and infantilize women just as well as men can. They know exactly where to stick the knife. Also, they do great ambushes. From men you're expecting it.

VII

Writing and *isms* are two different things. Those who pledge their first loyalties to *isms* often hate and fear artists and their perverse loyalty to their art, because art is uncontrollable and has a habit of exploring the shadow side, the unspoken, the unthought. From the point of view of those who want a neatly ordered universe, writers are messy and undependable. They often see life as complex and mysterious, with ironies and loose ends, not as a tidy system of goodies and baddies usefully labelled. They frequently take the side of the underdog, that flea-blown house pet so unpopular with regimes in power. Plato excluded poets from the ideal republic. Modern dictators shoot them. And as the germination stage of any *ism* ends and it divides into cliques and solidifies into orthodoxies, writers — seized upon initially for their ability to upset apple carts — become suspect to the guardians of the *ism* for that very reason. Prescription becomes the order of the day. If Rousseau had survived to witness the French Revolution, he would have been guillotined.

I have supported women's efforts to improve their shoddy lot in this world that is, globally, dangerous for women, biased against them and, at the moment, in a state of reaction against their efforts. But you pay for your support. The demands placed on those seen as spokespersons, either for women or for any other group under pressure, are frequently crushing; for every demand you satisfy, ten more come forward, and when you reach the breakdown point and say you just can't do it, the demanders get angry. Women are socialized to please, to assuage pain, give blood till they drop, to conciliate, to be selfless, to be helpful, to be Jesus Christ since men have given up on that role, to be perfect, and that load of luggage is still with us. This kind of insatiability is particularly damaging for women writers, who, like other writers, need private space and as women have a hard time getting any, and who are called by inner voices that may not coincide with the strictures of prevailing policy-formulators. I think of a poem by the young Maori poet Roma Potiki, addressed to her own constituency: "Death Is Too High a Price to Pay for Your Approval." Which about sums it up.

So — as a citizen, I do what I can while attempting to remain sane and functional, and if that sounds whiny and martyred it probably is. But as a writer — although it goes without saying that one's areas of concern inform one's work — I view with some alarm the attempts being made to dictate to women writers, on ideological grounds, various "acceptable" modes of approach, style, form, language, subject or voice. Squeezing everyone into the same mould does not foster vitality, it merely discourages risks. In farming it would be monoculture. In fiction, those who write from the abstract theory on down instead of from the specific earth on up all too often end up by producing work that resembles a filled-in colouring book. Art created from a sense of obligation is likely to be static.

I think I am a writer, not a sort of tabula rasa for the Zeitgeist or a non-existent generator of "texts." I think the examination of "language" is something every good writer is engaged in by virtue of vocation. I write about women because they interest me, not because I think I ought to. Art created from a sense of obligation is bound to be static. Women are not Woman. They come in all shapes, sizes, colours, classes, ages and degrees of moral rectitude. They don't all behave, think or feel the same, any more than they all take size eight. All of them are real. Some of them are wonderful. Some of them are awful. To deny them this is to deny them their humanity and to restrict their area of moral choice to the size of a teacup. To define women as by nature better than men is to ape the Victorians: "Woman" was given "moral superiority" by them because all other forms of superiority had been taken away.

VIII

There's been a certain amount of talk lately about who has the right to write what, and about whom. Some have even claimed that a writer should not write about anyone other than herself, or someone so closely resembling her that it makes no nevermind. What was previously considered a weakness in women's writing — solipsism, narcissism, the autobiographical — is now being touted as a requirement. Just for fun, here are a few women writers who have written in voices "other" than "their own" — those of other genders, nations, classes, ethnic groups, colours, other ages or stages of life, other times and other life forms: Emily Brontë, George Eliot, Beatrix Potter, Virginia Woolf, Nadine Gordimer, Mary Shelley, Kay Boyle, Adele Wiseman, Bharati Mukherjee, Marie-Claire Blais, Jane Urquhart, Marge Piercey, Louise Erdrich, Daphne Marlatt, Carolyn Chute, Toni Morrison, Audrey Thomas, Alice Munro, Nicole Brossard, Gwendolyn MacEwen, Cynthia Ozick, Anne Hébert, Margaret Laurence, Mavis Gallant, Alice Walker, Anita Desai, Blanche D'Alpuget, Rita MacNeil, Sarah Sheard, Nayantara Saghal, Katherine Govier, Nawal El Saadawi, Ruth Prawer Jhabvala, Susan Swan, Anonymous, almost all playwrights, many crime writers and all science-fiction writers. That's just a few that spring to mind. There are lots more.

Having said this, I'll say that if you do choose to write from the point of view of an "other" group, you'd better pay very close attention, because you'll be subject to extra scrutinies and resentments. I'll add that in my opinion the best writing about such a group is most likely to come from within that group — not because those outside it are more likely to vilify it, but because they are likely, these days and out of well-meaning liberalism, to simplify and sentimentalize it, or to get the textures and vocabulary and symbolism wrong. (For what it's worth, I think it's easier to write from a different-gender point of view within your own group than from a same-gender point of view from a different group.) Also, writers from outside a group are less likely to be able to do the tough, unpleasant, complex bits without attracting charges of racism, sexism and so forth. Picture Toni Morrison's *Beloved* written by a white person and you'll see what I mean.

But to make such a judgement *in advance*, to make it on the basis of the race, sex, age, nationality, class or jacket photo *of the writer* instead of on the quality of the writing itself, is to be guilty of prejudice in the original meaning of the word, which is *pre-judgement*. This is why, when I judge writing contests of any kind, I prefer to do it blind. Recently I gave first prize in a short-story-collection contest to Reginald McKnight, a writer of great verve and energy, who turned out to be black, male and American. One of the stories was written from the point of view of a bigoted white Southern male. Should this have disqualified my writer — that he was not writing with "his own" voice?

To lend support to an emerging literature does not mean you have to silence yourself. Being a good listener is not the same as not talking. The best thing you can do for a writer from a group in the process of finding its voices is to form part of a receptive climate. That is, *buy the work and read it*, as intelligently and sensitively as you can. If there's something new and valuable to be learned about form, symbol or belief system, learn it. But don't condescend. And never call anyone from such a group a token. For a writer, that's a big insult; it implies she can't really write.

Surely in the final analysis critical evaluation should be based on performance. I didn't give first prize to Reginald McKnight's *Moustapha's Eclipse* because its author was black, but because it was the best.

IX

For me, the dangers of dictatorship by *ism* are largely metaphorical: I don't have a job, so no one has the power to fire me. But for some members of what I now geriatrically refer to as the younger generation, things are otherwise. When younger women writers come to me, at parties or under cover of night, to whisper stories about how they've been worked over — critically, professionally or personally — by women in positions of power, because they haven't toed some stylistic or ideological line or other, I deduct the mandatory fifteen points for writerly paranoia. Then I get mad.

Over the years I've built up a good deal of resistance to such manipulations; in any case, those likely to be doing them probably think of me as the Goodyear Blimp, floating around up there in an overinflated and irrelevant way — just the Establishment, you know, like, who cares? But other, younger woman writers, especially those with academic jobs, are not so lucky. An accusation of Thoughtcrime, for them, can have damaging practical consequences.

If the women's movement is not an open door but a closed book, reserved for some right-thinking elite, then I've been misled. Are we being told again that there are certain "right" ways of being a woman writer, and all other ways are wrong?

Sorry, but that's where I came in. Women of my generation were told not to fly or run, only to hobble, with our high heels and our panty girdles on. We were told endlessly: *Thou shalt not.* We don't need to hear it again, and especially not from women. Feminism has done many good things for women writers, but surely the most important has been the permission to say the unsaid, to encourage women to claim their full humanity, which means acknowledging the shadows as well as the lights.

Any knife can cut two ways. Theory is a positive force when it vitalizes and enables, but a negative one when it is used to amputate and repress, to create a batch of self-righteous rules and regulations, to foster nail-biting self-consciousness to the point of total block. Women are particularly subject to such squeeze-plays, because they are (still) heavily socialized to please. It's easy to make them feel guilty, about almost anything.

The fear that dares not speak its name, for some women these days, is a fear of other women. But you aren't supposed to talk about that: If you can't say something nice, don't say anything at all.

There are many strong voices; there are many *kinds* of strong voices. Surely there should be room for all.

Does it make sense to silence women in the name of Woman?

We can't afford this silencing, or this fear.

Gilding the Dark Shades

Charlotte Gray

As I leafed through the letters, I knew I was eavesdropping. Each letter was part of a private conversation between the writer and its recipient. None was intended for a third party's eyes. The writer, Catharine Parr Traill, never imagined that her personal correspondence was destined to be part of Canada's literary heritage. But one hundred years after the ink had dried on Catharine's untidy, looped writing, almost five hundred of her letters are in the Public Archives of Canada. I slowly read through the correspondence of a lifetime.

At first, Catharine was simply an interesting historical figure, author of *The Backwoods of Canada* (1936) and *The Canadian Settler's Guide* (1855). There was no obvious overlap between the life she described and my own. She had arrived in the backwoods of Upper Canada in 1832 and struggled for everything that I take for granted: home, food, clothes, education for my children. I was an anthropologist, tracking a lost species of human being in a distant country. Catharine's catalogue of disasters appeared endless — and so foreign.

Harvests failed; babies died; her house was burnt to the ground. During the winter, she and her family were completely isolated. Catharine treated her own bouts of bronchitis by gargling with caustic quicklime. Her children's faces swelled and throbbed with "gumboils" because "they need more nourishing diet than I often have to give them." Before she left England, thirty-year-old Catharine had been a published author of some renown; now she was in a wilderness of illiteracy, desperately trying to persuade Toronto's handful of hard-faced publishers to take her seriously. "I want much to go up to Toronto this next month but I have not the means either for supplying myself with decent outer clothes . . . or to pay for a week's board and lodging at some decent house."

A prurient historical voyeurism welled up in me as I read on through the letters. "We were exposed for several hours to the full fury of the storm, the mare going at footfall and with great difficulty breaking through the deep snow drifts that blocked our path," wrote Catharine to a friend in early 1852, describing a bitter journey from Cobourg, on the shores of Lake Ontario, to her house thirty miles north. "The snow and ice froze upon us so that I hardly thought I could keep life in me from the intense cold." I sat back in my warm, well-lit room and imagined the white-on-white, bone-chilling scene. Catharine's son James tugged at the bridle of the raw-ribbed nag. The sleigh slid jerkily through the swirling snowflakes as Catharine pulled her threadbare shawls and blankets around her. The air was so cold it hurt to breathe. Darkness came, the wind rose, and Catharine was still miles from home. She was snowblind and frostbitten by the time the sled finally drew to a halt outside the Traill farmhouse, and she unbent her frozen knees and clambered awkwardly down. I rose from my chair and turned the thermostat up two degrees.

Yet as I immersed myself in another woman's life, I began to inhabit her skin. I gradually learned how Catharine's mind worked. I knew that every year her spirits would lift when spring came and she could start tramping through the woods, collecting ferns. When I discovered that her daughter-in-law was pregnant, I flipped through the next few weeks of correspondence, knowing that neither torrential rains nor extreme poverty would dampen Catharine's eagerness to hold her first grandchild in her arms. Sure enough, Catharine's joy spilled off the page. "The babe is really a fine fellow, so fat that his little hands and elbows and knees are full of dimples . . . I am head nurse washing dressing and taking care of the little fellow and really am almost as proud of him as the mother and father are." As she entered her eighties, and then her nineties, I winced at every mention of her aching back, knowing that she still tended the vegetable garden at her cottage in Lakefield.

No amount of empathy, however, could eradicate one of the greatest gulfs between Catharine and me. All her life, others had made the choices that governed her existence: her father, Thomas Strickland, had moved his family from London to Suffolk; her husband, Thomas Traill, had decided they must emigrate; her brother Sam Strickland had arranged the purchase of land for the Traills close to Peterborough. Catharine was swept along, deferring to the men in her life. When things went wrong (as they always did) she relied on her firm belief in a benevolent God to sustain her through hardship. She was drenched in a nineteenth-century faith that is almost incomprehensible today, and that shored up her remarkable stamina. She thanked "My God for that which in his wisdom he withholds as well as for the mercies he bestows." What self-respecting writer today would allow others to shape her life? Which woman today would swallow so many reversals with such a surrender of will to the deity? Even a confirmed churchgoer would not accept fate quite so passively. Like most of my post-Friedan contemporaries, I need to feel that I have at least some control over my own destiny.

But at a more fundamental level, I began to appreciate the

continuum between Catharine's life and my own. It was no longer the exterior details of Catharine's life that caught my attention; it was her preoccupation with those around her. Catharine Parr Traill always put her family first, her writing second. Catharine poured into her letters all her anxiety about her husband's gloom, her children's lack of schooling, her eagerness to see her four sons and three daughters satisfactorily married. Her concern went far beyond her own flesh and blood. She cared about everybody else's happiness. If she saw troubled waters, she felt personally responsible for smoothing them. She couldn't relax herself until all her nearest and dearest were safely settled. How human, I thought, how timeless. And how utterly infuriating. Catharine was driven by an entirely female compulsion that I share with her, and labour to suppress: a gnawing need to ensure that everybody is comfortable.

Is it wrong to want everybody to be happy, and to feel guilty if they're not? Well, yes and no. It is not wrong to observe the common courtesies, to look after people's physical needs, to be civil to each other. But it is wrong when it diverts too much attention from other pursuits, and it may be counterproductive. In Catharine's case, it meant she was never able to spend as much time writing as she wanted. It meant that she was irresistibly drawn to the emotionally needy, whose broken spirits she tried to mend. She spent twenty-seven years valiantly battling her husband's chronic depression, never allowing herself any disloyalty or exasperation, even in letters to her confidantes. As I read and reread the letters, her ingenuous enthusiasm for beautiful views or newborn babies sounded more and more brittle: the desperation of a woman who has taken upon herself the family duty of (in my own mother's words) "keeping the show upon the road."

In my own case, I have decided that my need to feel responsible for everybody else's happiness absolves other people from doing the job themselves. I certainly don't have Catharine's pioneer problems: no bitter storms of freezing winds disrupt my marriage, family, or home. Yet I observe my own antennae acutely attuned to other people's moods. If I see a scowl in a business meeting or at someone else's dinner party, I feel the maternal impulse to seize a metaphorical jug of oil and start pouring. But it can be a treacherous and arrogant impulse. It is foolish to think I can make it better. Often the situation requires that spurt of anger, that clash of wills, or vision, or whatever you want to call it.

Mothers must stop small children punching each other: my three sons heard me repeat like a mantra, "physical violence never solved anything." But walking away from a physical fight has nothing to do with pursuing an argument as an adult. And too often the altruism of self-styled peacemakers becomes the suppression of self. It smothers emotional currents: it allows old men to be cranky, so they can be soothed, or sisters to be wilful, knowing they will be forgiven. How often, in my attempts to ensure that everyone is feeling comfortable, have I watched a pall of polite behaviour settle like sawdust on the gathering?

The compulsion to chivvy everyone into happiness is a female trait, but not every woman shares it. Catharine's sister Susanna Moodie didn't. The author of *Roughing It in the Bush* made others (especially her husband) dance to her tune. She felt no obligation to keep relations sweet. She saw herself first and foremost as an author rather than as the centre and motor of a family. I know women today who can observe confrontation without rushing into soothe; several revel in a good fight. This attitude can make them seem cruelly disdainful of others' feelings. But it also allows them to take risks. Susanna Moodie snubbed her neighbours, then caricatured them in print in a way that Catharine Parr Traill could never do. The people in Susanna's books about Canada are as fresh and alive today as they were when she dipped her quill into the sooty ink. The characters in Catharine's books, on the other hand, are impossibly sweet and well-meaning.

Women who lack the selfless gene take risks because they

like to rock the boat. They want their lives to be potent and dangerous. They walk out of marriages to explore other lives; they change careers; they take up flying or scuba diving in middle age. Neither Catharine nor I would launch ourselves into such dramatic new directions — there are too many other people to think of. We have chosen predictability and reliability; but sometimes the scaffolding of our life creaks. We stand in a centuries-long line of women who have sighed ruefully and tried to pacify. We want to keep our citizenship in the country we have made for ourselves. We watch Susanna and her fellow risk-takers with doubt and longing.

Yet we can enjoy the deep contentment of the known, past and present. Catharine's determination to plaster over the cracks in her own family relations enabled her, as she grew old, to look back with satisfaction over a life that spanned the nineteenth century (she lived from 1802 to 1899). "Time seems to lay a hallowing finger on the past, smooth all the rough points and gild the dark shades of the picture," she wrote to her best friend. "I think that I have a happy faculty of forgetting past sorrows and only remembering the pleasures." From where I sit, Catharine made the best of a bad job because, by circumstance and temperament, she had no choice. And she was much happier than ornery, quixotic Susanna, who was never satisfied with what she had and was haunted until death by regrets for lost opportunities. I realize that I *do* have a choice: I needn't pay so much attention to everybody else's feelings. These days, it is easier and more acceptable to be a Susanna Moodie than a Catharine Parr Traill. But I wish that I had realized earlier that women do not have to be universal soothers.

Mrs. Jones

Lily Redmond

The first time I heard the word "abortion" it was 1977. Mrs. Jones, our neighbour across the street, was in her early forties. She and her husband had had three children but their eighteen-year-old son had been killed in a car accident a couple of years earlier. They had recently adopted a nine-year-old girl who was troubled and was proving very challenging to raise. Mrs. Jones was constantly upset. I remember overhearing my mother and one of our other neighbours gossiping about Mrs. Jones, saying that she had adopted the little girl because she felt guilty about an abortion she'd had not long after her son was killed.

I would have been about thirteen at the time and didn't understand what the word "abortion" meant. Later I asked my mother to explain. I never looked at Mrs. Jones the same way again. Though we were not strict Catholics in my family, we did go to church most Sundays and I knew the Ten Commandments by heart. *Thou shalt not kill.* But even then I knew that sometimes I, too, took these matters into my own hands. I had spent summers swatting flies around the house and burying armies of ants by plugging up the holes in their sandhills. And worst of all (my darkest secret), I once got tired of caring for my pet turtles, Coke and Cola, and starved them to death.

In high school I remember the hushed rumours about girls who had "gotten into trouble." The word "abortion" was so potent; it sounded bad, and by extension, so were those girls. In Health class the subject of unwanted pregnancy never came up. We learned about reproduction and birth control, of course — how babies were actually *made* — but we never talked about what options you had if a pregnancy happened accidentally. This wasn't the 1950s, either; it was a relatively liberated time — the mid-1970s — but abortion was still illegal, though I suspect that wasn't the only reason it never came up in class.

Having sex leads to having babies. This is something most of us know at a fairly young age, but until you actually become pregnant, the acts of making love and of getting pregnant can seem disconnected. Theoretically you know that by having sex you risk becoming pregnant, and yet somehow it still feels removed from what you are doing — expressing affection, giving and receiving pleasure. So what a truly shocking moment it is when that reality comes crashing in: you have conceived a child.

It is a humid day, one of the dog days of summer. I've just finished serving the lunch crowd at the diner where I work. In a few weeks, I will begin my second year of university. I am twenty-three years old. I live with my boyfriend; he is a student, too. I push my quarter into the telephone box and dial the number of the birth control clinic. I ask for the results of my pregnancy test. I am numbed by the answer. I flee work. I ride my bicycle down the street to the restaurant where my boyfriend is working. I don't say a word but I don't have to. He takes my hand and says he will be home as soon as he can. I get back on my bike, just as the skies turn black, then open up. I peddle furiously through the torrential rain. I am frightened. My tears are mixing with the water lashing at my face and the pain of it feels good. When I reach home I call my sister. I am standing in a puddle, unable to say the words. She guesses my news, and then says to me, "How. Could. You. Let. This. Happen?" And I am deeply ashamed.

We talk about a pregnant woman "having a baby." That is, unless she is not planning to carry the baby to term. Then we speak of "a pregnancy," and call what she is going to do "terminating the pregnancy." This woman is not referred to as a mother, for she has decided that she does not want to become one. When a woman miscarries, we say she "lost her baby." But when she aborts, we use very different language. We don't use the word "baby." That would perhaps make it too human, too painful.

Pregnancy, for a woman who is going to have her baby, is an experience that manifests itself outwardly as well as inwardly. The world opens up to her. She is congratulated and celebrated. I imagine that sometimes it can be *too* much of an outward experience, especially when people (oddly) feel entitled to touch her growing belly without being invited to do so. She becomes, in a sense, public property; her pregnancy is shared by those she comes in contact with.

But a pregnant woman who is going to have an abortion withdraws, turns inward. Her pregnancy is hushed, shared with very few people. She is having the same physical experience as the mother-to-be but she cannot talk about it. In fact, she will never be able to join in conversations about pregnancy. The mother-to-be, if she wishes, can openly talk about how she feels, while the woman awaiting an abortion does her best to deny her symptoms, to forget that she is pregnant, to act as though she weren't.

I make my decision instantly; I do not waver for a second. I want an abortion. My boyfriend is sad but accepting, and we do not discuss other options. In the following weeks, during the waiting period when a group of three doctors will decide whether or not I am allowed to receive an abortion, we rarely speak of my condition. I am angry that my fate is in the hands of these doctors, who do not know me but who possess the power to deny me a safe abortion. I try to forget that I am pregnant but I cannot ignore the changes that are taking place in my body. I am different. I want to throw up whenever I go into the diner kitchen and smell the chicken wings being fried. I fight to stay awake much past eight o'clock every night. I am exhausted. Though I am losing weight, my breasts are fuller, in preparation for the child that will never be nursed. Sometimes I look in the mirror at my naked body, trying to believe that I am pregnant, that there is actually something growing inside me, something with a heartbeat. It seems so unreal, yet once or twice I feel what I can only describe as a kind of secret pride that I have conceived, that I am able to procreate. And this feeling is immediately followed by remorse and shame. I see the doctors at the clinic several times. Finally, my case is approved and a date is set. I do not want to have the abortion on the date they give me but if I postpone it I will be into the first week of the new school year. I say yes. It is three weeks away.

One of the things that perhaps defines us as women is our need and our ability to be emotionally open — honest and intimate with one another. To tell each other our stories in order to make sense of our lives. We will talk about almost anything, including abortion. And yet discussions about abortion usually take place within a political context, not a personal one. When it comes up, I freely and firmly give my opinion, or, rather, state my position. I am pro-choice, I say, and I believe unequivocally in a woman's right to choose what happens to her body. I rarely, however, add that I think abortion is a tragedy. And I never say that I have been through it myself.

I am getting dressed. The phone rings. It is my mother calling. She asks me how I am going to spend my day. I lie. I tell her I will see her in a few days. She tells me that she loves me. She tells me that she is proud to have me for a daughter. My heart breaks. And before she hangs up, she wishes me a happy birthday. My boyfriend holds my hand tightly as we walk to the hospital, but his presence barely registers with me. I am lost inside myself, inside the hugeness of this moment, which I will attempt to bury as soon as it is over.

Abortion is cloaked in silence. After I had my abortion I desperately wanted to know how other women who had had abortions felt about their experience. I combed bookstores and libraries searching for material. I found nothing. Certainly it is a very private matter, but that is not the only reason women are reluctant to talk about their personal experiences with it. Few people know that I have had an abortion. I have asked other women I know who have had abortions why they, too, are reluctant to disclose this fact about themselves. Our reasons are almost always the same. We are afraid of being judged. As careless, as selfish, as reckless, as heartless, as a slut, as amoral. In a word: bad. Like those girls in high school. And how do you justify your decision to have an abortion when you are white, middle-class, healthy and privileged? The fear is of being judged for rejecting the most natural thing in the world: motherhood.

Anyone can make a mistake, even one of this magnitude. We are, as they say, "only human," and we are complicated beings. And sometimes we repeat our mistakes.

I am twenty-nine years old, I am single, and my period is late. I am ignoring this fact. There's no way I could be pregnant. No. I think back to the night four weeks ago when I went to dinner with a former boyfriend. I loved him once, and I still care for him, but we are not meant to be life partners. I know this, and he knows it, too. But it felt so natural, so comforting, to fall into each other's arms at the end of an evening spent reminiscing about everything that had been good about us, and none of what had driven us apart. I have not seen or talked to him since that night. I was certain that it was a safe time in my cycle, yet I can't explain why I took the chance. I decide to buy a pregnancy test. I stare at it on my bathroom shelf for a day. I cannot avoid this any longer. I open the kit and pee on the stick. It takes less than a minute for the little window to reveal a "+" sign. I rush to the nearest pharmacy and hand over my urine sample. They retest it while I wait. It is, of course, positive. "Could there be a mistake?" I ask. But the only mistake is mine. Again.

Sometimes I find it hard to believe that I am a woman who has had two abortions. On the rare occasion when I do confide in someone about my experience with abortion, I usually tell a half-truth. I confess that I have had an abortion. Two, somehow, seems unforgivable.

Every day the pendulum swings in the opposite direction. One day I tell myself I will have this baby. The next day I panic and fear that I am not strong enough to handle it alone. I feel myself becoming crippled by my indecision. Two weeks have passed. I am in a daze, lying on my bed staring up at the ceiling and all I can think is how much I do not want to face this. I see my doctor and she gives me a due date — June 6 — which makes it feel very real. On June 6 a baby will begin its life, and my life will be changed irrevocably.

We do not call it what it is: destroying life, life that, if left in the hands of a benign Mother Nature, would result in the birth of a baby. It is not a baby — not yet — but it is *life* nonetheless.

Time is running out. My ambivalence prevails. I feel like a failure.

It took me years to forgive myself for not being strong enough to have that baby. Nothing has marked me more. I am now thirty-six years old. I do not have children. I remain single. My greatest fear is that I will miss my chance to have a family — that time will run out on me — and that I will look back on the two occasions when I actually could have had a baby and regret that I didn't. I hope I will remember that I made the best decision I could at the time.

The streets are still shrouded in darkness as I slip into the hospital. It is six a.m. I register and take a seat in the waiting room alongside a half dozen or so other women. I have seen them all before at the clinic. We didn't talk to each other then and we are not talking now. We are locked in our silent worlds. The only sound in the room is the clock ticking. I look around at these women and I wonder what their stories are and what has led them to their decision to be here today. I wonder if any of them feel the way I do. Are they scared too?

My name is called and I am taken to a little change room. I put on a hospital gown and climb into a bed. A nurse starts an IV drip and the last of my waiting begins. I see the nurses come for us — one by one — at about twenty-minute intervals. I feel wretchedly alone. I am aware that it is not too late to change my mind. Part of me wants to leap from the bed and run, but the bigger part of me is frozen and will not. I want this to be over so there is no longer a decision to be made. At the same time I know that in some way it will never be over, that I will carry this with me for the rest of my life. It will become a part of my story, a piece of the puzzle to be shared with those few people in my life that I love and trust completely. This time my mother will be waiting for me when I am ready to leave the hospital. She will take me home and we will have tea. We won't say much, but her simply being there with me will be enough. I will feel immense relief but it will be tempered by an equal measure of sadness. Finally, the nurse comes for me and leads me down the hall. I lie down on the operating table and put my feet in the stirrups. I say a silent prayer and a heaviness seeps into my body as I slowly begin to count. "Ninety-nine, ninety-eight, ninety-seven ..."

Edited Version

Isla James

It's her night to stay up with the child. The woman and her husband take turns: one sleeps in the child's vacant room across the hall; the other stays up with her in their bedroom, keeping watch. After the six a.m. feeding, the woman unplugs the portable suction machine beside the bed — an act of bravery she rarely allows — and replaces it with the wicker rocker. That way, she can reach the child's face with one hand and keep her body angled towards the window, her eyes on the streaks of moonlight inching over the carpet towards the bed. The moving light anchors her, provides neutral territory for her gaze as she traces the child's features with her fingertips: around the eyes, down the nose, to the lips, and then back up the cheeks. Her hands know the way, at first circling gently over the tiny, Braille bumps then flattening over the hairless side of the head, her open palm feeling for the raised scar.

The woman closes her eyes then and retreats into the cool, sightless space of her head where she finds a circle of white heat she can stretch and spin into a thin current. She imagines it burning down through her body, out her hands, straight into the child where it can heal and reverse the damage. Her body arches forward and her face is red from the effort and the heat she is directing. Often, when this ritual ends she tries to hang on to the sense of power by keeping her eyes closed until she turns away from the child. But on this night, she has a surge of hope and opens her eyes while still curved over her daughter, expecting a change, some sign from the child locked behind that still face, now lit up by the light that has moved in over it.

Why is the sight always a shock? Maybe because of a contrast that hangs before her, the memory of her husband's teasing remarks about wearing out her eyes when the children were newborns. Back then, she couldn't stop gazing at the parcels of soft, scented flesh that had split off from hers. She had expected to love her children; she hadn't been prepared for falling *in love* with them or for the overwhelming urge to study perfection in their features.

This face in front of her now is foreign with its features ashen and taut, the skin a thin, transparent membrane stretched over a network of tiny, blue veins. The eyes are the most difficult to take in; they're open and expressionless with pupils wide and fixed. The mother feels a rush of anger; she should have known that these little black discs wouldn't respond to the light or her efforts. Drained of purpose, her hands drop to the child's body, where even with the nightshirt and blanket between, they fall on sharp bone.

Next she's at the bedroom window with her back turned. She's looking up at the early morning winter sky where the setting moon is full and smug, hanging over the shingled horizon of the neighbour's garage roof. She watches the burnt orange disc being sliced to a half circle then sinking behind the roofline. *Good. Disappearance is good.* Her head swivels at the sound of the sharp words escaping from her, sensing that someone is behind her. It's her husband, his expression smooth and free of judgement, there to trade places with her so she can see their son before he leaves for school. She's heard both of them earlier across the hall, her husband calling their son from sleep in a rich and comforting voice, and then the sound of genuine laughter — something she tries with the boy these days in an attempt to be normal. But the laughter falls from her like cracked ice, hard little pings of fake sound that alarm the boy and cause him to slide away from her and search out his father.

She's losing them all as a result of some terrible error, a fundamental flaw in character or a blazing sin that has slipped by her unnoticed and is now damaging everyone around her. This conclusion is her latest one, a heavy clunk of knowledge that keeps her rooted in the silent kitchen after her husband and son have left. She's trying to remember what she's doing there in the centre of the room, maybe counting the tiles again, the cream-coloured ones. She recalls that her husband had wanted bright colours; she had insisted on neutral tones. Why? Why had she cared? There's an invisible wall between then and now. No going back.

She pushes herself through the weight of these thoughts to the fridge and opens it, closing her nostrils to a putrid smell. *Tomorrow I'll check.* The words float through her mind with no will attached to them as she takes out an egg and a glass jar full of a brownish herb mixture and places them both on the counter. She remembers now that she needs the blender from the corner cupboard. The door of the cupboard refuses to pull up; its horizontal wood slats hold tight at one corner. She smashes the heels of her hands against the bottom of the door and pushes upwards. Still no movement. She pounds both upper corners. Her hands are stinging but the door hasn't budged.

How she comes to have a hammer in her hand, she's not sure. The sound of smashing wood satisfies her though, opens a river of power that surges through her. The gaping hole in the corner of the door allows her to hook the claws of the hammer into it and pull it up with ease. She retrieves the blender from inside and slams the door down. Later, when her husband discovers the jagged hole and fixes it, silently and painstakingly, with a board from the basement, she has to turn sharply from the sight of the soft curve of his neck as he bends over his redemptive task.

Back in the bedroom, she pours the liquid food into the syringe she's connected to the feeding tube taped to the child's nose. She's careful to lock her eyes on the liquid as it flows down in a slow stream, leaving the occasional splat of brown herbal substance clinging to the sides of the plastic syringe. Whatever these herbs aren't doing, they're enabling the child to hold down more feedings. Some of the panic over her starving has lifted.

So how will it come?

The doctors had sat them down, kept sympathetic eye contact when explaining. *There are certain things you should be prepared for if you want to keep her at home until the end.* They had a pamphlet, it turned out. *When Death Is Near* was the title. She had plunged the leaflet into her purse. It was still there, never opened. *Don't watch her die; watch her live*, her mother had said those first few days. She was determined to do just that, whenever she could watch. She hadn't known how much of the time she'd have to keep her eyes closed, or how death wasn't a single act but a series of silent takeovers.

Looking back, it was easy to see when it had all started. The initial signs were the tripping and the watery eyes, then the drowsiness, so unusual in a child just two. At first the doctors were fooled: *Just a virus, keep an eye on her and call if the symptoms persist.* Then it asserted itself more. Alarm. Tests. Then, an abrupt end of reassuring words, consoling looks. The avoidance began: *The doctor will be in to speak with you this afternoon… this evening… tomorrow morning.* When the doctor finally did appear, he closed the door to the room and pulled the curtain around the child's bed, sealing all four of them in, cutting them off, she discovered, from the rest of their lives. His words fell out, straight, specific, ice sharp: *third-degree malignancy, inoperable.* Then, the naming — *death* — with its agenda — *six months.* At first, these words hadn't parted the space between them or moved inward into sense; they had just hung there mid-air, deposits of a crazed Hermes, who then slid swiftly through the curtain and out the door.

What had they said to each other? Who cried first? That's not clear. What remains is a memory of the floor falling away from her and a hollow growing inside, pressing all the air out of her lungs, and she remembers looking at her husband, just in time to see the light go out in his eyes. In reaction to their sounds, the child's eyes had widened then dropped closed, responding to the mounting pressure inside her head.

Gradually, the shades of death had grown deeper, more distinct, especially on the child's face, at first puffy and blotched from the treatments, all the delicate features submerged. The only defense the woman had was not to look. Her husband's days passed from bargaining with a God, who had slipped beyond imagining, to a frantic search for alternatives: faith healers, herbal concoctions, laetrile smuggled across the Mexican and American borders. He spun out his impotence into a stream of outward action; she ravelled hers into tight knots of energy that fuelled her daily tending; both were acts of defiance against an expanding black hole.

Time expanded too. Six months had stretched to a year, to a year and a half. The clamour had seeped out of both of them over that period. Yet her husband still moved with a purpose, as though what force and action had failed to do, his gentle absorption of everyone's pain could accomplish. She feared his splitting wide open and tried at their night meetings to hold his cracking shell together. Other times, the two of them were parallel lines, strung out waiting, sometimes with impatience, for the end they dreaded.

There were other times when they escaped, or were pushed by a life force, to a space where their life was a small patch of intense darkness at a distance. They'd dress up, clear off a broad expanse of cement floor in the basement, and dance — for hours, it seemed. He'd put on Creedence Clearwater Revival tapes, old grooves of sound that called up wild, swooping body rhythms that left them dripping with sweat and exhilaration. They knew what waited for them upstairs; for breathless moments they could dance it off. But not on days like this one.

In the afternoon she probably moved the child to the living room as she usually did. Most likely she plugged the phone in beside the sofa, placed one of the books she was reading within reach and sat holding the child to the heat of her body, stroking or rocking automatically when movement asserted itself. Maybe the phone rang. He husband would have called, he always did, and her mother, the substance of both voices filling in some of the cracks that would have started to open in her because of the long afternoon, and the sounds of children playing on the front street. She would have had the window opened a bit even at that time of the year. Was it to receive those sounds?

Did anyone drop by? Not likely, or if someone did it would have been the neighbour from down the street. She was one of the few who could turn her face fully to a view of their lives. Often, during those afternoons, she'd crouch by the sofa, and, in unison, the two women would stroke the child's face, their fingers moving and circling in a slow dance of care that was never accompanied by words.

Or maybe there had been phone calls from others, voices oddly buoyant with little balloon words to keep the talk floating away from dark corners. *But I'm there,* the woman would call in her head, knowing she had to speak other words, reassure them she was positive, hopeful, blessing the goodness of her own strength, her husband's caring ways, their son's bright mind, which had taken on — she understood why — an edge of compensatory brilliance. She received these over-the-phone buoyancies as gifts that couldn't be refused, like clothes that didn't fit and had to be packed away in a box under the bed.

Others may have called to explain their absences, or

appease their guilt. *The flu's going around here … don't want to bother you … mustn't intrude … if you ever need help, just call.* The fine hairs at the nape of her neck would have risen at the last phrase, if it had come. Probably, it didn't. No hard little bullet of memory shoots up from that part of the day.

Later that day — it's Thursday, and this nest of routine still holds them — she transfers the child to her husband's arms before going to her evening class. There's a clear picture of him, home early from work, dropping his suit jacket over the chair near the sofa, scooping the child up into his arms and carrying her to the rocker where he immediately starts rocking and singing, his face dipped close to hers. There's no memory of what went on in her class. It must have been the one on science fiction, where the space to hide was double layered: she could disappear into the guise of student and then sail off to extrapolated worlds, universes ruled by god computers or by Martians who could shape-shift into live versions of dead family members. One thing for sure, she did go to class that evening even when, *surely*, there must have been signs during the day.

The time after her return from class has permanent memory grooves; every moment is clear. She walks into the house, closes the door and remains standing in the back hall, squinting into the darkness as the air, pungent with the smell of Lysol, hits her nostrils.

He's cleaned the suction machine; I hope he remembered to plug it in. These thoughts shift her focus, call her body back to its grooves so that her movements down the hall to the bedroom area are again automatic. The bathroom door is partly open, allowing out a slash of light that angles into her son's room. She lets it direct her into the bedroom where the rhythm of breathing is outside her, swirling around in the half darkness.

Her eyes adjust and she can make out her son splayed out on the bed, covers kicked off, legs folded at the knees in a wide vee and arms thrown back in a posture of supplication. His face is turned away from the wall, into the room and the small space lit by the burning red glow of the numbers on his bedside alarm: 9:59. As the number flap turns over, a wave of light passes over his face. Still, firm, calm — something else — unbroken, remarkable in its wholeness. She stands watching his body move to the rhythm of his breathing until she is inhaling as he exhales, then returning the air in a smooth push as he draws in. She allows, even welcomes, the ease of that exchange.

All this time her body and face have been angled away in resistance to the other sight that pulls at her, but the tug is too strong. On the floor beside the son's bed is an encampment of two other bodies. The daughter lies in the scoop of the father's right arm; his other arm curves over her and up onto the bed where his hand covers his son's in a soft mound, holding the surge of life in. He breathes in and out in strong, regular gusts. He has fallen asleep there while singing to them, sliding the son into sleep on the deep, round notes of his song.

A warm wave is spreading inside the woman, widening the cracks, but she doesn't try to block its advance. It will open a space for him to enter later when at two or three a.m. he will probably wake, cramped from his protective posture on the floor. He'll carry the child back to their room, cradle her shift back to bed, place the pillow between her knee bones and cover her with the blanket. As always, he'll arrange the satin edge to rest on her face. Then, he'll glide over those same tiles she counts repeatedly and enter her room — and then her. She will wake to a rhythm of theirs that has risen, unbidden, and find herself moving with him, circling him with her arms and legs, holding in all the shards of feeling that eventually spill out, first in sharp gasps and then in a wide, muffled cry that rolls through his body. He'll stay there with her until a movement, some need of the child in their bedroom, calls him, often soundlessly. (He seems connected to his daughter at a level from which the woman is absent.) He'll wake with a jolt and slip gently from her circled limbs. Before leaving, he'll stand over her, tuck the top sheet around her body, then lift the hair from the back of her neck and kiss the soft hollow of flesh. Usually the sensations that follow will carry her into sleep. Sometime though, they are too strong an intrusion and cause the pain to surface again, swell and widen until the only response possible for her is a sharp cry she tries to mute by biting into her pillow.

That night, he doesn't come to her.

She doesn't know what sound alerts her or whether the silence does. She finds herself awake in a sitting position with her head arched toward the hall. The fall of his voice catches her as she moves to the bedroom door. *Oh no, no, don't, don't.* By the time she is at his side, he has the child half out of the bed, his arms lifting her to his chest, his forehead pressed down into her still, blank face. A syringe half filled with clear liquid hangs from his limp right hand. The mother doesn't have to ask; the change in the air tells her *it* has come. She wraps her arms around them both and leans in, moving with the father's sobs and the rhythm of his broken voice.

The pain had broken through — she couldn't — her breath — the suction machine … unplugged … I couldn't ... She's gone. All that loveliness, gone.

She knows. *I know, I know.* The woman has vaporized, is without substance, yet is able to hold him — them — tighter. The child's body is still warm, pliable, one arm falling free and swinging in a purposeless arc. And her face. The mother lifts the father's head up, uncovering the child's face and sees, for the first time in days, the beauty, the sheer sculptured beauty of the face of her dead daughter.

Lora stops there, the hum of the computer taking over as she leans back in her chair, resting her head on the cushioned rim.

One of those last images had stopped her, left her chasing breaths in short, quick gasps. She had planned to go on, to describe how she — the woman she was then — kept blindly to the movements etched out in the air before her, how her husband Charles had slumped over their daughter's body and vowed he'd never forgive himself. How they had lain the dead child down, washed her cooling body — she sponging with a cloth dipped in warm, scented water; he following her movements, patting dry with a towel, their soft, breathy sobs mingling as, together and separately, they did their final tending. How, then, she had gone to Kyle's bedroom, kissed him awake, carried him in to see his sister and say good-bye. *Where has she gone?* he had asked, pulling away from the sight. They hadn't been prepared for the horror on his face or what to do next, when he ran from the room. Should they have done that, she wondered for years after, forced him to see? His sister's colour had started to change, and he was only six.

They were also unprepared about what to do next, whom to call, what to say: Come pick up our daughter? Our dead child? The body? Language had failed them then, as it fails her now.

Lora sits up and shakes the mouse to bring the print back on the screen. Her hands continue to tremble as she moves the cursor up to the print icon. Then she pauses, thinking about the press of ink on white paper and the release of these images for other eyes.

The previous week at a Y Neighbours' meeting, during a presentation on "Living through Grief," Lora had first seen the young mother. She was sitting at the back of the room, half-covered by a large, plastic fig tree, weeping silently throughout the talk. When Lora was leaving, dodging her way through noisy knots of reunited mothers and children, this young woman appeared at her elbow. Somehow she knew. She clutched Lora's arm and unhinged her with an account of a young son, home from the hospital, dying. Then with her direct, desperate plea:

"When did it come? Were you prepared? The doctors say we should be prepared. What should we do? How can we? How did you — watch your child die?"

Lora hadn't expected these queries; she didn't have time to arrange her face or her story. The old lie had surfaced: "We didn't; we watched her live, every precious moment." As soon as she spoke she knew that camouflage was for other times, other needs; she shouldn't have given the young woman the edited version. She should have prepared her, at least for the guilt. Warned her not to absorb it all the way Charles had.

Charles... Of course. With him gone, the words had dried up, no one in the same loop of memory, inhabiting the same need. Now this young mother and her question, the hook into the skin of the wound, peeling it back and letting her bleed. Amazing how the flow was print — black lines, curves and crosses rising up to contain all that history.

The printer cuts in with a series of clicks and whirs. It's ready. Lora stares at the words on the screen and then turns her head to blot them out. Even with her eyes closed, the image that's been chasing her forms inside her head — the little, dead arm, swinging. Then the young mother's face floats forward, eyes round and struck with knowing. Lora reaches down and switches off the computer. The words wobble, shimmer momentarily, and disappear.

She gets up and walks over to the window where the shades are stripped back to a clear view of the night sky. The stars are out, and the new moon, a thin thumbnail piece of gold perched in the sky waiting for her. *There you are.* These words rise up in Lora as a greeting to an old friend. She'll watch it grow this week and then call the young mother — she'll find her number somehow. As she turns from the window, she pictures herself kneeling beside the mother and her son while keeping her face turned fully to the child.

Outside, the curved moon climbs to the exact angle needed for its light to slip through the branches of the naked trees, casting alternate strips of light and shadow on the soft snow in the woman's backyard.

just a part

Deborah Schnitzer

It is four in the morning and I am roaming the main floor, looking for some hard surface that will take my weight. How many of us are there tonight, I wonder, standing in front of kitchen windows scouring night gardens, opening and closing fridges, pulling at the covers of memory trying to imagine endings unbelievable and yet entirely possible? Middle-of-the-night sifters of sorrow, we live with those who are chronically ill. We are awake well before dawn and we will fall back into sleep. But first, we pick up the plot of a story we have been telling inside ourselves from the moment illness first found our loved one. I think of it as a series of stages, of images I pull out and hold in my hand like cut glass, examining them over and over again. How can this be me? You?

I find some fat-free chocolate ice cream in the freezer and some chocolate sauce full of fat. I mix the two together in the middle of words and images I can barely comprehend. I stand in the kitchen tasting this concoction, then putting it away, tossing the spoon into the dishwasher, taking the ice cream and the sauce out once more, trying a new spoon, digging in, playing with the cool sweetness in my mouth, closing the lid, opening it. I look for signs and, pushed awake as I am, I race upstairs to the computer and try to find a way into its heart so that I can write down what is on my mind as you lie snoring at four thirty-two in the morning. I have been thinking of this story in stages for ten years. Here is one way I tell it.

I remember walking down a sunlit road at the family cottage just before the final diagnosis. We were arguing. You were optimistic; I was bleak. We were unable to look at one another. I knew what lay ahead, even when there was no actual confirmation. You reached out so that I could feel the strength in your hand. You had a big, strong hand that I had put my life into, saying, full-throated, at the age of eighteen: "Here, you are so sure of what is real, so sure of what we can do." Twenty years later, hurrying toward an unimaginable loss, the diagnosis has reconfigured your hand, our hold.

We walked, for that last time, through the woods to Anne's cottage and you told me not to worry, that we would come this way again, laughing, recovered, that we could beat this. I have never forgotten the strength in your hand. You were full of well-being. Your body had always worked. You were strong and made for summer and shorts and odd jobs. You could fix almost anything.

I watched families at the holiday concert the following winter. I watched people who did not know about the ending of things between them, who were not awake at four in the morning bracing themselves at the kitchen sink, heavy with loss, tear-stained. I didn't know this about them; I presumed it. There were children all about and a potluck with occasional wonders. Our own children were young, three and four feet tall. I watched these families and I said, "We are not a part of them any more. We know something that they are not living. We are living a diagnosis whose complexity shadows us."

How do people in movies end things? We often make the

mistake of renting the ones where some beloved one dies, and you start to cry and I start to get angry, especially at the really brave parts, where maybe a mother says goodbye to her children and says it really well and doesn't just become one large teardrop they all drown in. The last one we saw — I didn't know that what's-her-name was going to die. Can people really look that beautiful in the last stages of cancer?

There have been ten years of these kinds of comparisons, poignant, sometimes silly, sometimes unfair. And I say to myself and to your snoring self in the middle of the night, I hardly recognize you now. Your hand, big as it is, is not as strong, and the colour of your skin is different. Your eyes are swollen, and when you move to get up from a chair, you hesitate, often wince. And still, I think to myself, you are with us, and today you finished spring cleaning the last window in the second floor porch. Six years ago, you had enough energy to climb the ladder to our bedroom window, and you were determined to finish washing that one before you let somebody teach you how to hook your catheter up to bags of fluid so that you could flush your system out four times a day. I was no Rapunzel and you were no Knight in Shining Armour.

Your rituals mark the passing of the stages of this disease that has destroyed your own kidneys. They have seen you through dialysis, a transplant, the failure of that transplant, and now the waiting to go on dialysis again. Again and again, so many stages and mutations in the stages, so much ravaging by the disease and the drugs that trick your body into keeping you alive, that prolong the dying of this transplanted kidney. Numbers and checkups and biopsies and charts and complications. Grief. Guilt. Fear. So many words unspoken between us because sometimes we feel we will die if we name it, if we think about the time when we will not be together, when the children and I will remember you.

You're not supposed to be dying, really — just living with a terminal illness. The paradoxes make and unmake sense. We were raised on plots that had beginnings, middles and endings. Our middle is our end, as far as we can tell. Yet meaning is not contingent upon position or cure. It is made inside of "maybe" and "what if." We are surprised, like Mr. Stevens in *Remains of the Day*. He thinks back through his life and remembers a "turning point" when he did not act, when he did not say what was in his heart, and he says, quite simply, that he always thought that he would have more time, time to say what he could not say, time to try again, and it has come to him, now, at the end, that he has no more time.

We are surprised, often daunted, speechless. And I worry. Will I have said the things I should have said or done the things I should have done? And I know I won't. Sometimes I can live each day as if it were our last one together. I can see how nuthatch and treebranch could not have been more exquisitely suited to each other; am grateful for the treatment that is available that has kept you with us against the odds; can stand still and think of how much love we have lived in what might be too short a time. I can do that, yes, I can. I can also say, "Nothing has prepared us for this; nothing ever will, for I cannot imagine a world without you in it." Then, I do. Sometimes I want an ending even when the ending kills you off. And when you die, I won't know the world any more and I will have to spend the rest of my life building it anew.

People need to tell me that you look cute. Prednisone increases hair growth, and there was a period this past year when you found out that you were in chronic rejection, and you grew this incredible beard and let your hair fly out like a ring of fire. People figured that you'd just climbed off some Moses mountain. You look prophetic — and you are. When people who don't know about the illness see you, they say inappropriate things as if you had a particularly rotten flu. You know: "God, you look awful; I had it last month. Nearly did me in." What are we going to say in return? I want surtitles running across my forehead so that when people stare, they can read the plot that you and I are living. When I am in the middle of a meeting, I want some flashing lights, some way to say, "Oh, I am full of broken glass from living with someone who has been dying for a long time."

But when you say that out loud, even to the best of friends, they try and shush you, a partial lullaby to soothe that which cannot be soothed. They tell you about the advances in medicine, and that any one of us could be hit by a bus, and that we are all living on borrowed time, or they ask you if you've heard about Grace and Tony and their little boy who has leukemia. These are contexts. My sane brain says that what they are telling me is true, but my sad and heavy heart wants them to see that we have been hit by a bus, and we cannot get over it. Part of us wakes up every day overwhelmed by what we know, even as part of us gets on with the living of the day.

Sometimes, when you are very sick, you seem more dead than alive. And then, some adjustment in medication brings you back to life, or the virus runs its course, the thrush retreats into the forest, the cramps subside, the swelling moves from one part of your body to the next, lumps are removed and their biopsies are friendly.

Our children live in the present tense. They know that you are here, that your strange appearance can sometimes startle them, that they have names for when you behave irrationally. They call you Erg, even Tomatohead. We are redolent with gallows humour. The youngest is learning to drive. The oldest is driving you crazy. He has read *The Wealthy Barber* (he claims you have bought him three copies) and knows about financial planning and saving for the rainy day, but he's only nineteen, artistic, and doesn't want all the advice you give him.

You have been saving for a rainy day your whole life. Child of survivors of the Holocaust, Poland-born, you want to leave a legacy for your children because you will not see them into their future. And I tell you that your legacy is now and always, forever and immediate, and that it is raining. You meet with your financial advisor. To be perverse, when I am more angry than sensitive, I talk about remodelling the kitchen, or buying a big house with a fortress around it and a moat, so wide we can defend ourselves against the bad stuff that is out to get us. I search for that house, often, the one that doesn't look like illness can live inside its 3000 square feet, the house that celebrates an immunity from disaster. I know that I can't have this house — that it doesn't really exist.

You have finished cleaning the window in the sun porch, all four panes. I am reminded of the way some ancient stories begin: "Once upon a time, there was and there was not." And so I adjust my understanding. I am Rapunzel and you are a Knight in Shining Armour and we are living with dying and no one told us it would be this difficult. We are not living with a cure. There is none. We run out of words just as we will run out of time.

There you lie. I make meaning at four in the morning, mixing the taste of chocolate ice cream and tears with the sound of your snoring self across the way.

A Father's Faith

Miriam Toews

On the morning on May 13, 1998, my father woke up, had breakfast, got dressed and walked away from the Steinbach Bethesda Hospital, where he had been a patient for two and a half weeks. He walked through his beloved hometown, along Hespeler Road, past the old farmhouse where his mother had lived with her second husband, past the water tower, greeting folks in his loud, friendly voice, wishing them well. He passed the site on First Street where the house in which my sister and I grew up once stood. He walked down Main Street, past the Mennonite church where, throughout his life, he had received countless certificates for perfect attendance, past Elmdale School where he had taught grade six for forty years.

As he walked by his home on Brandt Road, he saw his old neighbour Bill sitting in his lawn chair. He waved and smiled again, then he continued on past the cemetery where his parents were buried, and the high school his daughters had attended, and down Highway 52, out of town, past the Frantz Motor Inn, which is just outside the town limits because it serves alcohol and Steinbach is a dry town. He kept walking until he got too tired, so he hitched a ride with a couple of guys who were on their way to buy a fishing licence in the small village of Woodridge on the edge of the Sandilands Forest.

The sun would have been very warm by the time they dropped him off, and he would have taken off his stylish cap and wiped his brow with the back of his hand. I'm sure he thanked them profusely, perhaps offering them ten dollars for their trouble, and then he walked the short distance to the café near the railroad tracks, the place he and my mom would sometimes go for a quiet coffee and a change of scenery. He would have been able to smell the clover growing in the ditches beside the tracks and between the ties. He may have looked down the line and remembered that the train would be coming from Ontario, through Warroad, Minnesota, on its way to Winnipeg.

A beautiful young woman named Stephanie was just beginning her shift and she spoke to him through the screen door at the side of the restaurant. Yes, she said, the train will be here soon. And my dad smiled and thanked her, and mentioned that he could hear the whistle. Moments later, he was dead.

Steinbach is an easy forty-minute drive from Winnipeg, east on the Trans-Canada, then south on Highway 12. On the way into town there's a sign proclaiming "Jesus Saves." On the way back to the city just off Highway 12 there's another that says, "Satan is Real. You Can't Be Neutral. Choose Now." The town has recently become a city of 8,500 people, two-thirds of whom are Mennonite, so it's not surprising that about half of the twenty-four churches are Mennonite and conservative. There is a Catholic church too, but it's new and I'm not sure exactly where it is. A little way down from the bowling alley I can still make out my name on the sidewalk, carved in big bold letters when I was ten and marking my territory.

My town made sense to me then. For me it was a giant playground where my friends and I roamed freely, using the entire town in a game of arrows — something like hide-and-seek — for which my dad, the teacher, provided boxes and boxes of fresh new chalk and invaluable tips. He had, after all, played the same game in the same town many years before.

At six p.m. the siren would go off at the firehall, reminding all the kids to go home for supper, and at nine p.m. it was set off again, reminding us to go home to bed. I had no worries, and no desire ever to leave this place where everyone knew me. If they couldn't remember my name, they knew I was the younger daughter of Mel and Elvira Toews, granddaughter of C.T. Loewen and Henry Toews, from the Kleine Gemeinde congregation, and so on and so on. All the kids in town, other than the church-sponsored Laotians who came over in the seventies, could be traced all the way back to the precise Russian veldt their great-grandparents had emigrated from. They were some of the thousands of Mennonites who came to Manitoba in the late 1800s to escape religious persecution. They were given free land and a promise that they could, essentially, do their own thing without interference. They wanted to keep the world away from their children and their children away from the world. Naturally it was an impossible ideal.

As I grew older, I became suspicious and critical and restless and angry. Every night I plotted my escape. I imagined that Barkman's giant feed mill on Main Street, partially visible from my bedroom window, was a tall ship that would take me away some day. I looked up places like Hollywood and Manhattan and Venice and Montreal in my Childcraft encyclopedias. I begged my sister to play, over and over, the sad songs from her Jacques Brel piano book, and I'd light candles and sing along, wearing a Pioneer Girls tam on my head, using a chopstick as a cigarette holder, pretending I was Jackie Brel, Jacques's long-lost but just as world-weary Mennonite twin. I couldn't believe that I was stuck in a town like Steinbach, where dancing was a sin and a serving beer a felony.

There were other things I became aware of as well. That my grandmother was a vanilla alcoholic who believed she was a teetotaller. That seventy-five-year-old women who had borne thirteen children weren't allowed to speak to the church congregation, but that fifteen-year-old boys were. That every family had a secret. And I learned that my dad had been depressed all his life.

I had wondered, when I was a kid, why he spent so much of the weekend in bed and why he didn't talk much at home. Occasionally he'd tell me, sometimes in tears, that he loved me very much and that he wished he were a better father, that he were more involved in my life. But I never felt the need for an apology. It made me happy and a bit envious to know that my dad's students were able to witness his humour and intelligence firsthand, to hear him expound on his favourite subjects: Canadian history, Canadian politics and Canadian newspapers. I remember watching him at work and marvelling at his energy and enthusiasm. I thought he looked very handsome when he rolled up his sleeves and tucked his tie in between the buttons of his shirt, his hands on his hips, all ready for business and hard work.

Teaching school — helping others make sense of the world — was a good profession for a man who was continuously struggling to find meaning in life. I think he needed his students as much as they needed him. By fulfilling his duties, he was also shoring up a psyche at risk of erosion.

Four years before his death he was forced to retire from teaching because of a heart attack and some small strokes. He managed to finish the book he was writing on Canada's prime ministers, but then he seemed to fade away. He spent more and more of his time in bed, in the dark, not getting up even to eat or wash, not interested in watching TV or listening to the radio. Despite our pleading and cajoling, despite the medication and visits to various doctors' offices, appointments he dutifully kept, and despite my mother's unwavering love, we felt we were losing him.

I know about brain chemistry and depression, but there's still a part of me that blames my dad's death on being

Mennonite and living in that freaky, austere place where this world isn't good enough and admission into the next one, the perfect one, means everything, where every word and deed gets you closer to or farther away from eternal life. If you don't believe that then nothing Steinbach stands for will make sense. And if life doesn't make sense you lose yourself in it, your spirit decays. That's what I believed had happened to my dad, and that's why I hated my town.

In the weeks and months after his death, my mom and my sister and I tried to piece things together. William Ashdown, the executive director of the Mood Disorders Association of Manitoba, told us the number of mentally ill Mennonites is abnormally high. "We don't know if it's genetic or cultural," he said, "but the Steinbach area is one that we're vitally concerned about."

"It's the way the church delivers the message," says a Mennonite friend of mine, "the message of sin and accountability. To be human, basically, is to be a sinner. So a person, a real believer, starts to get down on himself, and where does it end? They say self-loathing is the cornerstone of depresson, right?"

Years ago, the Mennonite Church practised something called "shunning," whereby if you were to leave your husband, or marry outside the Church, or elope, or drink, or in some way contravene the Church's laws or act "out of faith," you could be expelled from the Church and ignored, shunned by the entire community, including your own family. Depression or despair, as it would have been referred to then, was considered to be the result of a lack of faith and therefore could be another reason for shunning.

These days most Mennonites don't offically practise shunning, although William Ashdown claims there are still Mennonites from extreme conservative sects who are being shunned and shamed into silence within their communites for being mentally ill. Certainly Arden Thiessen, the minister of my dad's church, and a long-time friend of his, is aware of the causes of depression and the pain experienced by those who suffer from it. He doesn't see it as a lack of faith, but as an awful sickness.

But I can't help thinking that that history had just a little to do with my alcoholic grandmother's insisting that she was a non-drinker, and my dad's telling his doctors, smiling that beautiful smile of his, that he was fine, just fine.

Not long before he died my dad told me about the time he was five and was having his tonsils out. Just before the operation began he was knocked out with ether and he had a dream that he was somersaulting through the hospital walls, right through, easily, he said, moving his hands in circles through the air. It was wonderful. He told me he would never forget that feeling.

But mostly, the world was a sad and unsafe place for him, and his town provided shelter from it. Maybe he saw this as a gift, while I came to see it as oppression. He could peel back the layers of hypocrisy and intolerance and see what was good, and I couldn't. He believed that it mattered what he did in life, and he believed in the next world, one that's better. He kept the faith of his Mennonite forebears to the very end, or what he might call the beginning, and removed himself from this world entirely.

Stephanie, the waitress in the café in Woodridge, told my mother that my dad was calm and polite when he spoke to her, as if he were about to sit down to a cup of tea. She told her that he hadn't seemed at all afraid. But why would you be if you believed you were going to a place where there is no more sadness?

My dad never talked to us about God or religion. We didn't have family devotion like everybody else. He never quoted out loud from the Bible or lectured us about not going to church. In fact his only two pieces of advice to me were "Be yourself" and "You can do anything."

But he still went to church. It didn't matter how low he

felt, or how cold it was outside. He would put on his suit and tie and stylish cap and walk the seven or eight blocks to church. He always walked, through searing heat or sub-arctic chill. If he was away on holdiays he would find a church and go to it. At the lake he drove forty miles down gravel roads to attend an outdoor church in the bush. I think he needed church like a junkie needs a fix: to get him through another day in a world of pain.

What I love about my town is that it gave my dad the faith that stopped him from being afraid in those last violent seconds he spent on earth. And the place in my mind where we meet is on the front steps of my dad's church, the big one on Main Street across from Don's Bakery and the Goodwill store. We smile and talk for a few minutes outside, basking in the warmth of the summer sun he loved so much. Then he goes in and I stay outside, and we're both happy where we are.

One Woman's Experience with the Ecstatic

Martha Brooks

I was born with a deep hollow in the centre of my chest. Instead of supporting my rib cage, the breastbone pushed inward, affecting heart, lungs and stomach. This deformity was corrected by surgery when I was eighteen; but all during my childhood it had a profound impact on how I navigated in the world, altering breathing, eating habits and ultimately my physical health. Simple colds frequently turned to pneumonia, which at the time, the late 1940s, was difficult to treat. Mom and Dad were medical people, skilled at keeping the human body alive. Even so, I often drifted close to the line. Whenever that happened, and this is a particularly vivid memory, the only remaining part of me that seemed to be aware was the essence, the spirit. In this state, unencumbered by the physical, I sailed from my second-storey bedroom window, past the tangle of trees with the hilltops peeking through. I would hover briefly over the garden, and see the grape arbor that overlooked a deep ravine and the lake beyond.

During times when I was well, I would be drawn back

to those places of spirit. It was in this landscape that I first discovered another dimension of being and understanding. Here is my earliest memory of ecstasy: I'm not quite three years old, standing out of doors. It's early spring. The snow has melted away. I'm surrounded by winter-withered prairie grasses near the swing our surgeon father has fashioned for my sister and me out of two grey telephone poles. Below, beyond a stand of oaks and chokecherry bushes, is our wraparound verandah. Above is the top of a favourite hill; the view from there will appear in many later personal visions. But to my toddler self, standing near the bottom, the hill is a living companion in this first remembered spring. The sun warms the newly thawed earth. The south wind whispers against my flesh. Yellow light gathers all around me, its energy palpable, pushing against my fingers. I fall back into the grasses, against the hill, and feel so much love that it cannot possibly be contained within my body. A breath, or two, more flooding light, and finally all else disappears. What remains in my vision is light and only light. Scholars call this kind of experience numinous. Shamans deep in a Central American jungle might call it the Great Spirit. I, who have no knowledge of such things, only understand that something seems to be cradling me.

Another memory involves the lake, snaking through the belly of the prairie valley where I grew up. It's summer. Probably Sunday. I am wearing the pink cotton dress that Mom dressed me in earlier that morning. Even now I feel her warm hands carefully buttoning up the back before releasing me. The skirt twirls. I'm spinning on the dock down by the water. Dad and his companion, a young medical student, are readying the sailboat for a late-day sail. Somehow, in their distraction, I'm pushed off the dock, onto my back, into the water. In the slanting light of day it is vast and warm, its surface golden. The pink dress balloons gently around me. I feel disappointed when, all too quickly, I'm fished out. I protest. I wanted to float there forever! I was in no danger. I trusted the deep lake.

In the hills behind our house, wild plants sprang up bewitchingly, spring and summer, and always in the exact spot they had been found the year before. Rocks, old and mute in their standing places, grew speckles of orange lichen. An ancient bur oak tree, with the gaping mouth of a ghost, sprouted leafy fringes every year. My father and I, joining hands, could barely encircle its trunk. He said that people, perhaps three or four hundred years before, may have walked past, touched the bark, or rested there to look out at the lake. Listening to him, I swam in the mirage of the tree's youth, my eyes, my whole being, filling with brilliant green.

Only when I grew up and moved away to the city did I lose this particular way of glimpsing paradise. Yet my longing for it didn't die; it simply became subverted, like an underground river. When I turned fifty, I made a retreat from the city and went on a four-day spiritual quest back to the landscape of my childhood, the prairie valley in southwestern Manitoba where my husband and I now spend summer weekends at the family cabin, in two acres of bush overlooking Pelican Lake. It was the first week of September, and I was finally able to be there alone. I had been feeling a growing hunger for solitude. It was like a deep spirit ache. I was aware that in preparing to write my novel, *Bone Dance*, I needed to honour the beginning of that journey. But on another, more intuitive level, I sensed the need to mark the rite of passage from middle years to the youth of my old age. In doing so I also thought it might be possible to shuck off time and get back some of that early childhood connection with the divine, in Nature.

I fasted, honoured the rising and setting of the sun, lived by natural light and spoke to no one — not even uttering thoughts out loud. I took five-hour walks where head and body and feet floated between sky and sage-smelling earth. After a couple of days, something sweet started trickling in, and my spirit, like my shadow on the gravel road, seemed to become elongated. Each morning I headed for the other side of the valley, down along the road, and on up into the hills which had been my childhood's heart's home.

I found the tree that Dad and I had spanned with our arms forty years before. It looked the same. The view was the same. The tree and I were still here, though my father was not. I lay back in the grass under the tree, overwhelmed by memory, willing Dad's spirit back to tell me, once again, about the people who had been here before us when the tree was young.

Later, coming back to fall on my bed, I began to notice the sounds: the heightened rasp and whistle of insects and birds, and my own percussive heartbeat. The tree beside the window also emitted a kind low-grade hum. Only one other time did I actually hear a tree — one of the mightily vascular ones in British Columbia's Cathedral Grove.

Rising from my bed, I held a small stone I'd picked up on the road that morning. It quickly warmed in my hand and emitted a surprising low kick, like fetal energy. The sun went down; the wind came up; the lake flamed with light. Then the sky slowly changed and night came on.

On the last night, the fourth night of my retreat, I gathered up my sleeping bag and went outside to sleep on the deck. I had fasted for the first two days but ate moderately during the last two, so it wasn't hunger that made me reel under the power of the stars. I lay down, cocooned in the soft bag, my head surrounded by cotton flannel, and I gazed upward. I had never seen desert stars, but had imagined them, somehow, to be like these in the prairie sky, forming a vast and sacred wilderness cathedral, where you could lose yourself. And it was at that point that the stars seemed to gather closer and surround me. I felt myself leave the earth, as if being pulled right up into them. It was a moment of utter revelation, terrifying because it was also irresistable. It would have been so easy to go with them. No trick at all to leave without a trace.

A few months later, deep in the heart of January in the coldest Manitoba winter for a century, I witnessed my mother's own experience with the void. She was slowly, inexorably cracking, going away to wherever people with Alzheimer's disease go. She phoned, terrified, in the middle of the night, to tell me that she was worried about "the dark."

"I keep looking out my window," she told me from her eighth-floor apartment, "and it just keeps rolling in. I can't sleep." I told her it was night. Time to go to bed. Long after she was admitted to a personal-care home, that conversation haunted me. I remember standing in my kitchen, by the little light that shines from the hood fan over my stove. I can still see the pattern of roses on my pajamas bottoms, my feet on the cold floor, and feel her helplessness and her loneliness. Perhaps because I was so gripped by that memory I eventually chose to use it in the opening chapter of the spirit-driven *Bone Dance.*

Two years ago, as Mom lay dying at age ninety-four, I thought about the night of that phone call, and also about her hands buttoning my dress the day I fell backwards into the warm summer lake. A small candle, with a flame floating at its centre, sat at her eye level beside the bed. Once again, it was the middle of the night. The recording we played filled her room with the sounds of nature: waves, rhythmic as heartbeats, crashed to shore; birds twittered from treetops mingling with her sporadic breaths. At the moment she left us, a single tear pooled in the corner of her eye, then rolled down her face.

During my childhood illnesses, I left my own physical body. The grape arbour in our garden formed a portal of entry for my spirit. I would float down to the grass, feeling its velvety wetness. Quickly lifting off again, my spirit moved up into flying position. The opening of the arbour closed over with spirals of searing light. It was the centre of light I had to go for, at its most raw but brilliant place. The moment of breaking through was simple release, easy. Then I was on the other side, moving high as crows in spring who travel across the tops of trees, far above the ravine, their shining wings in love with new green and beckoning skies. I flew with them, effortlessly, eyes closed, and behind closed lids saw colours of great intensity. That's why, I think, they make that sound in the air, the wild cawing crows. Their experience of flight is beyond exquisite. It is a sobbing ecstasy.

Memory is the force that links all life. It makes us pay attention even when it is painful to do so, marking us in ways that can sometimes leave us mute or howling. But consider the moment after we are released from extreme pain. What happens next? No one ever told me that in order to feel ecstasy I would have to experience its opposite.

Seeing

Sharon Butala

When I was about ten years old, I was sick a lot and spent most of one winter either in the hospital or at home in bed, usually lying on the couch in the living room so that my mother would not have to add running up and down stairs to her many tasks. She had four other small children, and women in her situation around 1950 had none of the tools that now make the management of a household easier. I remember that once, to entertain me, she made a ouija board out of cardboard and pencilled the letters of the alphabet around its outside edge. She explained to me that I was to ask the board a question, then put my fingers lightly on a small piece of cardboard bent into a table-like shape and concentrate very hard on a question I wanted answered. The piece of cardboard was supposed to move and spell out the answer to my question. I remember trying very hard, but failing to make it work on my own.

But I also remember, at least once, her leaving the bubbling pots in the kitchen for a few moments to come and sit beside me on the couch where I was propped up with cushions, a quilt covering my legs, the ouija board balanced on my lap. She told me the question she was going to ask the board: I think it was something about her brother, our uncle Donald, who died a year or two later in 1952 of cancer when he was still a young man, and who at the time was gravely ill. Then she placed her fingertips so lightly on the cardboard piece that they barely touched it, closed her eyes, and while I watched, fascinated, the cardboard piece slowly moved, apparently of its own volition.

When she was finished — or the piece seemed to be finished, having spelled out the answer — she leaned back as if tired out, breathing deeply from her exertion — although, except for slowly moving the cardboard piece, she'd been absolutely still. Recovering in a moment, she seemed to be suffused with satisfaction. She went back to the meal she was cooking in the kitchen, telling me that she was busy and I'd have to entertain myself now.

All of this was deeply interesting to me. It didn't frighten me, or even seem particularly strange. Certainly it never entered my head to disbelieve what happened; I merely wished to have her powers, to be able to contact whatever it was that moved the cardboard. I had no conception of what this might be, for I knew very well that when it moved for me, I was pushing it myself.

My mother never commented on what she had done, or how. No one older than I am at any time ever spoke to me about the psychic powers of women of "a certain age," by which I mean just before, in, and beyond menopause. (My mother would have been in her early forties at the time of the ouija board.) Nor did anybody ever mention witches, except at Hallowe'en, when children dressed up as the ugly, big-nosed, warty, broom-riding kind in the tall pointed hat — but that was mostly little kids, since children my age didn't want anything to do with being witches. Ghosts were better, or bunnies, or nurses or fairy princesses. No one ever spoke seriously to us about witchcraft, or even of a more honest increase of intuitive abilities, yet our folklore is full of stories about witches, about mysterious, dark powers, about women's connection to them.

Our literature is full of these stories too, from Shakespeare's *Macbeth* to Goethe's *Faust*, from Fay Weldon's *Puffball* to John Updike's *The Witches of Eastwick*, from fairy tales to the Wicked Witch of the West of Frank Baum's Oz books. Having lived well over twenty years in a rural community where gossip is life itself, I have joined the school that believes where there's smoke there must be fire. Any undertow in society that powerful and long-lasting must be about *something* real, and this "something real," is always — with the exception of shamans — attributed to women.

Why did no one ever bring this subject up to me as something I should know? After all, the burning times from the fifteenth to the eighteenth century represent an important piece of female history. I think the reason has to be that we were raised in a patriarchal, Christian society, where we women are taught to think of ourselves as the weaker sex, where our powers have been systematically, deliberately reduced from the time, thousands of years ago, when God was considered to be a woman, until now, when most of us no longer know we even had, or have, power.

And, too, with the advent of the Age of Reason, which has led directly to our current society's deep faith in science — I am tempted to put quotation marks around science — and the wonders of technical solutions to all problems, we women ourselves forgot about that side of our natures. Our powers withered and shrivelled and were thus easily subdued in horror, fear and shame whenever they popped up without bidding.

But I don't know about all of this because my mother told me, or friends my own age (nearing sixty), nor because of family anecdotes — at least, not that I can remember. But then, there was much our mother wouldn't tell us; there was a point, often, when she would grow silent and reflective and when we asked her why, she would dismiss us with a brusque "Don't bother me!"

There was never a whisper of "pricking thumbs," or bent spoons, or herbal concoctions or healing hands. Although, come to think of it, I recall that the women of my family did some interesting dreaming.

Not only did none of them even mention special powers except jokingly, as if they were laughing at themselves for even repeating such foolish old wives' tales, they didn't try to teach us girl-children anything out of the ordinary either. But I remember my stern and genteel Scots grandmother, rarely, reading tea leaves. And, somewhere along the way, all we girls heard of ways to tell the gender of a fetus, although we were also told this "nonsense" was associated with "lower-class women."

But the fact that the women of my family never mentioned these powers to me, or demonstrated them except briefly and in odd circumstances, doesn't mean they didn't exist. And the strength and wisdom of older women was undeniably commonplace: the memorable unmarried or widowed aunt, or the grandmother who exudes a silent serenity and deep wisdom. They are the people in whom family life is anchored in rural areas, and even community life, although no one seems to notice this at the conscious level. It is anchored there, I'm guessing, because old women have hints of the magical about them, of the mysterious, no matter how phlegmatic and silent they might be. Because they are a living connection to the past. Because it is understood that they know women's mysteries.

Things have changed since my grandmothers' and mother's day. Now growing numbers of people are unafraid to say out loud the word "magic" or "witch." They come from nature-loving groups, who recognize the power in the land ("the earth is our mother"), as Amerindians do or did, and are trying to connect with it; they come from feminist consciousness-raising groups, who are discovering women's history in an effort to connect with the lost status and power of womanhood; they come from among the "new-agers," who tend to be more frivolous people seeking personal power and a nonexistent easy way out of life's tribulations. Now I sometimes hear of this person or that who is said to be — or claims herself to be — a "white witch" — a claim, I can assure you, that in the forties and fifties, or even early sixties, no woman in ordinary society would have made out loud for fear of being ostracized, dismissed as completely crazy or possibly even stoned by small children.

The powers I am talking about are an increasingly strong and accurate intuition, a more meaningful and richer dream life, and the occasional mystical experience of one kind or another, from hearing a "voice" (usually soundless in the normal sense) to seeing a vision, however briefly. Incidents of clairvoyance — "seeing" something true that is beyond the range of normal vision, and having predictive dreams — are also a part of this package of possibilities. I know about them because, like many of my friends, I've begun to have them with some frequency.

Sometimes these experiences are religious in nature. More often they can't be construed as having anything to do with God, but are simply about an intensified experience of life. Walking in an isolated field once, in a highly charged emotional state because I had quarrelled with a close friend and felt that our disagreement had revealed that we could not be friends any more, I felt someone behind me. I turned, and there the friend stood, her hand held out to me beseechingly, her face full of the pain I felt myself. The friend shimmered there for an instant, then vanished.

Or often I feel that the phone will ring an instant before it does, or find myself thinking strongly of someone only to have that person suddenly call. Or some strongly felt presence urges me to turn around and go back home from a bike ride just begun, and when I do I find my husband standing there, telephone in hand, because I have a call I wouldn't have wanted to miss. Several times, when having a private tutorial with a writing student, I've so acutely felt her desire — so strong it's actual pain — that I couldn't stand it and had to put more space between us. Or an idea will pop into my head about someone miles away and the idea will turn out to be true. (One morning a thought hit me so suddenly and with such clarity that I stood stock still with a cup of coffee in my hand. The thought was that a certain child with a mild illness might die in the night. In fact, the previous night the child had had a choking episode so severe her terrified mother thought she was dying.)

I could go on: small, meaningless visions in dreams that the next morning actually happen; dreams of people I don't know, have never met, that I recognize the next day in a meeting. There are other events, much more extraordinary and awe inspiring, but not of a kind one is able to speak of, for fear of being thought crazy or a liar, for fear of being called a witch. And there are those events have been told me by other women: a woman visiting an elderly relative in another province, as she is saying good-bye, bends to pick a dropped item from the ground, and in that bending sees a funeral cortège going by. She thinks she will never see her relative again, but when she gets home she discovers another relative has died and was buried in her absence.

What have such abilities to do with women? And why do they seem to surface around menopause? Recently I was lucky enough to stumble across the unpublished doctoral thesis of a Unitarian Universalist minister. Unitarians pride themselves on their rational approach to matters of religion; indeed, no other church does so to such a degree. The title of the thesis is "Subjective Religious Experience Among Unitarian Universalists: A Generational Study" (by Linda Smith Stowell, for the School of Theology at Claremont, California, 1995). Dr. Stowell found in her admittedly rather small study that women between the ages of 52 and 65 had the highest number of what we might call "mystical experiences" of all age groups and of both genders. Especially surprising is the fact that all her subjects were either laity or clergy of this most rational of churches. With the exception of the over-65 age group, who said they never had such experiences, just under 50 percent claimed to have had mystical experiences. In her summary, Dr. Stowell says

> Experiences in the first cluster (oneness/harmony, light/joy, intuitive certainty) were experienced by about 95 percent of the total sample population. In the second cluster, sense of "felt" presence, was significantly more common, with about two-thirds of the population reporting this kind of experience at least "rarely," while "voice" and "vision" were significantly less common, at about 45 percent of the population.

Dr. Stowell also reports that "the highest mean [for 'voice,' 'vision' and 'sense of a felt presence'] was for "older mid-life women." Men in all categories reported a lower incidence of such experiences.

I offer this small study as some verification of my thesis that mid-life women seem to have a more open conduit into what we call the supernatural. If a sample of people who can be expected to be unusually rational about these matters reports such a high incidence of "mystical experience," we might, therefore, infer that at least half the general population has them. If this inference is accurate, then there is a huge aspect of many people's lives that which we choose to ignore, to deny, never to talk about.

Why these experiences should be strongest in a certain age group I don't know, nor does anyone else I would trust to make a pronouncement. Suggestions so far have included female hysteria, evil spirits or too many hormones (or not enough of them) circulating in female bodies at this time of our lives. These notions seem to stem from the dark and ugly threads in society that consider women "unclean" (because we are so indelibly physical — bleeding every month, giving birth, nursing babies). Our supposed "evil" seems to be connected somehow to this "uncleanness."

Such notions about women strike me as absurd. When I watch the television news about riots, looting, battles or even parliaments and government committees in session — great mobs for whatever purpose — what appears on the screen is a sea of male faces. Rarely do I see women. Hysteria thus strikes me as a good deal more likely to be a male symptom than a female one. To condemn women for seeking power through their psychic abilities (always equated with evil powers) is also laughable. For no one has made greater Faustian bargains on this earth than scientists — with their atomic, hydrogen and neutron bombs, with their efforts to create human life by cloning, and with the killing of one human being still clinging to life to give organs to another. And the world of science is still a largely male one.

I can see why we women aren't told about the powers most of us will become aware of as we go through menopause, since our churches equate such abilities with Satan and Satanism. It may even be a good thing that we aren't told, because too many of us would think of such abilities or powers as being of our own making — and that is where evil begins.

I no longer have doubts about some of the claims of so-called "white witches," having seen what pops up without prompting or effort in my own life. I strongly suspect I might harness some aspect of these abilities if I were so inclined. After all, let's not forget that female witch-like powers are part of a tradition going back to the beginning of recorded history. Nonetheless, I do have serious misgivings about deliberate witchcraft. History has taught us over and over again how quickly powers of any kind, pursued and honed, are turned to revenge, or to acquiring material goods. It is "unfinished" people, I think who create evil in the world — people consumed by rage or by neediness of one kind or another, people who are wounded and unable to overcome their wounds, or even to accept them. But these people represent the extreme — at least I hope they do.

It seems clear to me that my own unexplained experiences involve making contact with some power, or with the "collective unconsciousness," or, as I like to think of it, a manifestation of spirit that flows through the universe behind daily life and is available to all of us. Not that I do anything to get in touch with it; either it touches me spontaneously or else I make contact of sorts simply by remaining as open as possible, by stripping my thoughts of any kind of personal aggrandizement, such as desire for personal power or the accumulation of wealth or prestige.

To be available to such wisdom, one must learn to wait, as all the great religious traditions say — wait in the right way. One must hold truth as the highest good, and be open to truth, searching for truth, willing to accept truth — no matter how hard or personally painful it may be.

Maybe this is the reason why older women experience more of this manifestation of spirit: Older women, their child-rearing days over, are less likely than men to be deeply involved in affairs of the world, and less likely also to be personally arrogant as a consequence of a life of wielding power over others. These women in their middle years may be closer to what Jung called "individuation," closer to having a firm, true idea of Self. For having a stronger understanding of Self makes it possible for one to open wider, without fear, to the universe. Dr. Stowell speaks of women of this age as having softer personal boundaries; perhaps they are merely more humble.

Most of us who recognize the strengthening of our intuitive abilities, and who begin to have experiences of the unseen side of life on Planet Earth, have no desire to use such abilities for any reason except the improvement of our own emotional and spiritual life — that is, in the necessary pursuit and understanding of Self. But we also are amazed at the way our heightened intuition works to expand our conscious knowledge not only of the world itself, but also of what exists in the universe. Just what that is we don't know, though we might make private guesses. And we realize that we waste certain normal human abilities — those that the few remaining societies still largely without modern technologies remember how to use.

These abilities teach us not how to *create* humans but how to *be* humans. They help us understand our own souls: what they are, where they came from, and where they are going. It, whatever "it" is, has the power, not me, not us. When you are certain of that, you are humbled rather than inflated by your encounters with it. *You are filled with awe.* And you do not turn away from it.

I have wanted to use whatever this is that happens to me as a way of opening up to the wonders of the universe — those wonders closed off to us by scientific orthodoxy, by the murders of women thought to be witches, by the general loss of women's status and power.

I think of my mother, who knew so much she never said, but whose wisdom darkened and deepened her eyes as she gazed at me.

Birth, Death and the Eleusinian Mysteries

Margaret Shaw-MacKinnon

Twelve years ago, after giving birth to my daughter Margaret Eve, I wrote a piece about my shock, my sense of not having been prepared for this essential female experience. I wrote this diary entry and put it away in a drawer. So often in women's lives, our thoughts fall like seeds into the rich loam of privacy. It is here that they blossom, exotic hybrids never to be viewed by the public eye. And yet, it is in these private musings that we can potentially find the quick of our personal, countercultural truths.

Looking back at this diary entry, I find my halting recognition of an aspect of childbirth absent from any discourse I had had with my mother, with other women, or in the communal childbirth preparation. After naming this absence for myself in my diary those twelve years ago, I found myself scanning my world to find others who knew about this unacknowledged aspect of birth. I found resonance in the most unexpected places.

Over the years, the aspect of my relationship with my mother that I came to cherish most deeply was our ongoing, ever-changing, ever-fascinating conversation. In my earliest memories, we talk together. She holds me on her lap. We look into each other's eyes as she listens to my stories. "Big eyes, and big ideas," she says lovingly.

Given the usual openness of our communication, I felt confused by Mom's teary silence when I first announced I was pregnant. When I asked her what was wrong, she quickly regained her composure, and we shifted our focus onto plans for the baby. But in spite of her reassurances, I had the sense that she was deeply afraid for me.

This fear, I suspected, was rooted in fragments of family lore I had heard over the years. When asked why Gram had only one child, Great-Aunt Olive told us that Gram's labour with Mom was so difficult that she never had another child. Mom herself almost died of toxemia twice when she gave birth to my two older sisters. And then there was Gram's Aunt Janet in Scotland, who died in childbirth. She slipped on a patch of ice while wearing a fur muff, couldn't break her fall and went into premature labour. She died with her baby.

Death and birth, then, were inextricably entwined in Mom's mind. Both were coloured with fear. The person whose wisdom I most trusted, and whom I naturally expected to prepare me for the complex challenges of childbirth, held back for emotional reasons beyond her own control.

Well, if I was not initiated into the mystery of birth by my mother, I was nevertheless not without information. My husband Brian and I took a childbirth class at the hospital. We got pamphlets illustrating the physiological process of birth. We practised breathing. We watched films.

Twelve years ago, Brian and I, along with other expectant mothers and fathers, watched a video titled *The Miracle of Birth*. The sound track was melodic, pleasant, relaxing. There was a red-haired mother in a rocking chair. A balding father counted as she breathed and rocked. The father got her a glass of orange juice. They went to the hospital. It was time.

The nurses had concerned faces — eyes that looked at the mother earnestly, mouths that spoke words about what to expect. If her pain was too great they would offer Demerol or an epidural.

The father's face was full of compassion. The voice-over told us that he couldn't stand to see his wife in pain. He fed her ice chips, patted her brow with a cold, wet, facecloth. The mother looked at him, murmured "I love you."

And so it went, until the mother's cervix dilated to 10 centimetres. The doctor came into the room. The mother drew up her legs, grimaced horribly.

The baby's head appeared in the vagina opening. The mother pushed. The baby slid out. It was a girl, covered in blood. Her little face was suctioned. She was handed up onto the mother's chest. The father and mother kissed and cried.

In the class, I noticed that many of us squirmed throughout the video. Some of us held hands. At the end of the video, many of us had tears in our eyes. I felt strangely violated for reasons I could only guess at. I thought of the men or women who had made the video, who had stood behind the cameras and gazed at "the miracle of birth." Now prenatal classes everywhere gazed at this same "miracle." This is what to expect, we were told.

In my diary entry, after I gave birth to my daughter Margaret Eve, I re-visioned "the miracle of birth" through the lens of personal experience:

> Why is it that the experience of birth is not at all like the video? The video gives a false impression. A camera's experience of birth is represented — not a woman's experience, or a man's. Or mine . . .
>
> In the hours before the birth, I close my eyes, keep them shut. My body takes over, moves inevitably through a process of pain. I give myself up to an orchestration of agony — this tightening

over my belly, this searing, ripping sensation in my side, this breathing that I do — drawing in when pain is there, exhaling when it subsides.

I hear my husband count somewhere in outer space. Feel my teeth clenched. Feel my eyelids squeeze, see black and red, and shooting stars. I give myself up to a nurse who inserts a needle into a vein in my hand; feel hopelessly upset about it. Feel diarrhea come — my shame and dependency and gratitude as a nurse quickly, efficiently cleans it away.

I hear the music on the tapes Brian and I chose to bring. I resist the Beatles — their crude "twist and shout, let it all hang out." They don't fit here. They intrude in this space. I hide in Beethoven's "Ode to Joy," in the prodigious repetition of themes, the momentous contractions, expansions, deliverance.

I care that my husband is beside me, watching a nurse miss my vein, watching my warm red blood spill onto white sheets. I care that he cares enough to want, naïvely, to shield me from his desire to faint, his nausea, by saying, "I think I'll lie down now." I murmur, "Yes . . . rest before the baby comes."

I feel disembodied, floating in a field of boundless pain. I think of what patriarchal mythologies have wanted me to believe. The woman is the body. The man is the spirit. Not here, not in this place. The man, Brian, remains attached, grounded in the comfort that is his body. It is I, the woman, who hides and flies where I can, who feels the difference of this body that marches ahead in its movement of pain. Brian whispers in my ear, "I love you," because he wants to be close to where I hover like a spirit-woman in the house of pain. Where can I settle, where can I rest, when inside, in darkness and nowhere, searing, ripping fire is my only foothold? A woman, tied to the body? Or feeling the excruciating difference that is the body?

The birth is a drug-induced numbness, a metallic tug under a glare of light.

And after the baby is born, I open my eyes, and in the mirrors above me, I see the doctors bent over a huge, bloody wound, stitching up a tear. I see again my own difference. The mirror says "this is you," but in the media mirror my culture has set before me, I have never appeared this way. I have seen myself constructed in fashion magazines — a body, autonomous, a female, clothed or not, sleek hair, lipsticked mouth, long, black-mascara eyelashes, shiny eyes. I have seen myself represented in this way on television, in newspapers, films — a woman, of course.

What a shock to awaken to an image of myself as mutilated genitalia.

The baby is placed in my arms. My daughter. This complete other. This wailing form calling me forth. I cloak myself in a new and fragile wholeness. Mother. Father. Baby. Baby.

In this diary entry there is the sense of an event sadly bungled and misunderstood, an event for which I was ill-prepared. From a spiritual perspective, there is the sense of a missed opportunity. I could not surrender to, or engage in, the spiritual intimations I so clearly felt, precisely because there was no cultural preparation for this. Here I was, on the threshold of my human existence, feeling myself "a spirit-woman hovering in a house of pain with no foothold but fire," and the only preparation I had was to watch a woman in a video giving birth. Birth was presented to me as a purely external happening, with no recognition of the profoundly inward and spiritual nature of this event.

In our present discontinuous culture, knowledge often comes to us in a piecemeal manner, and we find insight in the most surprising places. It was not until several years after my first childbirth experience that I began to understand that the great transitions in women's lives had not always been misconstrued and marginalized. There were, and are, cultures that celebrate females and the feminine. Out of all the possible woman-affirming cultures, it was ancient Greece that came to my attention first.

In a Myth and Literature class at the University of Manitoba I learned about the Eleusinian Mysteries that had held sway in Greece for over two thousand years. These were essentially feminine ceremonies centred around the goddesses Demeter and Persephone. I discovered that, in contrast to our present meagre treatment of the female mysteries, the Greeks spared no effort in honouring women and their divine representatives. In celebration of the goddesses they created myths, rituals, and works of art characterized by profoundly felt, far-ranging emotion, a keen aesthetic sensibility and a complex spirituality. In the rituals surrounding the Goddesses, there are deeply entwined patterns of symbol and experience, extending from the human realm into the divine. These patterns revolve around the concepts of mother, daughter, loss, grief, death, transformation, birth and rebirth.

Initiates into the cult of Demeter, men and women, went through exacting observances that took a year to perfect. At the end of that year, they engaged in an agonizing, but ultimately ecstatic, nine-day immersion into the lives of the goddesses through ritual. These initiations were so powerful that the classical writer Pindar exclaimed of them: "Happy is he who, having seen these rites, goes below the hollow earth; for he knows the end of life and he knows its god-sent beginning!"

In contrast to the one dimensional aspect of the birth video, I found in Eleusis a thorough preparation for and rich appreciation of the physical, intellectual, emotional and spiritual aspects of the threshold experience of birth. In Eleusis, the whole human being was embraced. Had my mother and I lived in Eleusis, our fears might have been eased. We would have found ourselves wrapped and held in a communal blanket, woven of female experience, myths, rituals and ceremonies. As folk wisdom would have it, sometimes even mothers need mothering.

The connection between birth and death that seemed so frightening in Mom's experience attained a new significance and meaning for both of us when Mom was dying.

She died of leukemia, slowly, over a period of five years, but it was only in the last three months that she really suffered. Towards the end, in the hospital, she grew rapidly frail, devastated, until at the last she was confined to her bed.

My diary entry from that time reads as follows:

> My mother, with all her layers collected in this life, lies like a baby, vulnerable, and all I want is to hold her, rock her gently, so gently, but I haven't been able to because of the chemotherapy. The chemotherapy knocked out her immunity, made her susceptible to any germ or virus that we might carry. So we wash our hands with anti-bacterial soap, sit back from the bed so that we don't breathe any stray germs onto her, hold her right hand beneath the covers.
>
> It is always the right hand. Poor left! The left is blocked by the intravenous tree, by tubes that extend from hanging bottles.
>
> I can't hug her because if I do, I am afraid of dislodging her main line, the tubes embedded in her chest, tubes that have kept her alive these past weeks with blood, plasma, potassium, antibiotics.
>
> But I want to lift her onto my lap and sing

> and tell her "wheesht, wheesht," and pat her hands and cup her face, and let her rest her sore and broken body in my arms, head on my shoulder, chest.

The intensive chemotherapy did not work. Strangely, Mom did recover just enough to have a reprieve at my sister's home. Sandra had prepared the room for her. A quilt — peach, blue, green, handmade by Sandra — lay on the dark wood bed that had once belonged to Mom's parents. It was the bed in which Mom was born.

The blossoming that happened to Mom at Sandra's seemed almost physical. We began to believe that there, in the lap of love, she could recover. All day Mom listened to the sounds of family life — adults talking, children laughing, the phone ringing, a little grandson playing the piano with all his vivacity, wind chimes tinkling in a warm spring breeze coming in through the open window above the garden. Lying in bed in the evening, she was surrounded by loved ones — her son, daughters, friends. And at bedtime, the cherished grandchildren tiptoed in with their blown kisses and wishes for Grandma's sweet dreams.

It was in the bed she was born that Mom died. We daughters — Janet, Sandra, Margaret, Irene — were with her; her son, Edward, was in the air, trying to reach the mom he so loved. That night was terrible, yet comforting, each daughter taking a turn curling up beside Mom to sleep, or sitting in the bedside wheelchair, keeping vigil in the moonlight. At some point, in the darkness, Mom turned to my eldest sister and whispered that she thought she must go now to the others.

The death was like birth — the fear, the pain, the loss of control, the immense vulnerability, Mom's awareness that she was moving into the realm of spirit, the rhythmic breathing, the deliverance. We sisters were midwives. We knew that as her breath deepened, grew rhythmic, Mom gave birth to her own beautiful soul.

The myth of Demeter and Persephone reveals the endless manifestation and cycle of birth, death and rebirth in the world, and in our lives. As the poets suggest, our lives are not only circles, but also spirals. Climbing the spiral of my existence, I conclude with another diary entry about birth, written from a new vantage point, after my son Arthur was born. The spirituality of birth that came as such a shock in my first childbirth experience is here accepted, explored:

> A woman is a door. Never is this more apparent than when she bears a child. She parts her legs in blood and pain, opens the door to the world, to a being of flesh and soul, a baby, an infant, her baby.
>
> A woman is a door and she knows this, when, after the birth of her baby, her body creaks and the winds blow through, and she has a rounded belly, dripping, sagging, ever-full breasts, stretch marks, where chaos and dissolution have loomed large. She has been close to the blackness of space. Her skin, pulled taut, stretched, was broken, but the winds have not torn her to pieces, yet. She knows her own greyness, her own silvered fragility. She accepts how she opened like a silver flower to let into life a pink, round-cheeked, perfect human infant. She welcomes his scowl and lusty cry, his sucking at her tender breast.
>
> Everything is alive with the sighs and flutters of the infant in the bedside cradle. The world is renewed, animate.
>
> A woman is a door. She holds her infant's hand and walks with him, through herself, into the hopeful new world.

Speechless

Eleanor Wachtel

Around the time of the sack dress, 1967, I began to lose my body. And my voice — or at least the confidence to speak in public. The dresses themselves were great. My sister and I, ages twenty-one and nineteen, roughly the same weight and height though different in style and walk, shared all our clothes. We'd go shopping together, speaking quickly *sotto voce* in the changing rooms, and the salesladies would ask where we were from, thinking we were foreign, talking an exotic language. That pleased us, of course.

It took me a long time to connect these things: body, nerve, rhythm.

The story probably goes back much further, like everything, to early childhood. My childhood is something I keep thinking about in connection with this piece. Everything else someone has written about. Even my childhood they've written about. Except it's not mine.

The youngest of three, I was allowed, not to say encouraged, to perform. I'm told that "Put Another Nickel In" was a favourite as I would lisp, "muthic, muthic, muthic." Or I would beak my hand on my brow in imitation of the metal sun visors of the early 1950s cars. My dream at age three or four was to hang on their running boards. When I was five, I could shuffle a deck of cards. I could play canasta and rudimentary bridge at age eight, taught by my Great-Aunt Fanny from Florida. (I didn't learn to read until the usual age of six or seven at school.) I don't think I was totally obnoxious, but as the little performer I did learn to enjoy an audience.

At primary school, I'd sing "The Wayward Wind" when called upon. When I brought home riddles or jokes, I'd often have forgotten the punchline, but discovered that this usually produced a bigger laugh. In high school, I joined the Public Speaking and Debating Club, and while it didn't come naturally — I needed detailed notes and I got nervous — it was manageable and something that seemed worth putting myself through. I represented the school at a city-wide girls' public speaking contest. My knees shook but not my voice. I didn't expect to win. I didn't. I also remember emceeing a folk music fundraiser for Foster Parents' Plan through the student council.

Yet a few years later, I couldn't speak at a university seminar without panic seizing my brain. Everything shook — my voice, my hand, spilling the glass of water as it knocked against my lips. My sister was married and I was buying clothes on my own now — all in sizes that were too big. I couldn't dance any more, couldn't find the beat, I — who had cha-chaed with my older brother since grade school, jitterbugged and twisted through high school — was hopeless.

I suppose the nadir, for someone who ended up in live radio, was at a meeting of the Canadian African Studies Association in Victoria, B.C. I had nervously read a paper about Margaret Laurence and Audrey Thomas, two writers who had lived in Africa and writen about it, both from inside the culture and as expatriates. My anthropologist husband and I had recently returned from East Africa so I was intensely curious about this bifocal experience. I was looking for connections, for a way to feel less marginal, especially now that I was back in Canada. In Kenya, it had been appropriate to feel like an outsider, since I was one in every way: neither African nor Asian, not settler nor contract worker nor volunteer, neither British nor American, I slipped through every category and felt completely comfortable.

Back in Victoria, after I had anxiously delivered my paper, a reporter for Radio Canada International approached us for interviews. We went up to his room in the Empress Hotel. He set up his tape recorder and began to ask my husband about his talk. That was fine. Obviously this was being taped — it could be edited, no pressure. The journalist asked me one question. I froze.

Now, there are a few things I don't understand. Music, my delight in dancing — what can I say? rhythm! — came back to me as if by magic at a disco in Nakuru, Kenya, in 1974, having gone AWOL in 1967. By the time of the African studies meeting in late 1975, my clothes were starting to fit. And, despite having decided that radio was something I could never do, I went looking for work at my local CBC station in Vancouver.

The job I had heard about at CBC Radio was behind the scenes, as a producer, but it turned out that the position was already filled. I could freelance, they said. But I had to do something that the regular studio host could not do, something a little unusual — quirky was probably the word.

I brought in a list of ideas and the producer checked off half a dozen. I went out with a home portable tape recorder and interviewed a Mexican mime who was performing at the Art Gallery. Next, I talked to a sociologist at UBC who was studying sign language in sawmills. Because of the excessive noise, the workers had developed a sophisticated system of communciating with each other, even telling jokes in sign language. Clearly, I had not exactly grasped the medium of radio.

My third attempt succeeded: an interview with Frances

Adaskin, who had accompanied her violinist husband Harry all her life and was making her solo piano debut at age seventy-two. She was gracious, charming, articulate.

But the real transformation occurred in Banff in 1978. It was the annual general meeting of the magazine publishers' association and I fell in with a congenial crowd, many of whom were running for the board of the organization. I was nominated from the floor and had to make a brief speech. The only way I could combat my fear was to think of amusing things to say, phrases that diverted me from terror. I spoke, they laughed. A comedian manqué was born.

It was all so mysterious how these things came and went and then returned. It wasn't simply a case of self-esteem; in fact, it seemed completely unrelated to what was going on in the rest of my life. It's as if the voice was dormant, no, worse than that, it deserted me, went into hiding to grow a new skin or something. What's odd is that while I was certainly dismayed (and surprised) when parts of myself vanished, I wasn't as alarmed as I think I would be now. Maybe the unexpected was more normal then; there hadn't been as many years for a reliable personality to accrete. Who knew anything with any certainty? Was this what happened in life?

Initially, with a carefully crafted script, I could do a bit of live radio for the local morning show, to accompany my tape clips. I learned to write the way I speak, so I had the reassurance of the words in front of me. That seemed to assuage my nerves somewhat. When I became the theatre critic for the local CBC morning show, I had to be on the air the morning after the night before. After a play, I'd go home, eat something to feel awake, and sit at the typewriter, creating a tiny play — a dialogue between the host and me. I'd bring in the script: an introduction and questions for them, answers for me. I remember one host who would read the newspaper while I delivered my lines; she'd look up when I finished and pitch the next question.

For me, "finding my voice" wasn't simply a human

growth cliché, but then I've always been literal-minded. On a good day, the little entertainer is back; but instead of singing about the nickelodeon, I tell jokes. Groucho Marx, Bob Hope. I'm shameless.

Juliet

Helen Fogwill Porter

"Your hair looks lovely," Sandra says, passing me the hand mirror.

"Smells nice, too," I say. "Remember how the old perms used to stink?"

Sandra nods, smiling, then asks me if I have a rake.

"A rake," I repeat. "You mean for raking up leaves and grass?"

Sandra laughs. "No, no, a comb. Like this one." She holds up a purple comb with a handle and wide spaces between the teeth.

"Oh, yes, I've got one of those somewhere. I didn't know they were called rakes."

As Sandra explains to me how to lift my hair instead of combing it in the usual way, I keep thinking about the word rake. It's an appropriate name for that kind of comb. And I must have heard it used in that way before.

I've never been able to do anything with hair, my own or anyone else's. When the girls were small I always kept their hair cut short, the way I'd worn mine as a child. "Unhandy," that was my mother's word for me. Whenever she said it she'd follow it up with praise for my high marks at school.

My father always took me to get my hair cut. We'd walk to Murphy's Barbershop at the crossroads, and he'd have his hair trimmed at the same time. I liked the feeling of the clippers on my neck, the swish of the brush and the smell of the green liquid floating in the air.

In their teens Janet and Abigail let their hair grow, curled and styled it themselves. They both inherited Doug's manual dexterity, thank God.

I pay Sandra, and she reminds me to come back in six weeks for a trim. When I'm halfway home I realize that I didn't give her a tip. I've never forgotten to tip Sandra before.

Rake. That word keeps repeating itself in my head. Rake. A simple four-letter word. As I continue walking home a shiver runs through my body. The weather is warm for May. What in the frig is wrong with me? I was fine when I got up this morning, fine when I left the house. Fine right up to the moment Sandra said that word. Rake.

Last night I heard an interview on the radio about recovered memory. I can't resist listening to programs like that. As I often do these days, I talked back to the radio. "God, she was thirteen when the abuse happened. How could anyone ever forget something like that?"

I'm home already. Remembering nothing I saw or heard on the way. Is this what it's like to be in a fugue state? It often happens to me when I'm lost in thought. It can be wonderful, when something good has just happened or is about to happen. Or when you're falling in love: "I know how it feels to have wings on my heels / And to fly down the street in a trance." I haven't felt that way for a long time.

After school I'd walk along LeMarchant Road with Nadine until we reached her house. Then I'd walk on alone. Sometimes I wouldn't know where I was until I got to the Parkers'. I'd always stop there, just to look at the long graceful cream-and-white house with windows that someone later told me were made of antique mouth-blown glass. In the fall there were piles of leaves outside the Parkers' gate, from the maple and chestnut trees that grew just inside the wrought-iron fence. I'd kick my way through the leaves till I got to the graveyard. Then I'd cross to the other side of the road.

Today my walk home was fraught with — fraught with what? Something I don't want to think about? Something I don't want to remember.

Sometimes when I'm with Lucy and Charlotte and Liz one of us will say, "Well, you know, one in four women has been sexually abused as a child. So which one of us is it?" We all laugh then, and change the subject. We were surprised when Charlotte told us about her cousin Susan. It was Susan's grandfather. Not the one she shared with Charlotte.

My father has been dead for ten years, my mother for fifteen. I was the first-born of five; Dad said he learned from me how to be a father. He was inconsolable when anything bad happened to one of us. "I can't stand it, Amy," he told my mother after I hadn't been chosen for a speaking part in the operetta at school. Eventually I gave up telling him things like that.

My father loved Shakespeare and had introduced my mother to the play when the Glossop-Harris Repertory Company came regularly to St. John's from England. "He'd always buy a big box of chocolates for us to take to the T.A. Hall. That's where the plays were put off," my mother told me. "I don't know where he got the money."

My father had already resolved to name their first daughter Juliet. Fortunately, my mother also liked the name. "Not Juliette," he told me many times, wrinkling his nose.

I'm sitting at my kitchen table now, a cup of strong tea in front of me. I'm not sure how it got there. I take a sip to warm myself. Why am I so cold? The sun is streaming through the window; the kitchen is the warmest room in the house.

Rake. Juliet. Juliette. The three words are circling around each other in my head. Damn that Sandra. What has she started? Poor Sandra, such a gentle person, painstaking in her work, kind to the children who come to get their hair cut.

It's not Sandra. It's me. Am I turning strange now that I've retired? When I worked at the library I had no time to dwell on myself.

I drink the tea, carry my cup to the sink. There's a slight sound from the hallway. The mail is late today.

Three letters and the phone bill. One letter is from my sister Jessica in Fort McMurray. Another from Nadine who lives in Little Rock, Arkansas. She married an American serviceman who was stationed at Pepperrell Air Force Base. Several of my schoolmates married Americans; they ended up all over the States. Doug and I were so young when we started going together that I never even dated an American. Once in a while I still feel sorry about that.

The third envelope is large and square, probably a card. It's not my birthday or anything. The postmark says Paris. But it's not the postmark that takes my attention. It's the "Juliette" scrawled in thick black ink. My back is cold, the way it feels at night when the duvet slips off me. "Cover over my left shoulder," Doug would repeat as he pulled the blanket snugly around me. "You'll be saying that when they throw the gravel on your grave." It's Doug who's in his grave, healthy, vigorous Doug who died suddenly of a massive heart attack.

Most people spell my name correctly. I make sure of that. Two or three times throughout my school years I had to correct teachers. In grade six Miss MacDonald patted my shoulder and said, "Don't worry, Juliet, I'll never spell your name that way again." Then she erased the offending "te" from the blackboard. Some of the girls laughed. I'd been reading Anne of Green Gables and identified strongly with Anne when Mr. Phillips left the "e" off the end of her name.

I pick up the envelope and study it. Then I tear it open. Inside there's a card with a picture of the Champs Élysées on it. "Dear Juliette," says the short note. "I remember you told me you've always wanted to go to Paris. This is my first trip and it's everything I thought it would be. Hope you make it over here soon." It's signed "Laura."

Letter. Juliette. Rake. The louse rake . . .

I'm fifteen years old, in grade ten at Queen Victoria Academy. Nadine and I are laughing as we walk up the school steps together. The bell is ringing for the start of afternoon classes. We run up two flights of stairs to our classroom on the third floor. I'm breathless when I sit down at my desk. I lift the hinged top to take my history book out. There's a large folded sheet of paper in there, with "Juliette" on it in big loopy letters. I open it and begin to read, my head holding the desk top in place. "Dear Juliette" — the name is in block letters, underlined — "Your face might look okay if you washed it once in awhile. And those long streely dresses you've been wearing, did you inherit them from your great-grandmother? As for your hair, why don't you comb it occacionally?" It registers with me that "occasionally" is also spelled wrong. "And don't forget the louse rake!"

There's more, much more, but I don't read it. I drop the letter back into the desk, take out my history book and sit back in my seat. My hands are trembling and my face is hot. I know it must be blood red.

Everyone in the classroom is unusually attentive to Miss Lambert's words about Alexander the Great. Nobody is looking at me. I hear a sound like a stifled giggle but I keep my eyes on the page in front of me.

After school, avoiding Nadine, I hurry to the girls' bathroom, lock myself into a cubicle and read the rest of the letter. It's more of the same. I look down at the blue-and-white polka-dot skirt I'm wearing, given to me by our neighbor, Mrs. Leary. Her daughter Pat bought a lot of new clothes before she left for nursing school in Halifax. Mrs. Leary also gave me several blouses, a slip and three dresses.

"I'll hem them up for you when I get a chance," Mom said when I showed them to her. "It's great for you to have something nice to wear to school now that you're allowed to leave your uniforms off."

I tear the sheet of paper into tiny pieces and flush them down the toilet.

"Juliet, is that you in there?" It's Nadine. She rattles the cubicle door. "What's keeping you so long? Monthly, is it?"

In the distance I hear a shout of laughter.

"No," I say. "No, Nadine, I just feel a bit sick to my stomach." I flush the toilet again.

"Sure you're okay?" Nadine asks when I come out. I go to the nearest wash basin and splash cold water on my face.

Several girls are standing together over near the showers. They're whispering and giggling. Louise is there, and Dorothy and Thelma. And Betsy Stewart. Betsy is doing most of the talking.

"So long, Nadine. Toodle-oo, Juliet," Thelma calls as we pass. She emphasizes the last syllable of my name. "Don't do anything we wouldn't do." They all laugh.

"Think they're it, don't they?" Nadine mutters. "They are, if you put 'sh' in front of it."

Betsy had come to our school at the beginning of the year. Her father was an officer at Pepperrell. Without even trying she had been accepted into the Louise Mercer crowd. They're mostly girls whose fathers are well-off — doctors, lawyers, businessmen. Thelma's father is not one of them. He works at the post office with my father. It helps that Thelma is very pretty, gets all her clothes from her sister in the States, and can coax her blond hair into any style she finds in *Seventeen*.

"You haven't said a word since we left the school," Nadine says as we pass St. Clare's Hospital. "Still feeling sick?"

"No, I'm fine now." I try to smile. Nadine starts telling me about Cliff, the good-looking fellow from Bell Island she met at the roller rink.

"And he's getting his licence next month," she finishes as we approach her house.

As I walk on alone, I try to think of a place where I can run to cry. No matter where I go at home someone will hear me. I still share a room with Jessica; Rosalind and Cordelia are always in and out. And Mom will want me to take Duncan off her hands while she's cooking supper.

I don't tell anyone about the letter. I especially don't want my parents to know. Dad would cry and Mom would get mad. And what good would any of it do?

It's years since I've thought about that day in grade ten, consciously, anyhow. Nobody knows about the letter except me. And the girls who wrote it. I know it was the work of more than one girl, even though only one hand held the pen. For a few years after I finished school I'd sometimes run into girls from my class. We'd stop and chat and all the while I'd be asking myself, "Was she involved, was she, was she?"

Back when I found that letter the meanness didn't bother me as much as my belief that those girls were right to despise me. I was dirty, sloppy, streelish, untidy, unhandy. Even lousy. I couldn't pretend that I'd never found a louse or a nit in my thick, tangly hair. That's the real reason I never told anyone.

I pick up Laura's card and read it again. I don't know Laura very well; we met at the yoga class Abby talked me into joining. I don't even remember telling her I'd always wanted to go to Paris. It was nice of her to write.

It's time to start supper. Janet and Bob and the boys are coming and I promised them beef stroganoff. While I'm taking the meat out of the fridge I remember a story my mother told me more than once about a woman in her church group.

"They never ask Mrs. Norman to bring anything homemade," Mom would say as she squeezed her shortbread dough into long curly fingers or chopped up the vegetables for her beet salad. She would always wear a clean pair of underpants on her head when she was handling food. "She'd be asked to bring a quart of milk or a pound of butter, something like that. Poor soul, they said she wasn't very careful."

I wash my hands and begin to cut the round steak into small cubes.

Hidden
in the hand

Renate Schulz

The Romans were the first to put wedding rings on the third finger of the left hand, believing that this finger had a nerve that went straight to the heart. Before taking a woman in marriage, a Roman man studied the palms of her hands, especially those flexure lines that circle the end of the palm like bracelets. If the lines pushed themselves into the palm in the shape of a tongue, they were thought to signal a deformity of the reproductive organs. But if the flexure lines were well shaped, the woman's ability to bear children was supposedly assured, and she was deemed suitable as a wife.

For thousands of years people have believed they could interpret the lines that feather out along the palm.

Those who have a square palm with three deeply engraved major lines, but no delicate network of fine lines surrounding the heart, head and life lines, are practical, loyal, hard-working, steady and dependable people.

Those who have narrow and fine major lines, criss-crossed

by a web of extremely fine minor lines, are sensitive and emotional. They are sentimental and very receptive. They love to have their birthdays remembered, and to receive loving attention, affection and approval.

Plato and Aristotle wrote about hand interpretations. Julius Caesar and the emperor Augustus were well versed as hand readers. The prophets of the Bible looked into the palms of their right hands to determine the length of their days. And Anaxagoras, an ancient Greek philosopher and scientist, was convinced that the hand was at the core of our lives. He proclaimed that the superiority of humanity was owing to the hand. However, his credibility sank and he fell into disfavour when he also claimed that the sun and moon were not gods but only hot stones circling the earth.

A lack of love and appreciation can create a health line that is very distinct and easily seen.

The mystical power of the hand is captured in the metaphors of our spiritual, moral and everyday language. We speak of the hand of God, the healing hand and the hand that rocks the cradle. We give our hands in marriage, lend a helping hand and sometimes let things get out of hand.

Automatically we use our hands in combinations of strength, delicacy, precision and grace. The dancer creates visual magic with her hands. The hands of a climber grip fiercely the face of a rock cliff, while the hands of a pianist deftly coax sensuous musical nuances from piano keys. Hands can comfort and command, beckon and menace, build and destroy. Hands make war and love at the same time. They can heal and they can kill.

"What, will these hands ne'er be clean?"

Our hands are both text and tool. Silently they hold our life stories: age is revealed in the brown spots and blue-grey veins; identity is inscribed in the pattern of whorls and loops on the fingertips, an unalterable signature, set well before birth. Even if the skin of our fingertips is accidentally removed through injury, it grows back in the identical formation.

Our hands cannot lie. If we want to hide our feelings, we can shape the expression of our face and smile while our heart cries. If we want to disguise our age we can pay for makeovers and endure tucks or lifts. But our hands are immune to those vanities. We cannot mask what they express. They speak their own stories and reveal us in ways we don't even realize.

Instinctively, when we clasp our hands, the left thumb covers the right thumb, or vice versa. The superposition of the right thumb is found in people who are realistic, who are rational thinkers and whose reactions are based on reasoning.

If you clasp your hands and the left thumb rests on top, this suggests that instinctive feelings and intuition act as major driving forces in your life and that your reactions are mainly based on emotional responses, not logical reasoning.

We are accustomed to locating feelings in the heart, and thoughts and logical reasoning in the mind. We speak "from the heart"; we talk of "what's on our mind." But the brain does not live only inside the head, even though that is its physical address. The brain reaches out to the body and directs the hand even as the hand directs the brain. We know that we can communicate with our hands, and that language is not restricted to speaking and hearing. The brain is indifferent to the specific input–output channel, and so hands can become the voice of the deaf. Deaf people around the world and throughout the centuries have invented sign languages, fully grammatical systems through which both concrete and abstract ideas can be expressed. Their spontaneous emergence confirms that communication through gestures is as natural as spoken language.

In a different way, Louis Braille made the hands see for the blind. For Helen Keller, blind and deaf from the age of two, the darkness lifted and the silence was broken the moment that Annie Sullivan's fingers traced language into her palm. She discovered too that she could listen to music through the vibratory sensations of the hand. She described the sensations she felt while listening to Beethoven's Ninth Symphony:

Yesterday evening, as the family at home listened to the immortal work, I placed my hand on the receiver and clearly felt the swell. Then the cover was removed for me and I touched the membrane. How great was my astonishment when I discovered that I could not only sense every swing but also the passion of the rhythm, the pulsation and swell of the music. I could distinguish accurately between the cornet and the roll of the drum, the deep tone of the cellos and the singing of the violins.

So it is that through the hand, the outside brain, we can hear, feel, speak and see. What of the other claims? Is there healing power in the touch of hands? Is there a reason for the unique configuration of crease lines drawn in our palms? Do they, as Aristotle believed, express our individuality? Or are they just curious fare for palmists, soothsayers and charlatans?

The quaint practices of another time make for entertaining reading. Chiromancy, or the art of hand reading, dates back over three thousand years. The ancient Chaldeans brought the practice to Egypt and India, and also taught it to the Arabic peoples. Eventually it found its way to the Greeks and Romans. A chiromancer would have been present at every important meeting or event in ancient Greece. Hand reading is rooted in the belief that our personality is physically represented in our hands. Hands grow naturally straight out from the wrist and fingers extend directly from the hand. Any curving or bending of the skeletal part of the hand is believed to be caused by the outside pressures of life, family, society or experiences. Just as we can examine trees to find how winds, storms and climate have affected their growth, so we can examine hands to detect early influences in a person's life. When a tree is stunted, it is from the tremendous pressure of great forces that prevented its growth. When any finger does not achieve its full growth, it is believed that powerful forces at work early in the environment prevented it from growing to its full potential.

It is said that our little finger represents our one-to-one relationships, our intimate connections. It is also the finger of communication. Long little fingers on both hands represent the ability to perceive the unseen and inaudible, making hunches reliable. If you have long little fingers, deep philosophical discussions fascinate you. You love conversations about the abstract and the unknown. A little finger curved toward the ring finger represents the ability to conceal true feelings. And if your little finger is short, you withdrew your antenna to non-verbal messages early, and your communication skills have not developed as well as they might. If you seek expansion and improvement in this area of your life, stretch and massage the little finger. Do this while you are fully aware of your purpose. Visualizing the end result you hope to achieve while stretching helps to reinforce your purpose.

Such prescriptions for self-improvement are harmless and easily dismissed. But healing acts rooted in alternative medicine can draw sharp responses from mainstream medical practitioners. Often the scientific community reacts with hostility to traditional practices because they are not based on the typical Western approach.

An ancient Chinese practice is to roll the herb artemisia into a cigar shape, set it afire, and hold it close to the little toe of a pregnant woman whose baby is in the breech position. The heat, it is claimed, stimulates an acupuncture point on that toe that increases fetal movement, helping the baby swim around into the proper position to be born.

More and more often we are surprised and rewarded when we submit such curious practices, rooted in traditional knowledge, to closer examination. In old manuscripts dealing with witchcraft and sorcery, the medical profession has found many a hint as to how certain herbs and plants, thought to be the hocus pocus of ancient times, can be used to help and serve modern science.

Italian medical researchers divided 130 women in two Chinese hospitals into two groups. Those pregnant women treated with the herb artemisia, in the ancient practice called moxibustion, had 30 percent more babies move out of the dangerous breech position that women left untreated.

There are more things in heaven and earth, Horatio, than are dreamt of in your philosophy.

Women have long been the keepers of much of our traditional knowledge. Wouldn't it be interesting if we returned with a new sense of wonder to explore some of the forgotten corners of our knowing? The hand, being feminine in all languages that assign gender to nouns, in a sense belongs to us. Do we know her well enough? We didn't know that we could be pianists, that we could make music with our hands in that way, until the piano was invented. What else might we discover in the unfolding of the hand?

Intrigued by the ancient belief that the lines in our palms express our individuality, I look there for confirmation of who I am or who I would like to be. The lines in my palms are delicate and fine, their configurations suggesting a sensitive and emotional nature. When I clasp my hands my left thumb rests on top, pointing to a strong reliance on feeling and intuition. But my little finger curves towards the ring finger, telling me that I am also adept at hiding my true feelings. Like a mirror my hands give back to me parts of who I am: pocket-sized pieces of me that have been tucked away, hardly used, almost forgotten, seldom called into conversation.

When I am asked to speak about myself, to talk about the things that have surprised me or disappointed me about my life's experiences, the things that move me, my answers are halting. My ideas shuffle about, startled by this request to go public. How should I begin? I am not practised in the art of shaping my feelings into words. I have lived no great tragedies, harbour no dark secrets. No stories well up. I have little to spread out before my listeners.

Maybe on some tomorrow I will be able to unfold my heart as easily as I now unfold my hands. That is my hope. This is my present.

Wild Roses

Katherine Govier

Lucy Gray's aunt had been a famous artist. Ruth Bentham was her name and she first painted the wild roses and the coulees of southern Alberta, where she had moved in 1937 as a young bride. She then graduated to interiors with a little narrative — letters on tables, hats on chairs, shawls hastily thrown over lampshades. The objects that caught her attention became lurid: they did not look like still lifes. Quite the opposite; they looked as if they were possessed. In the words of one critic, her work was "infused with a fearsome volupté." It was more likely she was going mad.

Yes, an artist. But famous she wasn't. In fact she had laboured in near obscurity, and such attention as she had found had been negative. In Ruth's day, the overheatedness of her images and colours gave offense. She put too much into her paintings, people said. Strangely, today, some sixty years after her death, Lucy's aunt had a modest following; she was a local feminist heroine. Sometimes people even showed up, carrying guidebooks, at Ruth Bentham's grave, which was on the side of a hill off Tenth Street in northwest Calgary. Although Lucy grew up within a mile of that grave, she had never visited it. Until today.

Lucy Gray had three children, a busy husband and a house, not to mention a job as a part-time teacher of children with learning difficulties and an increasing amount of responsibility as the caretaker of aging parents. She was grateful to get through the day, let alone create a work of art. She repeated this to herself while marching moodily up the grassy prairie hill beside Confederation Park. In her right hand she bore a nosegay of flowers, more appropriate to being thrust through a doorway by a shy suitor than placed on a grave.

Lucy had flown in from Vancouver to help her parents move into a condominium. In her hotel that morning a fax from home had been shoved under her door. Jason complained that he had too much homework and couldn't find his baseball hat, and Jennifer added two broken sentences demanding that Mummy come home. Mercifully the baby was too young to complain. The second page held a few lines of denial added by her husband: "Have fun! Everything's under control." This morning she read the fax as she sat at the breakfast table waiting for her parents to appear. When they did they looked unhappy. Her father's eyes were blood-rimmed and her mother fussed with her food. Feeling helpless, Lucy decided to let them oversee the carpet installation by themselves.

"I thought I'd go and visit your sister's grave," she said.

Marjorie's face livened, and the downward twist around her lips lifted for a moment.

"Oh!" she said. "I'd like to do that with you." Then she looked at her husband. His mouth was half open in protest already. She quickly backed down. "But there will be other days."

Lucy had intended to visit her aunt's grave; for years she had meant to, but had been put off because Marjorie was always going. What on earth did her mother get out of staring at some rectangle of ground that had swallowed her dead sister's body, that was what Lucy used to say. A child's cruelty, a child's jealousy. But now she was curious.

Long ago but not far from here, in a clapboard prairie house on a long street sloping upward toward West Hill, a slim vellum envelope pregnant with news pokes its triangular corner through the slot in the door. Inside this house are burgundy rugs, heavy forest-green curtains, doilies, antimacassars, African violets and dark wood trim that needs oiling and dusting every few days. There is a window overlooking the dry enclosure of a garden where a mountain ash stands. A French lilac raises its lonely midnight torches. The prairie can't be seen, only felt, the grass meeting wind in its huge, impartial coming and going. Inside this house, Ruth Bentham sees the letter fall and freezes in her steps.

This happens in the 1940s. Ruth is a dutiful wife and an older sister to the newly emigrated Marjorie. She makes Yorkshire pudding and ham with scalloped potatoes on Sunday nights. She used to go out on horseback for painting excurions down toward Fish Creek and Priddis, but now she stays in. She is lonely in this house. Ruth's husband Nigel is tired of Ruth's unhappiness which has been bred elsewhere; in the ghettos of Eastern Europe, in the rains of Scotland, in the secrecy, denial and drink here in her home. It is only cured by painting trips with cowboys, and these are not appropriate for a pregnant woman.

The envelope falls through the slot in the door and Ruth's cat jumps off the needlepoint chair. Ruth picks up the letter and sees that it is addressed, in a ladylike hand, to Mrs. Nigel Bentham.

It is her name. She still thrills to it, to being called after the tall, laughing man with the beautiful suits and the lacquered hair. Still feels flattered by the association, by the appropriation even, although he's been a disappointment — good to look at but not to depend on, and she has been forced to depend on him. He looks a bit like Fred Astaire. He will look more like

Fred Astaire as he grows older and the hair shrinks back from his creased forehead and lean, cheerful face. With his knife-edged pants and his Vaselined patent shoes he will look as nimble as if he could dance over the tabletop and down the wall. Nigel will drive the wrong way down one-way streets all his life without getting caught. But in the end, having left his chaos behind him, he will be buried in the cold earth alone, well-meaning and bewildered. Like the rest of us.

Before Ruth opens the letter she has time to look around the room, which, despite everything, she loves. She takes in her watercolour of the wild roses, and two sombre little reproductions of that English boy and girl you see everywhere. She has time as she unfolds the single page to note that the purple violet leaps unbidden out of its fuzzy leaves and that a red scarf over the chair back is glowing in a sinister way. And then she reads:

> Dear Mrs. Bentham,
> Be advised that your husband is not faithful to your marriage. He has been seen often in the company of a woman in his business. If you think about it you'll know who. He does not play tennis as you think, on Thursdays and Sundays. He goes off with her to her apartment on Fourth Street. I am tired of these prairie tight lips where everyone knows and no one says. Don't hide your head in the sand! I feel I must tell you. It is only right and proper that you should know. Go and look! You'll see his car.
>
> Sincerely,
> A Friend

This much of the story Lucy has been told. She has always been afraid to ask what happened next. Did Ruth "go see"? Was the "friend" shocked at that harm done? How long was it between when Ruth found out and when she did it? And the final question. Who found Ruth? Somebody must have found her. Not Nigel, of course, because he came home late, if at all. It would have been Ruth's sister, little Marjorie, only seventeen and recently come out from Scotland to find a husband. Still, little Marjorie survived; she went on to marry and to have children to replace the child Ruth had been carrying.

Lucy had trouble finding the grave. It was winter, and a light cover of dry snow obscured many of the inscriptions. But she was persistent and at length she stood before the grave, an unassuming granite stone, set somewhat on an angle. A sob rose up her throat and she wanted to cry out Ruth's name. She ignored the cold. It might have been half an hour before she saw the two figures. Lucy's feet and fingers were numb, her ears frozen too. Two women approached, behatted, sixtyish matrons, the type who made Lucy want to say "fuck" ten times over straight into their faces. On those faces were expressions of greed, of self-congratulation, of self-worship, even. They moved alongside the hillside, not deviating from their course.

Sidehill Gougies, thought Lucy. That's what they were. On Crescent Hill, across Center Street, where Lucy grew up, everyone knew what Sidehill Gougies were. No one had seen them, of course. They were the bogeymen who always loped in the same direction across a steep hill and hence had one leg longer than the other.

Once they arrived, the Gougies virtually shouldered Lucy aside. One of them stepped forward and began to swipe at the monument with her glove, dusting the snow off it. The other actually got down on her knees and attempted to scoop the snow away from the base.

Lucy gave a little gasp of outrage. But, suddenly conscious of the baggy khaki pants she'd donned this morning in anticipation of crawling around on the floor of her parents' condo, of her ski jacket and half-laced Kodiak boots, of her son's baseball hat, which she had pulled out of her suitcase, and of the ridiculous nosegay, gone stiff in her hand, she allowed herself to be displaced at the graveside. One of the women spoke first.

"Did you know this is Ruth Bentham's grave!" she said, over her shoulder.

"And look at the shape it's in," added the other, lifting her head from digging. "It's absolutely disgraceful."

"Not looked after! Ruth Bentham's grave!" repeated the first.

Finally Lucy found her voice. "I know it is," she retorted. "Ruth Bentham is my aunt. Who the hell are you?"

The women looked at her, astonished.

"You're nosey parkers," Lucy shouted. "That's what you are." It was another name dragged up from the past. That's what you'd have called them, back then.

The story of her aunt always ended with the words "She received an anonymous letter. . . ." Marjorie would close her lips, avert her face. Ruth died soon after. She had been ill, an invalid. Marjorie's voice would fade over the details. After an unspecified amount of time had passed since her sister's death, Marjorie herself had married Nigel. Yes, really, and the children were born. Marjorie was too lonely; her whole family, aside from Ruth, had stayed in Scotland. Lucy was the eldest. Marjorie had confided in her. One day she used the word "suicide": "My sister committed suicide." Never any more than that. Never the details. And Lucy couldn't ask; how could she ask?

Eventually, everyone knew. Some critic dug it up, some historian reading death certificates. The fact that Ruth Bentham had killed herself was part of the mythology, part of what brought out the art lovers. Did they know about the anonymous "friend," Lucy wondered? Because the friend had made another communication.

There on the snow-dusted hillside Lucy remembered the summer she was fourteen. In her shorts and halter top, free, wearing no underwear because she was young and brazen. She was turning cartwheels in the yard. Her father was out of town.

This morning her mother had received a phone call. Lucy did not know then, but now she can imagine what was said. The caller was unknown to Marjorie, and did not give her name. She simply said that someone had seen. Someone knew. The woman from across the street was with Nigel. Incredible but true. Going on for months. Go and ask your husband if you want. You could catch them red-handed if you went to see.

Marjorie had run to the bathroom. Lucy had heard sobs and did not know what to do. Later her mother came out and telephoned the airlines to book a ticket to Winnipeg. But she did not have money to pay for it. She did not have credit cards, not in those days. So she cancelled it. Then she ran into the den and stayed there for an hour. She emerged with an envelope in her hand. It was addressed to her husband at his hotel in Winnipeg. "Take this letter and mail it," she said to Lucy. "Right now before I change my mind."

Lucy trotted across the meridian, waited for the traffic to pass, then ran across the wide asphalt road toward the mailbox. Lucy practised her grands jetés along the grass bank to the red mailbox. Pushed aside the metal gate over the slot and dropped the letter down into the darkness.

There was a moment of terror when it was gone. Had she misunderstood? Her mother had seemed very certain but Lucy knew her too well. She knew about the fear her mother lived with, the shakes and the tears and the regular screwing up of courage required even to go shopping. She peered into the slot. She could see nothing, after the brilliance of daylight. What did the letter say?

> Dear husband of mine. You are in trouble big-time.
> You've given me grief once too often and I'm here-
> by telling you to shove off. Love, Marjorie!

Wrong. Her mother would never write such a letter. Not just because it was the fifties and women didn't leave their husbands and go out to work, not in Calgary. But because Marjorie was Ruth Bentham's little sister.

The letter was truly gone. Into what? A pile of other envelopes. Or did it lie alone? Lucy checked the schedule printed on the drawer. Mail would be picked up at nine o'clock a.m. and at one o'clock and five o'clock p.m.

Heading home she stopped on the grass and did more cartwheels. She had spent the entire last summer learning how to do them. Her mother could do them too. That was the good thing about Marjorie. She was like a sister in many ways. Lucy waited until, across the street, she could see the post truck. The mailman got out. He was cute, with a moustache and sideburns; he was a snappy dresser in his summer short pants. With his key, his great sack, he opened the hatch. He fit the sack over the opening and then tipped the internal drawer so that the contents slid together into the sack. He hitched the sack over his shoulder, and heaved it into the back of the truck. Bang. The metal door of the truck closed.

At home Lucy faced an apparition.

"The letter. Where is it?"

"I mailed it."

"Is it gone? Oh, no."

"The truck came."

Marjorie was rigid and staring. "Oh, no. I changed my mind. You can't get it back?"

"No."

Marjorie's face crumpled. Ruth Bentham's little sister.

Lucy wailed. "But you told me to!"

"Well, if you're family you ought to be ashamed of yourself!" cried one of the Sidehill Gougies/nosey parkers. She had clambered off her knees and was dusting her hands angrily on the sides of her thighs.

"I beg your pardon!" cried Lucy. "What right do you have to come here and — disturb — yes, disturb! — my aunt's grave?"

"Your aunt, if she is your aunt, is a public figure. And this grave is neglected," charged the other.

"It is not!" She held out her flowers. "Look. I've come to visit."

"Well, how do we know you're not a crank?" said one of the women. The other cast her a warning glance and spoke gently, as if to be conciliatory. The exchange only made it clear she knew she was dealing with a nutbar.

"Not only that. It's hard to find. We had to ask twice. The stone should be more prominent. And the epitaph, well, it doesn't say anything."

Lucy's heart was pounding. Her cheeks were in flames. She was enraged. The art critics were hard enough on old Ruth. Now the grave critics were onto the rest of them.

"I'm sure her husband and sister felt it was appropriate at the time," said Lucy with heavy irony. The epitaph read "Sorely missed."

The two women stared at her balefully. Lucy would never fully understand why she did what she did next. Was it the stress of moving her parents into the home that set her off?

"Get out! This is private property," shouted Lucy.

"It is not!" said the more belligerent of the two. "It's a public cemetery."

But nonetheless she backed off.

"This is private! This is the Bentham plot!" cried Lucy, getting shrill. "There is a space right here for my mother and my father and my sisters and me."

Lucy found herself crying with rage. She stepped forward and, quickly switching the nosegay to her left hand, pushed the shoulder of one of the women as they hustled away, clucking and spitting with disapproval, pulling their fur collars up around their necks. When they were gone she leaned against the gravestone, pulled off the baseball cap and ran her fingers through her hair. It was cold; she wished she had a fur hat like those awful women.

In the fifties there was a fox stole. It was basically a dead animal that lived in a long, thin pink box. It had ears, eyes, a nose and claws that dangled. The box lay in the bathroom drawer. It had belonged to Ruth. From time to time Marjorie took it out and wore it around her neck.

In the powder room off the front hall they both faced the mirror, Lucy behind and above her mother. Marjorie pulled the fox-box out of the drawer. As soon as the fox was out of the box, pain suffused the little room. Like a fog, it slid up mirrors, dampened the beige monogrammed towels, burrowed in the hole at the core of the pink conch shell. The pain was seeking exit, or refuge, but in the mirrow-walled powder room there was nowhere to hide. The whole place became, to Lucy, a tomb. The animal's fur was like part of an Egyptian mummy. The glass perfume bottles were offerings to the dead.

She touched the fox stole. The fur was soft, as if still living. Lucy was older now than when she had mailed the letter for her mother. Around that time she had began to do what her parents called "rebel." Her father had become authoritarian, distant and dumbly furious. Her mother had dealt with the rebellion simply by refusing to acknowledge that it was happening. Hence, although Lucy didn't actually help her mother any more, she still watched her get ready for parties.

The fox wound around Marjorie's bare shoulders, pliant and faintly dangerous. Lucy's job was to say how it should be draped, where the nose should be, and the claws. She reached down over her mother's shoulders and lifted the little fox face, catching the gleam from its glass eyes, letting the smooth black curved claws drag across her mother's collarbone. She put the nose facing down, into her mother's cleavage, then tucked up tight into the wraparound tail at her neck. Marjorie was complacent, staring into the mirror. As she stared, and as the fox settled on her clavicle, she seemed to grow. Her back straightened. Her shoulders broadened. Her face took on a distinct, mischievous character. Regarding herself in the mirror, she began to smile.

Was it just because Lucy was paying attention to her? Or did she feel that her sister had come back to give her love? The strip of hide with fur gave her the strength to get through one more evening. She would go out to a party with Nigel, who was pacing, elegant, in the hallway.

"Tuck the claws out of the way," Marjorie said. "We don't want them rattling."

"I think it's creepy the way fur hangs around long after the animals who grow it are gone," said Lucy aggressively. Her mother sprayed on perfume. "I can't stand that scent," Lucy said. And she ducked away from their joint image in the mirror.

Alone again, Lucy laid her nosegay at the base of the crooked stone and smoothed over the snow that the intruders dug up. She leaned against the tombstone, her forehead on the cold stone. Marjorie was so frail now that one hundred fox stoles could not restore the lustre, the love of fun in that mirrored image. Lucy could not ask. Perhaps the question was meant for Aunt Ruth, anyway. The question was no longer, "How did you do it? The oven? The knife? (I don't think so.) Something dramatic and public like the train station? (Not your style.) Drugs? (Impossible to get in those days.)" The question was not even, "Are you sorry now? Do you miss being alive? Did you imagine how much you would hurt your little sister and even, yes, her daughter?" That was obvious. The real question she had for her aunt was this: Why did you not write a letter? And if you did, would you have told your sister to avoid the man who would do the same thing to her, a man who would let her down? Or would you have had her marry him? Surely it was Ruth's duty to say something. It is you, Aunt Ruth Bentham, who are negligent.

Negligent, she said to herself.

The letter Lucy had dropped through the mailbox slot would never be discussed. When Nigel came home from his business trip in Winnipeg, detained only one day in the hotel room by the ardent neighbour woman, who soon left her husband and moved to Toledo, he brought a present for his wife. It was a white negligée, long, with a heavy lace gown that went over it. Marjorie did not seem overly impressed, but Nigel swayed Lucy to his side with that romantic gesture. From then on, she was her dad's girl. She went on trips with him; she played golf with him. He never liked any of her boyfriends.

Lucy took a long time to settle down. Her younger sisters married first. Each of them received a beautiful white negligée on the night before they left home. But when Lucy's wedding night came, she was disappointed. There was nothing.

For a long time Lucy believed that her father forgot her negligée because she was not a virgin. Her father knew what her "rebellion" was about; he had seen through her lies about the ski trips and sleepovers with girlfriends. Oh yes, he could spot a lie when he heard one, tell a liar when he saw one. And it was true, that she had lost her innocence. It had happened before her trysts with boys. She had lost it mailing the letter. She had lost it travelling with Nigel. She had lost it hearing about Ruth Bentham. Out of love she had become entangled. She hated that, but she couldn't blame anyone. The safest person to hate was Ruth Bentham. That was why she had never been to the grave before.

Sitting in the snow, Lucy pounded the stone. You couldn't hate the dead. But if only you could make them speak. What did Ruth have to say? Wild roses turning to hats, scarves, tables with opened letters — voluptuous and tragic, seductive and deadly, objects screaming out their wordless message. "Don't do as I did! Do as I did!" It was the same message she'd given her sister, and her sister had given her daughter.

Lucy stood with her parents at the check-in line at the Calgary airport, ready to go back to Vancouver. She and her parents hugged and kissed, laughed and wiped their eyes, gathering a few stares. It was always so hard to leave; they all cried at airports, a family trait. It was the sign of a good visit. Lucy was, when she thought about it, a little embarrassed about screaming at the visiting art enthusiasts, but not very. She liked the grave to be neglected. Ruth Bentham had earned her eccentricities. So had they all.

"I heard the strangest thing," said her mother. "When I was at the art gallery a woman came in talking about Ruth Bentham's grave. She said it was in a shocking state. They're going to get up a subscription to have it improved. They want a plaque."

"What would it say?" said Lucy. But just then they announced the gate number for Lucy's flight, and Marjorie didn't hear her.

"This woman had been out there to show it to a friend, and apparently ran into some woman pretending to be a relative. She claims this woman physically attacked her. Told her to get out. She asked if it was you."

Lucy smiled slowly. She opened her mouth to confess. But her mother was still talking. Her eyes were bright and smiling.

"I got quite huffy. I told her it was impossible. We all know you would never say anything like that."

Reflections from Cyberspace

Carol Hussa Harvey and Katherine C.H. Gardiner

. . . .

Sent: January 14, 2000
To: Karen McDermott (karen_mcd@home.com)
From: Andrea Howell (ahowell@messages.com)
Subject: New job

Hi Mom,

I know I promised to write and tell you more about this new position, but I haven't really known what to say. The excitement that the recruiters built has shrivelled to practically nothing, and the enthusiasm that the executives had for bringing my "exciting new ideas and expertise" has never translated into anything besides talk. Just over a month on the job and I'm feeling quite certain that I've made a huge mistake! I hardly know where to begin...

For the first couple of weeks I had niggling feelings that things were not quite right. Now, I am certain that this new environment and I are not a very good match. It began with Mel, my boss, introducing me around the office. Almost every single person asked if I was his "assistant." At a bit of a loss, I said that I was indeed working for him, but, frankly, the whole concept of being his assistant never dawned on me.

I knew when I started that agribusiness is a male-dominated arena, but I am floored by the attitudes I've encountered. The majority of women here are in support roles, and today I found myself in a conversation with my male colleagues about what their wives made them for lunch. I'm sure this must sound trivial, but it was absolutely bizarre! No one actually said it out loud, but the whole tone of the conversation seemed to imply that I (the only female in the department) should naturally be supporting my hard-working husband in the same way.

The most frightening part of this is that these attitudes seem to affect how others view my work. So far I have been assigned a number of support tasks to fill my time and haven't received any of the data or internal support for the projects I was hired to champion.

To be fair, the potential of my position is still very interesting to me, and I still think that my finance background is perfect for the job. I've always wanted to be part of the big picture, and working in the corporate office does that. Mel is full of energy and is infectious in his enthusiasm for having me here. He has acknowledged that there are stumbling blocks, but he is sure that once I "prove" myself I will be able to get the challenge and diversity that attracted me in the first place. So, I'm trying hard to throw myself into my work and ignore what's been going on around me.

Rob thinks things will get easier with time, so we shall see . . .

Love to you and Dad
Andie

....

Sent: January 19, 2000
To: Andie Howell (ahowell@messages. com)
From: Karen McDermott (karen_mcd@home.com)
Subject: Re: New job

Hi Sweetie,

I was so glad to get your e-mail address and hear about your new job, though I'm sorry you were feeling so aggravated. Actually, I noticed your company has been getting good press and seems to be having an impressive growth spurt. Should be a good opportunity to apply your talent — don't get so upset that you fail to remember its good aspects.

Things here are going along as usual. Been doing a fair bit of reading in the evenings, as I don't feel much like fighting the weather outside. Dad religiously keeps up his running at the track, but I don't seem to be going with him as often as I was last fall, even though it's indoors.

Work is going well, though it's getting routine after 21 years. I can't believe I have been with the government that long. I get a good feeling when I look at what I have accomplished here: I think my work has made a difference. And the people I work for have largely been supportive, so, all in all, I can't really complain.

Saw on the news last night that you folks had another snowstorm; hope that hasn't caused either you or Rob too much hassle.

Dad says "hi!"
Love, Mom

....

Sent: January 26, 2000
To: Karen McDermott (karen_mcd@home.com)
From: Andrea Howell (ahowell@messages.com)
Subject: Re: New job

Hi, Mom

Good to hear from you! Sorry it's taken such a long time for me to respond, but the past week has been full. We made it through the storm OK (it's amazing to see how quickly the city deals with Mother Nature's little surprises) and are now coping with everyday life. Rob's taken over most of the work on the home front, keeping things together there while I put most of my energy into work. I don't think he minds too much, as he's quite happy to finally have me working and out of student mode!

As for how I feel about work, the jury's still out. Per Mel's suggestion, I have launched several proposals that highlight my abilities. Most have been met with varying degrees of success, so that helps.

Cheers,
Andie

Sent: February 9, 2000
To: Andrea Howell (ahowell@messages.com)
From: Karen McDermott (karen_mcd@home.com)
Subject: News

Hi Sweetie,

I was sorry to miss you when we called last night. Tell Rob that Dad and I really enjoyed our visit with him. We were amazed that you two prairie-raised people are going to take up downhill skiing... Terrifying, if you ask me!

I was thinking about the workplace after you wrote a while back. A given location certainly can be influenced by the gender of its employees. Working for the Province, I find many people at my level are women, so the male dominance thing doesn't apply, thankfully. Regardless, I don't think anyone here really cares whether a person is male or female.

You know, even though you've had some trying times, Dad and I are both really proud of what you're doing. Your grandfather would be so impressed! Little did he know when he was farming on the Saskatchewan prairie that his granddaughter would be working in agribusiness.

Dave called last night from Nepal. He met a fella from England who will be his travelling buddy, so I'm relieved he's not alone. They are off "trekking." Did you ever dream your timid little brother would be so adventurous? Drop him a line if you have the chance. He's travelerguy@hotmail.com

Hugs,
Mom

Sent: February 17, 2000
To: Mom (karen_mcd@home.com)
From: Andrea Howell (ahowell@messages.com)
Subject: Needing to vent!

Hey, Mom,

Well, again I've got myself all worked up and thought it'd be best to drop you an e-mail rather than lose my cool at the office. I feel as if I'm living through a 1950s flashback!

I was at my desk waiting for a conference call when one of the program managers appeared. He was going to a meeting and held a diskette towards me, saying, "Could you do me a favour?" I told him that I was expecting a call any minute but said I'd help if I could. Turns out he wanted me to edit and print one of his documents so it would be ready when he came back. I couldn't believe it — his position and mine are basically equal, yet here he was asking me to be his secretary!

Maybe I've just been lucky in my past positions, or else I'm naïve, but I thought these kinds of attitudes were in the past.

Love,
Andie

Sent: February 17, 2000
To: Andrea Howell (ahowell@messages.com)
From: Karen McDermott (karen_mcd@home.com)
Subject: Re: Needing to vent!

Dear Andie,

Wow, I'm sorry to hear that you're feeling so out of place. As Rob suggested, you may just need to give yourself a little more time to get acclimated — you know, get to know everyone a bit better; let them get to know you... I'm sure that being mistaken for a secretary (when that isn't your job) is just an isolated incident. I suggest you don't rush to conclusions. Things have a way of working out all right, so have a bit of patience.

I also think that rather than fretting about what's wrong, you should look at what you have going for you. You have a wonderful husband, a good relationship with him, friends, good health and a family who loves you. Take a deep breath and swoop down the ski slopes, perhaps worrying less and enjoying more. :-)

I'll phone you tonight; keep your chin up,
Mom

....

Sent: March 10, 2000
To: Andrea Howell (ahowell@messages.com),
David McDermott (travelerguy@hotmail.com)
From: Karen McDermott (karen_mcd@home.com)
Re: New news!

Dear Andie and Dave (whenever you tune in from cyberspace),

Am excited and want to share some news with you. Hope you have your laptop with you in Vancouver, Andie, so you get this message right away. I've applied for a promotion!

Sam, my boss who is retiring, has encouraged me to apply for his position. I replaced him last year when he was on sick leave, so I know I can do the work — even received a commendation letter after his return. This position is exactly what I've been working towards. I wanted you to know that my interview is tomorrow.

Will keep you posted,
Mom

Sent: March 15, 2000
To: Mom (karen_mcd@home.com)
From: Andrea Howell (ahowell@messages.com)
Subject: Job

Oh, Mom, I talked to Dad just now and he told me what happened. When we talked, you had mentioned that Peter had applied as well, but it seemed like you were more suited. Anyhow, I'm so sorry you didn't get the job. You must be disappointed. I'll try to reach you again tonight.

Love,
Andie

Sent: March 15, 2000
To: Mom (karen_mcd@home.com)
From: David McDermott (travelerguy@hotmail.com)
Re: No Job

Hey, Mums. Andie wrote to say you didn't get the job. Sorry to hear it, but I guess it just wasn't meant to be. Trekking is terrific — back to Kathmandu tomorrow. More later. **Love, Me**

Sent: May 3, 2000
To: Andrea Howell (ahowell@messages.com), David McDermott (travelerguy@hotmail.com)
From: Karen McDermott (karen_mcd@home.com)
Subject: Interesting developments

Dear Andie and Davy,

What happened to our resolve to write more frequently? I was actually meaning to send you both some chit-chatty type of message today, but now this e-mail is smoking... I've learned more of what went on behind the scenes when Peter got the promotion that should have been mine.

Basically, I got the runaround. The human resources officer who contacted me with the bad news said that Peter was transferred from the Feds to the Province, had more experience, etc. Turns out, that wasn't exactly true.

Since I'm a member of our public employees negotiating committee, I received the final draft of our next contract proposal. Looking through the analysis at the end, I was astonished to see it showed a lot of gender discrepancies in both pay and upward mobility. The union report interpreted the differences as a "glass ceiling," showing that women tended to stop at a certain rate of pay. I was incredulous. In fact, I believe I told you earlier that this didn't happen here.

Naturally, the report piqued my curiosity. I turned to the back, where the raw data were appended. Sure enough, there was information on my case (without names, of course). Peter actually had a lower rate of pay in his old job than I do in mine, and he also had less experience. Why, then, did I not get that job?! I'm furious and flabbergasted.

I brought it up with Sam, who shrugged and didn't really know what to say. What do you think? Dad says I should sue for what is rightfully mine.

Love you,
Mom

Sent: May 3, 2000
To: Mom (karen_mcd@home.com)
From: Andrea Howell (ahowell@messages.com)
Subject: Unbelievable

Well, Mom, I got your message and wanted to get back to you right away... I'm so sorry to hear about the politics at your office. You've always been so proud of the fairness and equity throughout the years, so this must be quite a blow.

I honestly don't know what to suggest about legal action. On the one hand it seems like the right thing to do if you're sure you were discriminated against. On the other hand, a lawsuit seems rather severe.

Not entirely helpful, I know, but I am thinking of you and sending lots of love!

Andie

Sent: May 4, 2000
To: Mom (karen_mcd@home.com)
From: Andrea Howell (ahowell@messages.com)
Subject: Thoughts

Hi,

After we got off the phone my brain was still going a million miles an hour. Rob and I had another big discussion about gender equity and now here I am e-mailing you. Fact is, I still can hardly believe that any of this is even an issue. Six months ago I thought that sexism was a thing of the past. No one in the Business Administration department (or anywhere else at the university) ever suggested otherwise.

I've always known that there were plenty of traditionally male jobs "out there," but it never seemed to have any effect on me personally. I had never felt that being female was any kind of hindrance. Now I'm not so sure. First, all the covert messages I run into nearly every day at my job and then the large roadblock you've experienced...

Rob was giving me the old "if you can't beat 'em" pep talk — change circumstances by moving into an executive position and then implementing the change from the top down. A great theory, but the thought of applying it in my own job? YUCK! Why would I want the stress of being a pioneer?

So, here I am in a catch-22 position: I want <u>someone</u> to change things, but <u>I</u> don't want to deal with all the headaches of being that person. I feel like such a hypocrite!

You and Dad set examples for us kids of how men and

women could both work and be active family members at the same time. You raised us to believe that we could do anything we set out to do. Whether we were male or female never seemed to be an issue. I'm not subscribing to the blame-your-parents-for-everything-that-went-wrong-in-your-life theory, but I'm starting to think that my perception of reality doesn't actually fit in the "real" world.

Cyber hugs,
Andie

....

Sent: May 17, 2000
To: Andrea Howell (ahowell@messages.com)
From: Karen McDermott (karen_mcd@home.com)
Subject: Davy's opinion

Dear Andie,

Sounds like your brother has a different opinion... see below. Dunno what to make of it.

Mom

> Hi Mums,
> Just a quick check of my messages before we sojourn to the holy city of Veransi tomorrow. Am anxious to see where the Buddha preached his first sermon. And I hear a lot of Indians bathe in the sacred Ganges there.

> You know, I am sorry you didn't get the job you wanted, but I really I think a lawsuit is over the top. You wanted the job, but so did Peter. AND he's got a family to support, and you have a share in Dad's income. It's not like you got fired or anything. Thing is, too many people

are out there crying "discrimination" when these days it's white men who can't get a job. Employers are so busy filling quotas that they don't care who the best person for the job is... Been thinking of how it will be for me to find a job when I get home and I'm not terribly optimistic... D.

Sent: May 17, 2000
To: David McDermott (travelerguy@hotmail.com)
From: Andrea Howell (ahowell@messages.com)
Subject: Yikes!

Davy,

I cannot even believe the message you sent Mom. She forwarded it to me and I've been stunned ever since. Did we actually grow up under the same roof?? You KNOW how important Mom's job is to her. It always has been. Just because Dad had a job doesn't make hers any less important! AND, the whole "poor me for being a white guy" is such a bunch of bull!

I don't know where you get your information, but all you have to do is look around and see that jobs for people fitting your "discrimination" list. I, personally, am the ONLY woman in my department. The company has 27 executives — only one is female. Two new people have been hired in the past month — both yuppie white men.

Give me a break!
Andie

Sent: May 20, 2000
To: Andrea Howell (ahowell@messages.com)
From: Karen McDermott (karen_mcd@home.com)
Subject: Time for a change

Hi,

Well, Dad and I always meant to set examples for you to be strong at work and at home, but I'm not going to act powerfully now. I checked with a lawyer, and though it appears as though I have an excellent case, fighting the Province and its bureaucrats would take most of Dad's and my savings. We've discussed my options and I've decided to ask for a transfer. This way I won't be seeing Peter every day, will get a new set of colleagues and will have some new projects on which to spend my work time. Not the morally righteous outcome, and for that reason this decision seems a bit cowardly. However, I can put the whole mess behind me after I transfer, and, at this time in my life, it seems to be the best course of action. Guess I should listen to my own counsel and start concentrating on the other facets of my life.

Honey, don't worry about Davy. He's young. He will see the world through a different lens when he's back home. He's probably a bit intimidated at the thought of looking for work — and seeing the poverty in Nepal and India may influence him right now into thinking of two jobs per family as a luxury.

Spring is lovely. We have daffodils in bloom, the ones Dad planted for me a couple of years ago. Having a Mother's Day chat with you and Rob, Andie — plus the flowers you sent me — and getting another call from Davy — all made my day feel wonderful. Thank you.

Love,
Mom

I Have Blinds Now

Sandy Frances Duncan

My mother never told me about lust. She never told me about curtains either. But then, we never lived in one place long enough to worry about curtains. I don't know what she thought about lust.

"Lust" was not a word of the 1950s. "Love" was — as in, "they're madly in love" — and "sex" was — as in, "he has sex appeal," of the Elvis or Marlon variety. The latter was frequently shortened to "S.A." so we girls could discuss it with giggly whispers in living rooms or parent-driven cars. But we had no word for the thrumming, throbbing, sinking, moist and breathless sensations lust so aptly describes. If we didn't have the word we wouldn't have the feelings, I suppose, was the ethos of the time.

When my class studied *The Canterbury Tales*, our teacher announced that "Gat-tothed was she," meant that the Wife of

Bath was lusty. The way our teacher pronounced "lusty" — loosty — did not have the open-mouthed expansiveness of lust, but no matter; all year, whenever we passed a gap-toothed person on the street, we nudged each other and giggled.

Throughout this time, my mother and I lived in one-bedroom apartments, unrelated to the white-picket-fence reality of *Father Knows Best*, for which I longed. We moved each year, sometimes to new cities, primarily, I think, because my mother was restless. The curtains were as boring as pots and pans to pack; we agreed the books were most important. In the new apartment, the curtains were shaken out of their folds, then hung up if they fit or replaced if they didn't, one year by crinkly plastic floral curtains that my mother, amazed at this peculiar invention, told everyone "looked just like real drapery!"

Through my adolescence, the set of *Father Knows Best* melded with the image of the Rose Covered Cottage in which the aproned wife served Tea for Two while living Happily Ever After. Robert Young, Gregory Peck, Cary Grant, Audie Murphy, dressed in shining armour, pranced around my mind on their white horses. I considered my thrilling bodily sensations to be naughty, shameful and too embarrassing to mention; no one, no book, ever said that girls felt this way. I eventually packaged the sensations under Love (as in "falling in") and Romance (as in lingering looks from the tall, handsome stranger, or Scarlett's full-skirted descent down Tara's stairs). As the dating books recommended, I practised "showing interest in his interests" and "asking him about himself," but had a difficult time if the boy's interest was football.

When I was twenty, my mother died. Grief swept all other feeling away. I knew parents could die; my father had when I was eight. But he'd been ill for years, while she was eating dinner one hour and dead the next. Other people dealt with the curtains and I certainly felt no lust. My only desire was to get back to before her death, to keep her safe, to fight death off. "If only!" I cried and, "Why her?"

I finished university and married my boyfriend. He fit my mental set and, since we moved into an apartment building, his aging Morris Minor was less trouble than a white horse. Lust there certainly was, damped occasionally with grief, but sanctioned. My husband. Forever after. Happily. Someone gave me an apron and someone else a teapot. I hung curtains and — familiarly — took them down the next year when we moved.

Eventually we bought a house with a picture window that required wall-to-wall curtains. Since it was the sixties we chose burlap, and since we could nearly afford it, had them professionally made. There they hung, opened in the morning and closed at night, while we got on with our lives.

A number of years and two children later, we had to repaint the living room. When I took the curtains down they shredded in my hands.

"Well, dear," my mother-in-law or aunt said, "What dry cleaner have you taken them to? The process can be too rough."

"Clean?" I squeaked. "You clean curtains?"

"Yes, dear," replied my mother-in-law or aunt. "You always clean curtains once a year and vacuum them as well."

"Why didn't you tell me?"

"But dear, I thought you knew. Everyone knows about curtains."

Everyone minus one. I saw my mother shaking curtains before folding them for their annual packing. Possibly she'd had them cleaned between moves and I'd never noticed. Possibly an annual shake was enough. I was chagrined, more at what I hadn't known — hadn't known and therefore hadn't asked — than at anything about curtains. When I told my husband, we both laughed, but then he wasn't an Everyone expected to know about curtains.

My mother had frequently quoted, "He who knows and knows that he knows is wise; follow him. He who knows not and knows that he knows not is young; teach him. He who knows not and knows not that he knows not is a fool; shun him." Yet to find out what one knows not one must know the questions to ask. Without information, the last category is too harsh. I would say, "She who knows not and knows not that she knows not is uninformed; inform her." And I wish someone had informed me.

"Lust" was not a word of the early eighties, of my forties. Yet all the hot throbbingness of adolescence that had been clothed by dailiness erupted, as if other curtains abruptly shredded. Trouble was, the sensations were not directed towards my husband.

I couldn't believe I was Having An Affair. He was not tall and handsome; he just smelled right.

I tried to place this in my old scenario. I was a Bad Woman. I had to be noble and do the right thing. Which was? Renounce the Lover, of course. Which I couldn't do: my feelings, his smell, were too strong. (Actually, my timeline was too short; affairs, like curtains, don't last forever.) Also, I wanted to be Bad. No, actually, I wanted an affair to be included in being Good.

Father Knows Best didn't have an affair. A husband was forever. I was to forsake all others. Knights rode white horses (or Morris Minors) towards Good women. June Allyson's apron never had a spot. Yet there was "Tea for Two and Two for Tea" — or a glass of wine, afterward —

My children were going about the normal, messy business of growing up. My husband and I went to work and came home and had lovely times together amidst frequently boring times. A working marriage.

I was scared. I didn't know what was happening to me. I wasn't supposed to be having these feelings in my forties. I was supposed to have had them to find a husband in my twenties and then the feelings were supposed to disappear unless directed toward my husband. Married matrons — mothers, yet! — weren't supposed to swoon round the house, throbbing and sticky with desire, unable to do more than weakly pass a dishcloth over the counter.

I thought of every adulterous married woman I knew of. Anna Karenina. Madame Bovary. Hester Prynne with her scarlet A. The French Lieutenant's Woman. None of them had come to a good end.

I renounced the Family and sought the Lover. Because, I thought, there was not enough room for all my feelings on the Family set. I felt I was so bad that I would contaminate my family. I thought it was nobler to go than to stay. "It is a far, far better thing that I do —"

If someone had said, "This is just lust and it will pass," if someone had said, "It's a common experience for women at any age," if someone had said, it had happened to her, if I had known what to ask, if I'd known I knew not that I knew not . . . .

"Lust" is a word of the nineties. A year ago a vibrant woman with grey-blonde hair and her life on her face told me that she'd fallen in love a few years before and what a struggle she'd had; that she hadn't been prepared for the feelings. We were in a garden and the early May sun picked out the tender green. Tulips were drooping and carnations perking. I had only met her an hour before and knew of no prompt for her spontaneous, ruminative admission. She was perhaps ten years older than I, and I studied her wrinkles for instruction.

She said he was bald and she was surprised; she'd never known how attractive a bald man could be, especially if surrounded by a fringe close-cropped like a putting tee. She said he was someone she'd known for years, and the feelings happened to her suddenly. "Did you limply move a dishcloth over the counter, wondering what to do?" I asked.

"Yes!" She looked at me with gratitude: You know? I nodded. She stared at a fading tulip, purple, as I recall.

I couldn't wait and blurted, "What did you do about it?"

"Nothing, in the end." She clasped her hands behind her back. "It was a dreadful struggle. I just didn't know what to do."

She smiled at me and it was the smile of woman who hadn't known what she never knew, and now she knew she knew it. I smiled back and touched her shoulder. "It's more comfortable to learn about some things than others, but I'd rather know than not."

"Yes," she laughed, "and won't we be wise when we're ninety!"

I've had blinds now for some years, not curtains. But, as everyone knows, they still need to be cleaned.

The Joys of Belly Dancing

Katherine Martens

When I was in my forties I enrolled in a belly dance class. It looked so easy and graceful, I felt I could do it too, with practice. How hard it was at first to move my body in unaccustomed ways. Unlike most Western dances, belly dancing works by moving one body part at a time, for example, moving the ribcage up and down or sideways while keeping the hips still. Many of the moves we learned were the kind our mothers had often warned us against — "Don't stick out your chest," "don't stick out your bum" — moves that drew attention to our female anatomy or were considered to be unladylike. I looked around nervously in class to compare myself with others and saw that some other women also seemed self-conscious about moving their hips and chests in unaccustomed ways. But seeing those who learned it easily made me blush; after one or two classes I gave up in dismay. A few weeks of dancing could not undo the years of conditioning that decreed my body should be seen as little as possible.

Many years later, at a woman's retreat, I went to a demonstration of belly dancing with a group of women of all ages, shapes and sizes. Our instructor asked us to move elastic waistbands down to our hips, which allowed our bellies to move freely. For much of my life I have been more concerned with how attractive I was to others than with how I felt about my body. Now the teacher inspired confidence. I hoped that what I had been unable to accomplish at age forty might still be possible. As soon as I could I joined a weekly beginner's class where, awkwardly at first, I learned the basic movements. Practising the movements in belly dancing helped me reclaim what I had learned to ignore or repress. After each class ended I observed the members of the more advanced class, who entered the room and immediately changed into their dancing costumes. Their wide skirts, veils and coin belts, sparkling with sequins, left me feeling ambivalent. "I won't get carried away and waste time and energy on dressing up. I am in it for the exercise, pure and simple," I rationalized. The voice in my head was the censor saying, "This is getting dangerously close to the wide road that leads to damnation."

However, by December, having observed that the clothing she wore affected the way a woman moved, I was getting my instructor's help in sewing harem pants. I saw my teacher transformed from the hurried housewife and mother she was when she came in from the street to an energetic dancer moving with fluid grace to the music. Through dance, she told the story of a woman who had faced darkness and pain, her face lighting with joy when she moved. I learned by doing that physical movement was the antidote to fear, to shame, and to depression.

Belly dancing is a way to relieve menstrual pain; there are also belly dance classes for pregnant women. In the countries where belly dancing originated, women companions model the movements of belly dancing to help a woman birth her child. Because we narrowly define the pelvis and breasts as the sexual areas of women's bodies, we see belly dancing, which emphasizes these underexercised parts of our bodies, as provocative and suggestive. Because of lack of exercise, most of us have tight muscles in the chest, pelvis and upper back; in belly dancing we use these parts of our bodies.

Dancing and giving birth are both defined as intensely physical activities, yet, paradoxically, they are also occasions when our spirit, body, and mind come together. Sometimes dance puts me into a trancelike state — in which the lines separating body, soul and mind are blurred and I am able to exist purely in the moment.

In a dream, I saw that dancing was opening a new body, one that I did not even recognize. The dream frightened me; the painful, stiff body I had grown used to was at least familiar. Again in a dream, I had been subpoenaed to go to court because of something I had written. There were several scenes, all of which ended in my not being able to talk to anyone. My teacher came to see me in the dream to offer help but I told her, "My hands are tied, my voice is stifled, I CANNOT TALK." Reflecting on the dream I wondered if movement and dance would be a new form of voice for me.

I moved to the advanced class against my will. After a few months I came to a hard place. The dance moves were becoming more and more difficult to master, and the review of the moves was over before I learned them and was confronted with new ones. I felt I should quit. A five-day flu mirrored my feelings of being stuck. Thoughts of not going back to the class brought on depression, but when I decided to go, I felt paralyzed. I talked to my dance teacher from the beginner's class about my frustration and self-consciousness. As I talked, I began to recognize that the instructor in the more advanced class, a gifted dancer and performer, focused on performance technique; because I had no intention of performing, I seemed to be failing. My decision to go to classes was a way of saying that no matter how uncomfortable I felt, I would persevere. I wanted to experience dance as an expression of spontaneity and joy before I quit.

At the beginning of a new session, our instructor

remarked that the performing dancer must be careful not to make suggestive or vulgar movements that could be construed as a sexual invitation. I pushed the remark away, but it stayed at the edge of my consciousness. The more I thought about it, the more angry and discouraged I became. Her seemingly casual observation had struck a nerve; would I allow it to inhibit me with the concern, "What will others think?" What if some of my movements looked overdone and vulgar? A woman of my age could easily look ridiculous. What was I doing here? My sore throat returned. I went back to being immobilized and restricted.

A door was closing in my face. When I put these feelings into words, my sore throat disappeared. I decided to tell our instructor how her words had inhibited me. In the class discussion that followed I was flooded with relief, because I had listened to my body feelings and not let her comments slide by without responding.

I was on the road to leaving my inhibitions behind. That same evening we were learning to do the gush turn. The effect of the turn is to move the upper body to the left while the feet move to the right. Dancers who learned it quickly practised it with the others. I tried it over and over, but my body refused to do what seemed to be contrary movements. At last my partner said, "You don't have to move from left to right if your body doesn't want to do it. Try moving from right to left instead." And after some more futile attempts I did it in reverse, the way my body wanted to do it instinctively, and suddenly we were laughing. It worked!

When winter fabric sales arrived I went — just to look. I fingered the flowing slinky fabrics and came home with yards of material for a circular skirt. I found, but did not buy, a body suit to complete the costume. I showed my fabric to a few classmates and told them about the black body suit I yearned for. "I can't spend this much money on a body suit," I said. "Of course you can," they told me. "It's only the price of two books. Do you feel this guilty when you buy a book?" asked one. In the interval between shopping trips my imagination had embroidered the body suit with beads, sequins and all manner of glitter. When I came back to the shop to buy the body suit I was surprised by how plain it was. Most of all I was shocked at how hard it was to honour my desire for sensuous materials in clothing. Most of my regular wardrobe consisted of casual, sporty clothes. I was starved for slinky, fluid fabrics.

A long time ago I dreamed I was in the Mennonite church of my childhood, which in my dream had curtains in the front for a stage. I saw several patriarchal male figures I recognized. I drew the curtains open and told the other furtive women who were hiding there that they could now dance openly and freely in church.

New awareness comes out not only in dreams but in mundane or momentous events, like the Winnipeg flood of 1997. The rising Red River was in the background during the spring term of my dancing classes. I live near the river and felt a shift in consciousness as I knew all my efforts had to go into preparing for the dreaded arrival of water into my basement or even main floor. I felt threatened as well as energized by my concentrated effort. I had an adrenaline rush as I focused on moving precious books upstairs. I was aware of existing on several levels; sometimes I saw myself from a distance. One evening, when my anxiety was at its highest, I looked for the symbolic meaning of water in *The Woman's Encyclopedia of Myths and Secrets* by Barbara G. Walker. Water is the first of the elements, both material and spiritual, embodying both female and male principles. "When the feminine principle is subjected to sustained attack," said the book, "as it was from the medieval Christian authorities, it often quietly submerges. Under the water...it swims through the unconscious of the dominant male society, occasionally bobbing to the surface to offer a glimpse of the rejected harmony."

The first evening in May, a group of us were at the house

of one of my teachers, Satori. In a few weeks Shahrazad, a belly dance performer and teacher from Germany, was coming for a visit to Winnipeg. Satori reported that Shahrazad was having trouble locating her music for the West African water goddess dance she wanted to perform here. We laughed nervously at the thought of the water connection. My intense involvement with dancing at the time of the flood merged with two images in my mind.

When Shahrazad came to perform I saw a ordinary woman transformed with colour, dazzling costumes, make-up and music into the goddesses of many different cultures and ages. I attended her workshop on chakras and dance. (Chakras are energy centres along the spine.) As we danced each chakra, we wore the colour it represented. We began with red for the root chakra at the base of the spine and ended with violet for the crown chakra. At the end of the day we danced the Sufi meditation dance, also known as the whirling dervish dance. We could choose to whirl in a clockwise or counterclockwise direction. As I danced counterclockwise I remembered the instructions and thought, why not slow down and try dancing in the other direction. When I did I quickly become dizzy and sat down next to the wall to get my balance. Shahrazad came to steady me. I was close to tears. "I don't want to miss any of the dance; I haven't got much time left," I said — meaning time left in my life! When the music ended, I felt as light as a child. I had danced away the stiffness and rigidity from my lower back. Shahrazad told us later that most people dance in a clockwise direction; the people who dance in a counterclockwise direction are often trying to shed a psychic or physical burden. The distinction between the dance and the dancer began to disappear for me in the dervish dance. Again, I learned that my body has an instinctive wisdom of its own and does not need directions from my mind. Like the powerful flood waters of the river, I had ignored my body for a time, but not forever.

Weeks later, driving down St. Mary's Road, I saw where

the river had coiled its way through the trees, leaving all manner of floating debris. I saw plastic containers of Avenge, a herbicide for killing wild oats, caught in the tangled tree branches. Water, the mother of all things, had risen from the deep, danced into our homes without permission, overturned pianos, pushed her way into cupboards, and entered the dark basements where we keep the hidden, unexamined parts in our lives. The flowing water, sometimes lapping peacefully on the shore, sometimes pouring over the banks of the river, remains an image of movement. The dancer merges with the dance.

Politics: Is it a Woman's Game?

The Honourable Sharon Carstairs

When I decided to run for the leadership of the Liberal Party in Manitoba in 1984, I assumed that I was in a new era of women in politics. In 1981 seven women had been elected to the Manitoba Legislature. We were coming into our own. I would not have to fight the battles of Agnes McPhail, the first woman Member of Parliament, who had to obtain permission not to wear a hat on the floor of the House of Commons when she was elected in 1921. Nor would I have to worry about wearing formal evening dress to be sworn in as did Senator Carine Wilson when she took her seat as the first woman in the Senate of Canada in 1930. I could even forget about the need for a large supply of white gloves, both in the office and at home, which our first federal cabinet minister, the Honourable Ellen Fairclough, had to put her mind to. I was a feminist, this was 1984, and other women, thank God, had already fought and won these battles and many more important ones.

It did seem appropriate, however, to take an inventory of my assets. On the plus side was my training. I had an undergraduate degree in political science and history and a Masters of Arts in the teaching of history. I had worked as a journalist during my undergraduate years and had written, directed and narrated educational television programming. I was as well qualified as others in the Legislature. On the negative side, I had lived in Manitoba for only seven years and my knowledge of the province, and more particularly its agricultural and mining roots, was minimal.

It was the cause of some surprise to me that none of the things I considered to be negatives were ever raised. But, boy, did I have other negatives!

My voice brought instant criticism and ridicule. I was described as Manitoba's new audio threat. I was accused of constantly swallowing helium. My voice was described by some as having a Minnie Mouse pitch and by others as having machine-gun delivery. After several years of voters getting used to "the voice," I began to be stopped and congratulated for the success of my speech therapy. I did not ever have any speech therapy, but that story has persisted throughout my political career.

What was it about my voice? I certainly can accept that it is loud when I want it to be. So too was my father's and that of my brother, Dennis. Apparently the shape of our mouths and our vocal chords contribute to this phenomenon. However, prior to entering politics I had always considered my voice an enormous asset. When no one else could get the attention of 1400 high-school students in the gymnasium, I could. I also knew that as a product of my Nova Scotia heritage I had a bit of a Maritime twang, and I certainly pronounced words like "aunt" and "about" differently than Westerners did, but that in itself did not appear to warrant the enormous ink that my voice generated. Was it because it was a woman's voice? A strong woman's voice? Was this disturbing to men who still believed a woman's place was in the home? Did it make women, who were still not sure of the roles they wanted to play in the last decades of the twentieth century, uncomfortable? Or was it really as bad as everyone said? I listened to myself on tape and honestly could not find anything wrong. I did try to slow down my delivery because I recognized that my nervousness before a scrum was causing me to speak too quickly. I then decided that Manitobans would simply have to accept me and my voice. I did my best to ignore the criticism and to laugh at the radio programs that made use of the voice to generate amusement throughout the country.

I think, had it only been my voice that generated criticism, I would have accepted the mockery, telling myself that the media likes to find the weaknesses of all politicians, both male and female. However, it was not only the voice. It quickly became apparent that my clothes (particularly their colour), the fact that I was quite content to let my hair go grey and the size and shape of my glasses were also subject to active discussion by both the media and the public.

The one aspect of my physical presence that escaped criticism was my size. I am certainly not svelte. However, being somewhat overweight actually seemed to be an advantage. I could not be dismissed as a lightweight since I was quite obviously not one!

Fifteen years have now passed since I began to question why I was subjected to such physical scrutiny. How much of this was a gender issue? How much of it was just plain stubbornness on my part? Why was I so unwilling to play the game? After all, I could have coloured my hair. I simply refused, and yet there is no question in my mind that a number of male politicians in their fifties and sixties are doing just that. To me it seemed to be an advantage not to look so young. I did not want to be regarded as grandmotherly, but I did want people to see that I was of "a certain age." I did change the shape and size of my glasses because I was convinced by television-camera technicians that they could not get a sharp picture of my face because the glasses created double images. The change seemed to make sense from a public image perspective, and therefore I accepted it.

I have come to the conclusion that most of what happened to me was because I was a woman. It was so much easier for the media to write about how I looked than what I was or what I had to say.

Sadly, I must state that I do not think there has been a great deal of improvement in the last fifteen years. The media are still writing stories about what female politicians are wearing. *Hustler* magazine recently tried to threaten the Honourable Sheila Copps into submission by sponsoring a contest surrounding sexual activity with her as the topic. The Honourable Anne McLellan's voice is called "piercing" and "grating" and "helium-dependent." More significantly perhaps, the women who get most of the other media coverage are the ones who most frequently act like men. It is when women are raucous that they get publicity, not when they are sound and reasonable. The critics are quick to point out they do not like the raucous behaviour from woman politicians. Rarely, however, are men criticized for such behaviour. Consensus-building skills, which are so often part of a woman's attributes, are both underrated and undervalued. Yet woman parliamentarians quietly go about their work representing their constituents — work that frequently goes unnoticed by the media. However, it does not appear to go unnoticed by the constituents, since female politicians seem to get reelected at the same rate as male ones.

Perhaps it is because the number of women in public office has not yet reached a critical mass that the skills of women remain, in my view, unappreciated. Scholars interested in the participation by women in politics argue that women will not be truly recognized until they form 25 to 35 percent of legislative chambers. At the present time, the only legislative chamber in this country to reach that magical number is the Senate, which is 31 percent female — and the Senate is rarely covered, except in a negative way, by the media of this nation.

For many female politicians, the frustration remains.

When will we be able to carve out our own style and when will this style be appropriately recognized? For me the most frustrating aspect of many of the stories written are that they are written by other women. Why do women in the media feel they still must pay lip service to the stereotypes? Why are they unwilling to write stories about politicians with styles and attitudes different from the norm?

When I announced my resignation from the leadership, I was extremely surprised that none of the women from the other political parties with whom I had served in the Legislature commented on my decision. When I questioned their lack of commentary, I was told I intimidated them. It is truly sad that women who are out there breaking ground together should be intimidated by one of their own. We should be supportive of one another. We should not be considered threats; we are walking a difficult road together, no matter what our political affiliation. We are, after all, sisters and we need the support and encouragement of one another.

Can we change as women in politics? Should we? Will we ever be accepted as equals, willing and able to accept criticism of our work and our effectiveness but not subject to criticism based purely on the fact that we are women? Will our daughters have an easier time? I believe the answer to all of the above is yes. But it will take time and dedication. It will require women to work together to reject the stereotypes.

It should not be expected that women will support only women candidates. However, we must, as women, learn to encourage them. We must ensure that the rules of our political parties do not put obstacles in their way. For example, while there are limits on expenditures during election campaigns, there are no such limits for nomination races. This is patently unfair to women and must be changed if the playing field is to be level. Election expense rules do not provide for child-care expenses or household expenses. How is a woman to campaign at the same level as a man if she is still doing up to 80 percent of the child-rearing and household tasks? Most female politicians need help to fulfill their responsibilities at home while they are on the campaign trail. By supporting electoral and party reform, we must find ways to make it possible for women to participate fully in the political sphere while at the same time meeting their family and child-rearing responsibilities.

We must challenge the reporters who comment on what a female candidate is wearing unless they have made the same comments about male candidates. When female politicians complain about gender bias we must support them, even when their political postures are different from our own. If we do not, then they will be called whiners and, by implication, so will we. Above all, we must be prepared to write cheques in aid of those female candidates we are able to support. Campaigns are expensive and, to date, the average amount raised by female candidates is significantly below that of male candidates. Their campaigns, then, cannot be as professional. Is that what we want as women? I hope not.

As women, we have special contributions to make to the body politic. Our life experiences are different from those of men because we have earned each one of those experiences as women. When we examine issues such as tax cuts, or the health and education systems available to us, our parents and our children, we do so as mothers, daughters and sisters.

In my view, the participation of both men and women in the political process ensures that a wider range of issues is debated, and that the debates reflect the full experience of both genders. If women do not participate in equal numbers, the debate will not be as rich, nor will it lead to true equality of all persons.

Each time a young woman says to me, “Thank you, you have made it easier for me,” then I know things will get better. I just wish it would happen sooner rather than later.

The Anger of Young Men

Blanche Howard

In 1951 a young scientist named Rosalind Franklin was caught up in the race to replicate the hidden molecular structure of DNA, a discovery that would revolutionize the field of genetic research. Three young men were her immediate adversaries: James D. Watson, then twenty-three, his partner Francis Crick, who was thirty-five, and Maurice Wilkins, who was Watson's age. Eventually in the 1958 bestseller *The Double Helix*, Watson chronicled the steps that led to cracking the code.

The book is gossipy and exciting even for the non-scientist. The struggle to beat out the other front runners, notably the Nobel Prize laureate Dr. Linus Pauling, reads like an amalgam of the search for the Holy Grail and an NHL game. Except that there has never been a part for a woman in either pastime, other than as idealized inspiration. And Rosalind Franklin did not, by any stretch of the imagination, fill the inspiration bill. The fifties code of acceptable femininity had simply passed her by.

In the book Watson lampoons Rosalind cruelly. He paints a picture of the forces of good — Watson, Crick and their rival

Wilkins — up against a formidable dragon, the hag-ridden force of evil — Rosalind Franklin.

Rosy, as the men called her behind her back, was a thirty-one-year-old crystallographer, trained to take X-ray diffraction pictures of the patterns made by molecules whirling around a central core. She was recruited by Maurice Wilkins to speed up his research, and she was aggressive in her claim to equal billing with the men.

Mere inspection of her, according to Watson, suggested she wouldn't back off. She looked so unfeminine! She never used lipstick to contrast with her straight black hair. She hadn't learned to dress with any flair. Probably the product of an unsatisfied mother who thought a professional career could save bright girls from marriages to dull men. Oh yes, she had a good brain, he conceded that — if she could just learn to keep her emotions under control. He attended one of her lectures and spent his time speculating on how she would look if she took off her glasses and did something about her hair.

Unfortunately for Watson and the forces of good, Rosalind's beautiful and precise pictures of crystallized DNA were vital to the research. Furthermore, he was correct in surmising that she wasn't about to hand them over without a struggle. On one occasion, according to Watson, she actually lunged at him when he was trying to bully her into discussing details of her X-ray work.

Watson and Crick procured Rosalind's data by other means, which Watson suggests may have been a tad unethical. Eventually they were able to build their brilliant model of the double helix of DNA. Watson was only twenty-five years old; Rosalind was thirty-two. To the surprise and relief of the men, Rosy accepted their conclusions at once, and Watson was forced to concede that her previous protestations about the importance of her X-ray pictures were not, as he had thought, the "outpourings of a misguided feminist." She had simply been right.

When I first read this sorry little tale it reminded me of something that happened to me when I was a young woman — or rather, girl, since I was still in my late teens. In high school I had been fortunate enough to have, in our small prairie school, a teacher who was in love with physics, and as we all know, a teacher in love with a subject is a sure bet to transfer that love. Girls, in our small high school, were given the same treatment and education as the boys; indeed, boys were in the minority since they were still such valuable resources on the farms that they often could not be spared for the luxury of learning.

After high school, we moved to Calgary and I was able to take enough courses at a college there to go directly into third year at the University of Alberta in Edmonton, choosing as my major physics, mathematics and chemistry.

At that time this choice was considered odd. Only 3 percent of women in Canada went to university, and it was assumed that they were there for husbands. They congregated either in the Faculty of Arts or, if they were interested at all in science, in Home Economics.

Since the University of Alberta was then a very small university, third-year physics courses had to be taken with engineering students. In a classroom of about fifty students I was the only girl. It sounds like a recipe for heavenly delight, but a week hadn't gone by before something in the air, a buzz like the circling of killer bees, warned me that romance was definitely not going to be a perk. The averted faces, the scowling visages, the blank seats beside me — none of my fellow students spoke to me. They simply pretended I wasn't there. When my lab marks were better than my partner's, he snarled that it sure helps to be a pretty young woman. When I topped the class on the Christmas exams, everyone crowded out the doors so fast that I had to wait behind until the room was empty.

What sin had I committed? What had I done? I didn't know. I was puzzled, an outcast, and for many years I occasionally mulled over the riddle of that anger, hoping to find its source. Then, fifteen years later as a young mother, I decided to augment the family income by going into the work force in a field I knew I was good at. This time I broke a double taboo: mothers didn't work in the fifties, and women didn't become chartered accountants.

The clients didn't care about the gender of their accountant as long as he or she saved them money on their taxes. And although initially there was scepticism among my peers, as the years went by uneasiness gradually changed to acceptance, even camaraderie. Except with one group — the young men. Aged twenty to early thirties. They reacted to taking orders from a woman with usually convert, but sometimes open, hostility.

Thinking back from the vantage point of our more enlightened decade, I might attribute all this to the restrictive social mores of earlier times, particularly the family values of the fifties, were it not for the spectacle we have had in the last few years of women in the armed forces encountering similar hostility in young males. Much of the publicity about this issue has centred on sexual aggression — as though sexual aggression were not a subspecies of plain aggression. As though it were the kind of spinoff we should expect when young men and women are thrown together without the sensible chaperone of earlier centuries. As though boys will be boys, and can scarcely be expected to hold their raging testosterone in check when in close quarters with bosomy foot soldiers. As though soldiers (and policemen and firemen) are a more hormonally fired bunch than boys who go into business, or teaching or law. As though they are from another tribe.

And it does smack of tribalism. The bonding. The unreasonable rage at the "other." Us against Them. Black versus white. Hell's Angels. World Wars I and II. All wars. The IRA. Communists. Aliens. Fundamentalists. Good guys versus bad guys. Men versus women.

Men versus women?

Why not? At puberty, young men and women all go through a metamorphosis as profound as Kafka's hero who, day by terrifying day, turns into a beetle. Each sex becomes intensely focused on the mysterious emergence taking place in the other. To the young men, young women are seen as intensely desirable, mysterious, threatening, withholding. Intimidating beings who can emasculate with a leer, quarry who can be captured or who can walk away, exalted beings who are transmuted with time into witches who should be, and have been, burned at the stake.

Who must be kept in their places.

By men. Especially by young men. Men of the age of the Montagues who crossed swords with the Capulets. Of the Indians who charged across the plains and the cowboys they charged at. Of the Palestinian youths stoning Israeli youths.

Blame it on evolution, testosterone, pecking order, injustice, deprivation, overabundance, male bonding or that bricked-up cavern of Oedipal rage in the corner of the Freudian cellar, but there it is: young men are angry rebels searching for a cause.

The status quo can become a cause. Society's rules, once learned, appear to be hard-wired into the brain, so that when titled ladies consort with their chauffeurs, when Untouchables touch and blacks sit at the front of the bus, when aliens are E.T. cuddly and women work while men cook, these defections from the old order threaten at some subliminal level. Which makes societies, like great ocean liners, cumbersome, requiring great distances to slow down and long stretches of time in which to turn around.

My own experience led me to believe that anger at women is a characteristic peculiar to young men, those I would put roughly in the twenty- to thirty-five-year age group. But my observations are many years out of date, so I consulted my two daughters, who are in their forties.

One daughter (and her husband) maintain that I've got it wrong — that such anger is a thing of the past, and that, except among a few subgroups who are having trouble getting into the new age, there is little or no resentment of this sort nowadays. The "sensitive, new age kind of guy," willing to share housework and professional life, they say, is replacing the stereotype of the formerly gender-structured world.

The other daughter totally disagrees. When she meets them in the course of her own work, she says, she finds that young men are as arrogant, insensitive and angry as they were when my own experiences were fresh.

Finally I decided to go straight to the front lines: my twenty-year old granddaughter. She grew up in the Air Cadets and, during her free time from university, she now teaches new cadets, so she is able to assess the diverse worlds of academia and the military.

Has the anger disappeared, I asked her? Not at all, she assured. It's more subtle now, but it's still there, just beneath the surface.

In every class of society? I asked. She thought about that. Yes, she said, but it does depend on upbringing.

So you think it is a learned reaction?

Absolutely, she answered. It all depends on what boys were taught in their homes. She thinks that the age group I found the worst, twenty to thirty-five, is no longer the worst — that the more extreme sexism is working through the population like a rat through a cobra, and that the worst is now to be found in men aged thirty-five to fifty.

Finally I asked, do you think it has to do with female intrusion on male territory? Definitely, she said. Men bond together in a different way than women do. Men bond around shared purposes, while women bond more through their feelings. And since women deal in feelings, anger is the weapon of choice against them.

Anger *is* intimidating; indeed, that may be part of its evolutionary function. An angry person can do you physical harm; an angry tongue can slice you into emotional ribbons. Either way, anger will leave you bleeding on the sidewalk. Anger gives its possessor control.

Watson, Crick and Wilkins were awarded the Nobel Prize in 1962. Of all the other combatants in the race to replicate the structure of DNA, most agree that it was Rosalind Franklin who came closest; she was, it seems, only two steps away from the solution.

Watson, in an epilogue to *The Double Helix*, says he came to appreciate her personal honesty, and that he realized too late the struggle that intelligent women faced in order to be taken seriously by the scientific world. Too late, because by then Rosalind Franklin was dead.

Still Life
with Power

Anne Giardini

Linwood, her husband, has stirred in his bed at the right. He gets out and puts on a robe, listening. Most often jovial, he has developed an iron repression of his exceptions to Willa's behaviour — he more than loves her, he admires her, as though her mercurial nature, her temper, her massive dreams and little cruelties, served him as only sharp reminders of the turbulent longings within her, longings which he shares but lacks the temperament to utter and follow to their end.

[...]

LINWOOD: . . . I don't say she's a great woman. Willa Lodam never made a lot of money. Her name was never in the paper. She's not the finest character that ever lived. But she's a human being, and a

> terrible thing is happening to her. So attention must be paid. She's not to be allowed to fall into her grave like an old dog. Attention, attention must be finally paid to such a person.
> — *Death of a Saleswoman*

These are excerpts from a play that has never been written. There is no Willa Lodam in either life or literature. It has taken me all of my life to discern what is so absent from the world that it has no true reflection in art, even as a allusive absence. Many random observations came into my conscious vision only recently, after two switches had been thrown. These two events were like a flint and steel; they infused the essential spark into an awareness for which I had spent my life accumulating, like dry kindling, the sustaining proof. Like Mary Shelley's monster, this idea, or way of interpreting the world, became vital only after it had been galvanized — not in my case by power, but by the understanding that men have it while women do not.

Arthur Miller's *Death of a Salesman* concerns — insists that the audience be concerned about — the ways in which the world can fail a man of "massive dreams and little cruelties." Miller knew what I have learned; that the only measure of great dreams is the dreamscape of men and that power and its attendant glory are a country inhabited only by men. Just as there is no Willa Lodam, there is no Queen Lear, no Stephanie Dedalus. There are no Mesdames Miller, Shakespeare or Joyce. No woman has ever been, in the fullest sense, messiah, explorer, builder, conquistador, founder, philosopher, creator, god. Men occupy two realms: one is the actual and the other is the possible, the abstract. They assume the role of leader — civil, domestic, business, spiritual — as if leadership were a coat cut just for them. Women are limited to the concrete. We are the stagehands, the handmaids, the helpmates and the typists. This is not by chance. It is the way the world is set up — and for good reason, since this is how women and collusive men ensure women's safety.

There is no greater tragedy than a man who has, like Willy Loman, missed the ring. Drama lies in men's getting and wanting of power, and tragedy is engendered when men lose or are denied it. Men want, need, lust for, seek, maneuver for and grow weak for and fat on power; if they are thwarted, the loss is significant, meaningful and resonant. They may not seek it consciously; they may consciously avoid it or put power aside, but even such acts of renunciation are potent, both in effect and in our discernment of what it means for a man to relinquish what could be his.

There is no sonority in the situation of a woman without power. We are not meant to have it in the first place. The division of labour did not begin with economic society. It began with the family, within which women are the smaller, weaker, more constrained partner, and became a social norm, so that women have been systematically discouraged or penalized for endeavouring to amass power, while men are selected and rewarded for pursuing it. Power enters into the life of a woman, in art or in life, only obliquely. Women are left unable to be tragic with respect to any abstraction. Her tragedies are always concerned with the concrete, such as the loss of her child, her home or possessions, her husband.

So obdurately fixed are our views of the inherent nature of men and women that we are blind to any instance of a woman actually wanting and striving for power. We imagine that the few women who have found themselves in positions of power came there by accident rather than design. When a woman achieves leadership of a country, political party or a company, we look for the man and we always find one: a husband or father, teacher or mentor. If we can't find the obvious or hidden man behind a woman's success, we conclude that she has achieved her position by use of wiles or, failing that, by accident. We are unable to see that a woman who has risen to a position of power may have done so intentionally, because there is no world view in which to frame such a narrative. We are unable to perceive that a woman may be motivated by, and plan for, power.

The first university class I ever attended was a political science class. (I was there wholly by accident. I registered for first year late [it was already September] and young [I was seventeen]. The helpful woman at the registration counter suggested that many first year students took "poli sci" and I enrolled, supposing that the phrase referred to an introductory survey course to all the different branches of science — poly sci — which is actually a course I would still be interested in taking.) The overall theme for the year was power. We began with the anatomy of a coup, and I was hooked. But, in hindsight, I wonder how I could have failed to notice that all of the actors in the examples discussed, and almost all of the theorists — from Aristotle to Voltaire to Marx to Trudeau — were male. Why was there no discussion of this absence? Could my otherwise insightful and engaging instructor have been as blind to this lopsidedness as I was?

The writers I remember from the English survey course I took that year are Shakespeare, Conrad, Eliot, Pound and Sinclair Ross. In my introductory course on economics, the concepts were male in both sentiment and language — competition, monopoly, demand and production. I went on to study economics for four years. I could see that capitalism was about consumption, but it did not become clear to me until recently that it is *only* about consumption. In the same way, I grew increasingly aware that politics, literature, economics, law, history were about men, but did not realize until recently that they are *only* about men. I took two law degrees, reading laws made and interpreted by (and for) men without asking myself where the women were in all of that. My first inklings of where the problem lay came when I became for a while active in the prochoice movement. "Why do people assume women are incapable of making a *moral* decision?" I asked my friends.

Three years ago, when I was making several starts on a

novel to be called *Assiniboine*, the protagonist was, in my conception, a woman. But as the shape of the novel came together in my mind, I began to realize that the novel concerned voluntary (rather than externally imposed) moral choice. That is, what I wanted to write about was an inherently moral person. At the same time, it occurred to me that the main character of this book should not be Ellen, but her husband. This husband stepped forward from the shadows of my imaginings, saying aloud: "I hear that you have put out a casting call for a novel about ethics and principle. I just want to tell you that I am your man." Why Eric and not Ellen, I wondered? And then realized — the first breaker thrown — that if I filled my narrative need with a man, half my work would be done. My readers would assume Eric to be capable of sustained philosophical thought, to have strongly held ideas and beliefs. It would take an enormously greater effort to create an Ellen whom readers would expect to act as a moral creature. More time than I had available for this novel. More time, in fact, than anyone has ever had for a novel. Understanding this, I could not go forward with Eric, noble though he was, and have made only a cursory start with Ellen. How can I start what cannot be finished?

The second switch was thrown when I was working on a project at the invitation of a colleague senior to me. Fairly early on in the process, a meeting was called in another city. A day or two before the meeting, it turned out to be impossible for my colleague to attend and he asked if I would go in his stead. This was to a certain extent an opportunity forgone for him; he balanced the importance to him against the difficulty of going, giving weight too to the possible advantage to me of being able to attend. I flew to the other city on the morning of the meeting and, due to difficulties at the airport, walked into the meeting room after everyone else had arrived and had started to work their way through the agenda. I opened the door and saw that the room contained about three dozen men. They looked up at me, and we all become aware of the awkwardness of the situation in the same instant. The culture I worked in was very stridently dedicated to equality of opportunity, to diversity, but none of it had trickled into this room where important decisions, affecting many millions of dollars and hundreds of people, were being made. I felt as naïve as a schoolgirl. It wasn't so much that I was surprised to see that the room was occupied by men, but that it was occupied *only* by men. Everyone froze for a moment, and I thought in that instant: "still life with power." The men at the meeting were not conspirators; there had been no consensus taken that women should be excluded. When it came time for important things to be done, each man in the room simply assumed that he was the best person to carry out the task. These men had all assumed their way to power. Women don't have any assumptions at all about power — except that someone else has it and if they want any of it they will have to work damn hard to prove to themselves and to the rest of the world that they merit some portion of it.

So here is my dilemma. Power is the stuff of society and women are excluded from it. What should I tell my daughter? Should I say to her what I was told — that she can be anything she chooses to be? Or should I tell her the truth? That unless she pens the book, she will never see her soul written out, that unless she barges into rooms uninvited, she will never be part of how decisions are made; they will be made without her knowledge and without considering her at all.

The Worth of Women's Work

Nina Lee Colwill

I was born during World War II into a fatherless world. Daddy was in Belgium and the Netherlands, fighting the war that would bring worldwide peace forever. Mum and I lived with her parents and sisters and brothers in Gaspé, Québec, in the little farming village of Wakeham. Central to that life was Grandma — Grandma, who, then as now, personified strength and wisdom.

My earliest memory is of creeping downstairs in the morning and hugging Grandma's legs as she lit the fire in the kitchen stove. Her braids hung freely then, and I'd play with them while she rocked me in the old green wooden rocking chair, waiting for the kitchen to warm for the day. She would scold me: "You should be in bed where it's warm, Nina Lee, not down here in this cold kitchen." But I always knew I was right where she wanted me, curled up on her lap.

Grandma could do anything. She baked the most delicious of breads, drawing sifter after sifter of flour from the deep bin that Grandpa had built under the kitchen counter — soft white bread with thick, hard, brown crusts. She made the most comforting of bedtime snacks — dried bread and cream and brown sugar. She taught me to play solitaire when I was two. She taught me not to cheat at solitaire when I was four. She solved an architectural problem that had plagued my grandfather and the other carpenters in the village for years. And she could kill a chicken in a trice.

Grandma belonged to the Women's Institute. Every couple of weeks she'd change from her housedress into her church dress and set a hat on her head, and off she'd go to the mysterious WI.

I'll never forget the day I discovered the photograph. Actually, I'd seen that group of women every day of my life, standing in four neat rows in their flowered dresses, right there in a black wooden frame in the livingroom. But one day, playing alone with a puzzle on the chesterfield, I looked up and spied Grandma in that group. It was then that she showed me her name printed neatly on brown paper on the back of the photograph: Ruby Jane Patterson, Wakeham. As we sat at the kitchen table eating blueberries and cream, she told me how she'd taken a train to Montreal to represent her district at the WI Convention. It was, I believed, the most worldly and sophisticated work a person could possibly undertake.

When I was older and the war was no longer foremost in our thoughts, when my parents and I had moved to another life and our family had grown to four, then five, then six, I would often visit my grandparents in Gaspé. Sometimes I'd sit cross-legged on the painted wooden floor and study that photograph, ruminating about the women and imagining their lives. All those women, all over Québec, with their own families and their own work. And Grandma was part of this illustrious band.

No one ever told me about the value of women's work. No one ever said, "To love your work is to love life." Yet a sisterhood of women, a mysterious train trip to Montreal, a grandmother with grey braids wound around her head, humming as she kneaded bread — these pictures arranged themselves into a complex collage of women and work. Grandma never told me that all work is a privilege, or that our integrity depends on the value we place on our work. But she treated her work as a calling, and silently she taught me that my work is a calling, too — that I've been chosen.

Yet there's a sombre side of work. To study women and work is to face sadness, is to confront a belief shared by every culture in every country on this planet: the assumption that men, the things men do and all things masculine are more valuable than women, the things women do and all things feminine.

I remember the day it struck me, overwhelmed me: the work of women is less valued than the work of men. I suppose I'd always known it at an intellectual level, for I'd studied women and work for half my life. But on the day I truly understood, with a logic beyond logic, that women's work is valued less than men's, I wasn't collecting a paycheque or reading in a library or consulting for some organization. I was in the Rijksmuseum in Amsterdam with my husband, Dennis, and we were viewing the work of the Dutch Masters for the first time.

The Rijksmuseum has erected a veritable shrine to the Dutch Masters, where people the world over pay homage to the likes of Vermeer, de Hooch and Rembrandt. In every room is a guard, well-versed in the history of each painter and each painting, for many thousands of words have been written about these brilliant men and their work.

One passage leads from the chambers of the Dutch Masters into a quiet, darkened room; eventually we found ourselves there, in the needlework gallery. There we could browse without attending to the explanations of guides or the murmurs of worshippers. We saw crocheting, needlepoint, quilting, embroidery. Ancient works — works from the days of the Dutch Masters. Exquisite works — works of brilliant artists. And no names.

You can imagine Dennis' shock when he found me in the

corner sobbing over a tablecloth, weeping for the woman who designed and created it without recognition, for the woman who didn't sign her name.

Yet, I like to believe they created with joy, these women. I like to believe their work was their calling, that they knew they'd been chosen. I hope their offerings were treated as precious, that people were generous with their praise and their payment. But most of all I hope they created with joy.

Because, when all is said and done, we must love our own work. If the historical and universal belief that men's work is more important than women's work is not to be perpetuated to yet another generation, we must judge our own work to be worthy. And we must value it so highly that we value the men who choose to emulate us.

Because women and men, who have much to learn from each other, do not imitate each other in equal numbers. For women to do the things men do, to do men's work, is for women to better themselves — a fine accomplishment in an achieving society. So women become ministers, fix their own cars and compete for Olympic medals in hockey, and most of us today consider such women to have achieved. But praise is not as loud for the men who become nurses or take on the family's housework and child care. To emulate one's superiors in an achieving society is to increase one's status. To emulate one's inferiors smacks of perversion.

No one ever told me that women would always be valued in proportion to the value we place on women's work. No one ever said that female physicians would never acquire the status of male physicians until secretaries are valued as highly as tool-and-die makers. No one ever explained that the father who needlepoints a birthday gift for his son must be accorded the same respect as the woman who wires her family cottage. But the status of women's work, I now know, is a measure of the value we place on women.

There's been monumental change in the past fifty years, in

the past twenty years, even in the past year. It didn't occur because large groups of people decided simultaneously and unanimously that things must change. It occurred because you and I decided to change ourselves a little bit. We didn't change our spouses; we didn't change our children; we didn't change our co-workers. We addressed the only thing over which any of us has any direct control: we changed ourselves. We faltered, we backtracked and we hedged our bets, but we changed our beliefs about the worth of women and men. The rest followed.

We're placing higher value on women's traditional art forms, the fibre crafts: quilting, weaving, embroidery, smocking, tatting. Women's work. Honoured in ways it's never been honoured before in written history — in shops, in competitions, in art galleries, in homes. The entrepreneurial styles for which women have become famous are lauded today: start small, with as much of your own money as you can manage, and do what you love to do. As women feel free to be themselves, to lead as they are comfortable in leading, women's management styles are recognized and men are emulating those styles. More parents are steering their children away from violent, competitive sports and into lifetime, co-operative sports. And child care, the chronic issue of every employed mother, is slowly being reconceptualized as a family issue, a corporate issue, a community issue.

Of course there is more we can do. We can tell the world by word and by action that women and girls are valuable people and the things they do are valuable as well. We can refuse to participate in the derision of men and boys whose voices or gestures or interests are described as feminine. We can ensure that the family policies of our organizations and our governments are as supportive of fathers as they are of mothers. And if men who try to use these policies are ridiculed, we can be vocal in our protest of their treatment. For if we cannot imagine a world in which men choose to emulate women, we will never create a world in which women and men are equally valued.

When I finished my B.A. at the University of Western

Ontario and was accepted into graduate school, Grandma sent me a note of praise and admiration — encouraging words, consistent with the support she'd given me all my life. But she closed her letter with a comment that enraged me: "Remember your husband and children and home." Thirty years later, I think I understand what she was telling me, and I now count these words among her wisest: "Never undervalue the work that your foremothers carved out as their special domain, for in doing so, you undervalue yourself."

AFTERWORD

I was twenty-one years old, and standing in line to receive my Bachelor of Arts diploma from Hanover College. Major in English, minor in history. It was June, and the temperature was 97 degrees Fahrenheit. Under our black academic gowns my girlfriends and I wore, by previous agreement, nothing. Nothing at all. This was considered high daring in those days, 1957. The night before, seven or eight of us had gathered in the woods above the campus and conducted a ritual burning of our saddle shoes. We were utterly ignorant of what lay ahead of us, but imbued, for some reason, with a nose-thumbing rejection of the suffocating shell of convention that enclosed us.

And yet most of us were prepared to inhabit that safe place our parents had defined for us. We married the same summer we graduated, joined our lives with men no older than we were, and within a year we were buying houses, having babies and planting petunias. Hardly any of us thought of a career other than wife and mother. No one had suggested such a notion to us.

The 1957 graduation address was given by a very popular

math professor at the college. He began his talk by telling us that we would remember nothing of what he would say that hot June morning. This was true; I sat dreaming of my wedding, which was just six weeks away, and of the apartment where I would live with my new husband. The charm of domesticity, its sweetness and self-containment, pulled at all my passions. But suddenly he broke though my daydreams. "I ask you to remember only two things," he said. "Remember the date, 1957, and remember the words *tempus fugit.*"

I had studied Latin, but even if I hadn't I would have known what that phrase meant: *time flies.* Our convocation speaker was reminding us that our lives would speed by before we had grasped them. It was our responsibility to seize each moment and fill it with accomplishment. Otherwise our life would be wasted, worn away with the turning years, and we would grow old and disappointed in what we had made of it.

The phrase haunted me in the ensuing years. I was occupied with babies and with the hard physical work that babies involve. We moved several times and so there were always new domestic arrangements to carve out. Cleaning, cooking, coping, running errands — my days were filled with such minutiae. It was in the calmer, cooler evenings that the phrase *tempus fugit* would return to me, beating at the back of my brain and reminding me that time was rushing by. I was spooked, frightened by what this meant.

And then, quite suddenly, I realized it meant nothing. Tempus did not fugit. In a long and healthy life, which is what most of us have, there is plenty of time. There is time to sit on a houseboat for a month reading novels. There is time to learn another language. There is travel time and there is stay-at-home time. Shallow time and fallow time. There is time in which we are politically involved and other times when we are wilfully unengaged. We will have good years and bad years, and there will be time for both. Every moment will not be filled with accomplishment; we would explode if we tied ourselves to such a regimen. Time was not our enemy if we kept it on a loose string, allowing for rest, emptiness, reassessment, art and love. This was not a mountain we were climbing; it was closer to being a novel with a series of chapters.

My mother-of-small-children chapter seemed to go on forever, but, in fact, it didn't. It was a mere twelve years, over in a flash. Suddenly I was at a place where I had a little more time to reflect. I could think, for instance, about writing a real novel, and I did. And then another novel, and then another. I had a desk in this new chapter of my life, a typewriter and a pile of paper that belonged just to me. For the first time I needed a file cabinet and a wrist watch, something I'd done without for a decade. I remember I spent the whole of an October afternoon working on a single sentence; I was not by nature a patient person, but for this kind of work and at this time in my life, I was able to be endlessly, foolishly, patient.

In 1985 I looked up from my desk and realized that the children had gone, all five of them. The house was quieter now. The days were mine to arrange any way I wished. I wrote a novel in which, for the first time, there were no children. It was a different kind of novel than I'd written before, with a more inventive structure. The publisher was worried about this innovation, but I was insistent. The insistence was something new, and it coloured the chapter I was living in, my early-middle-age chapter. The woman I saw in the mirror looked like someone else, but I knew it was really me, relocated in time and breathing another grade of oxygen. I was given an office and a key to that office. I loaded it down with plants and pictures, a soft lamp, a carpet. It felt like a tiny apartment, offering solitude and giving a new permission, another space in which to live my ever-altering life.

Friendship took time, but luckily I had time as I entered yet another phase. My women friends provided support, amusement, ideas, pleasure, wisdom. The two-hour lunch was a luxury I could afford during this period; moreover, it was a kind of necessary music. The more words we tossed into the air the closer we felt to the tune of our own lives. We talked about what we knew and what we didn't know. Our conversations were punctuated with the joyous discovery of commonalities, the recognition that the narratives of our lives bumped along differently, but with the same changing rhythms.

But one day, over a long lunch with my friend Marjorie Anderson, we spoke for the first time of all that went unspoken, even in an age of intense and open communication. There were the things our mothers hadn't voiced, the subjects our teachers had neglected, the false prophetic warnings (*tempus fugit*, for example) we had been given and the fatal silence surrounding particular areas of anxiety or happiness. Why weren't we told? Why weren't we warned? What contributed to the reticence between generations, between one woman and another?

We decided to ask some of our women friends to talk about the skipped discourses in their lives and how they had managed, at last, to cope with the surprise of self-discovery, stumbling on that which had been missing: an insight, a truth, an admission, a dark hole. The proposals poured in. This was an exciting time; Marjorie and I were exhilarated by the ideas that were suggested, and astonished that so few overlapped. The areas where woman had been surprised by lack of knowledge ranged from childbirth to working with men, to illness, loss, friendship and secrecy, to the power of sexual feelings, the frustrations of inherited responsibility and the recurrent patterns that haunt us.

The finished essays, which arrived like dispatches from the frontier, described these varied experiences and reported on how they were confronted or accepted. Each voice was separate, and yet each connected subtly with others, as though informed by an underground stream. The essays expressed perplexity at life's offerings: injury and outrage that could not be voiced (*Woman, hold thy tongue*), expectations that could not be met, fulfillment arriving in unexpected places, the need for toughness, the beginning of understanding, the beginning of being able to say what had once been unsayable. Or, in my case, the apprehension of a structure that gave fluidity and ease to a long life, the gradually (or suddenly) shifting scenes, each furnished with its own noise and movement, its particular rewards and postures.

We move through our chapters mostly with gratitude. Who isn't renewed by startling scenery or refreshed by undreamed-of freedoms? Surprise keeps us alive, liberates our senses. I thought for a while that a serious illness had interrupted my chaptered life, but no, it is a chapter on its own. Living with illness requires new balancing skills. It changes everything, and I need to listen to it, attend to it and bring to it a stern new sense of housekeeping.

But I have time for this last exercise. All the time in the world.

Carol Shields
March 2000

CONTRIBUTORS

MARGARET ATWOOD
I am the author of more than twenty-five books of poetry, fiction and non-fiction, and my work has been translated into more than 30 languages. My newest novel is *The Blind Assassin.* I live in Toronto.

JOAN BARFOOT
Juggling fiction-writing and journalism, as I've mainly done, can be problematic, but ideally they have in common curiosity and attentiveness — not to mention up-close exposure to some extreme choices people do, truly, make. So far I've written eight novels, seen one translated into film, won a couple of national awards. Only one novel has friendship as a major theme. People with friends are moderated by them, less likely to slice themselves on the real sharp edges that create extreme journalism or extreme fiction. In work, edges fascinate me; in life I like to know friends are holding the rope.

JANET E. BRADLEY

I am an Ottawa lawyer and not a writer, except as professionally required. I have had, by my own account, a privileged life with few past or present hardships or grievances upon which to draw. When asked to contribute, I responded with a topic that is currently occupying my over-burdened and middle-aged mind.

MARTHA BROOKS

Twenty-eight years ago, our daughter was born, and after that came the birthing of award-winning plays, novels and collections of short fiction. My most recent novel is *Being With Henry*. It is a fact, however, that singing was the channel through which I first discovered my voice as an artist. Six years ago I reconnected with that earlier passion and am now, as well, a performing jazz vocalist.

BONNIE BURNARD

I have written two collections of short fiction and one novel, *A Good House*, HarperCollins Canada/Phyllis Bruce Books, which had the good fortune of winning the 1999 Giller Prize. Writing gives me such a heap of pleasure and, aside from the haphazard, clumsy but love-drenched raising of three very fine children, it is the only contribution I've made. I do mean it to be a contribution, an offering of some kind.

SHARON BUTALA

I've been writing for more than twenty years and have just completed my eleventh book, a non-fiction work called *Wild Stone Heart*, recently published by HarperCollins Canada. My previous book to that was a novel, *The Garden of Eden*, (HarperCollins Canada, 1998). For the last twenty-four years, I've lived on a cattle ranch in southwest Saskatchewan.

JUNE CALLWOOD

I have been a journalist since I was sixteen and cub reporter on the *Brantford Expositor.* This bypassed not only journalism schools but a decent formal education. Since then I have written columns for *The Globe and Mail,* about thirty books and lotsa magazine articles.

HONOURABLE SHARON CARSTAIRS

I worked as a teacher until I was elected leader of the Manitoba Liberal Party in 1984 and was an elected member of the Manitoba Legislature from 1986 to 1994. I was the Leader of the Official Opposition in Manitoba from 1988 to 1990, the first woman in Canada to be elected to this position. I was summoned to the Senate in September of 1994 and from 1997 to 1999 served as the first female Deputy Leader of the Government in the Senate.

CLAUDIA CASPER

I'm forty-three, married with two sons, four and eight. They go to school, I drink coffee and write until I pick them up, by which time I'm hungry, speedy but spinning my wheels, and some combination of excited/depressed. To move I play squash or ride a bicycle. My first novel, *The Reconstruction,* published by Penguin, also sold rights in Britain, the U.S. and Germany and has been optioned for a feature film. My shorter work has most recently appeared in *Geist* magazine and *Best Canadian Stories* by Oberon.

JOAN CLARK

Born and raised in the Maritimes, I lived in Alberta for over twenty years before moving to Newfoundland, where I've now lived for fourteen years. I am the author of seven children's books, two short-story collections and two novels. A third novel, *Latitudes of Melt,* was just published by Knopf, and I am, of course, working on another.

NINA LEE COLWILL
I'm a born-in-Gaspé Manitoban, an ex-receptionist, a former professor, a management consultant and a grandmother. My favourite jobs are writing and laundry. I write a quarterly column in *Women in Management* called "As I See It" and am putting the finishing touches on my first novel. I've authored and co-authored three books of non-fiction and some 100 articles, and I've done 9387 loads of laundry.

LORNA CROZIER
I was born in Saskatchewan and now live on Vancouver Island, where I teach at the University of Victoria. My books have won numerous awards, including the Governor-General's Award for Poetry and two Pat Lowther Awards for the best book of poetry by a Canadian woman. I have sworn to remain a poet and never write fiction, but have discovered a growing attraction to the personal essay, which I think is an extended lyric poem with a few more rooms to wander in, a few more windows to let in the light.

SANDY FRANCES DUNCAN
Since moving to Gabriola Island, I have learned a great deal about my gardening ignorance. Now I'm learning what I don't know — and don't know how to ask — about computers. Who knows what I won't know next! Then there's writing — a fast track for learning what you never knew you do know. I am presently writing a grade six textbook and am revising a novel set in the Klondike Gold Rush.

HELEN FOGWILL PORTER
I was born and grew up in St. John's, where I still live. For about thirty-five years I've been writing professionally: fiction, non-fiction, poetry, drama and reviews. My book publications include *Below the Bridge* (memoir-history, 1980), *January, February, June or July* (novel, 1988) and *A Long and Lonely*

Ride (short-story collection, 1991). All were published by Breakwater Books. My stories, poetry and articles have been published across Canada and overseas. I'm now completing a novel titled *Finishing School.*

KATHERINE C. H. GARDINER
I am a marketing professional who spends my work hours planning corporate events. This career fuses my creative processes with my desire for measurable, attainable goals. Reading has been a passion for as long as I can remember; writing, however, had been a private endeavor until now. This is my first piece of published fiction.

ANNE GIARDINI
As a columnist for the *National Post,* I write about the vexing subjects of family, love, work, gender dynamics, the ingredients of happiness and sorrow, our purpose and role in the world. Among my many areas of interest is women and power. In a recent column on "alpha" woman, I wrote: "Alpha women may not be who you think they are. They are astonishingly energetic, and have a gift for taking charge and getting things done. But they are not driven by a desire for power or a need to dominate others, but by clarity of vision, resoluteness of purpose and a delight in accomplishment. Their need to govern does not apply to people but to circumstances." This is the kind of power I envision more and more women claiming for themselves. I am a lawyer, writer and mother of three school-age children.

KATHERINE GOVIER
I have published three collections of short stories and six novels, the most recent of which is *The Truth Teller* (Random House Canada). My collection of women's travel stories, *Without a Guide,* is in print in five countries. I was born in Alberta and live in Toronto with my two teenagers and a dog

called Rosie (no relation to the roses in this story). For my sins, I have been Chair of the Writers Trust, and President of PEN Canada. In 1997 I won the Marian Engel award for a Canadian women writer in mid-career.

CHARLOTTE GRAY
I am the author of *Sisters in the Wilderness: The Lives of Susanna Moodie and Catharine Parr Traill* (1999) and of *Mrs. King: The Life and Times of Isabel Mackenzie King* (1997), which was nominated for a Governor-General's Award. I came to Canada from England in 1979 and am married with three sons (who test my capacity as peacemaker!).

ANNE HART
I was born in Winnipeg and grew up in rural Nova Scotia. For the past 28 years I've had the good fortune to live in St. John's, Newfoundland, a place where the discourse is lively and many revelations occur. I'm the author of two books, *The Life and Times of Miss Jane Marple* and *The Life and Times of Hercule Poirot*, both of which have been translated into five languages.

CAROL HUSSA HARVEY
Writing this short story was a new adventure for me and I enjoyed working with my daughter, Katherine Gardiner, on it. I am a Professor of Family Studies, Faculty of Human Ecology, University of Manitoba, Winnipeg. My previous publications relate to academic topics such as family and work stress, intergenerational relationships and widowhood.

BLANCHE HOWARD
My first novel in 1972 elicited a savage diatribe from a male reviewer who took exception to a woman writing from a man's point of view. How times have changed! *A Celibate Season*, 1991, co-written with Carol Shields, is partly a male voice, but did not, as far as I know, outrage anyone. The protaganist of my

latest novel, *Penelope's Way*, is an aging woman. She is unlikely to be a lightning rod for the wrath of either sex.

ISABEL HUGGAN
Life has been one surprise after another since an uneventful childhood growing up in Elmira, Ontario: the only certainty has been my ongoing love of the English language, rather ironic now that I live permanently in France. Still, I manage by working as a mentor for the Humber School for Writers, and have every intention of adding another collection to *The Elizabeth Stories* and *You Never Know*.

MARNI JACKSON
I am the author of *The Mother Zone* and live in Toronto with my husband, *Maclean's* film critic Brian Johnson. My sixteen-year-old son, Casey, writes for the school paper, the *Jarvis Jargon*. This makes for cutthroat Scrabble games. Random House Canada will publish my next book, which looks at the science and culture of pain.

ISLA JAMES is the name I've given to the voice that has been composing stories inside my head for years. This particular story was over twenty years in the making, and the living. Now that it has been launched, others may follow — lighter ones, I trust. Winnipeg is my home where I teach, mother, love, dance, dream, and listen to Isla.

KATRINA KOVEN
My parents bought me a piano when I was five and a paint set soon after — creative outlets for my electric, passionate spirit, and tools that significantly influenced the shaping of my grown-up self. I am a pianist and co-owner of an alternative music school; a painter, an illustrator, a writer, the wife of a jazz musician and mother to an imaginative nine-year-old daughter who has her own piano and paint set.

SUSAN LIGHTSTONE
I'm a lawyer by training, a writer by calling, a sister by chance and a mother by choice. My writing ranges from features in national magazines, to essays in *The Globe and Mail*, to the bestselling *The Pig and the Python: How to Prosper from the Aging Baby Boom* and *When the Pig Goes to Market: How to Achieve Long-term Investing Success* (both co-written with David Cork). Currently, I'm working with Dr. R.V. Hodder on a medical book, *Every Breath I Take: Living with Chronic Obstructive Pulmonary Disease.*

KATHERINE MARTENS
I live in Winnipeg. My first book *All in a Row: The Klassens of Homewood* is a family memoir. I have published a number of articles in other anthologies — "Giving Birth"; "Sexuality and Childbirth: One Woman's Search for Emancipation." *Prairie Fire* published "An Encounter with Maria Reimer" co-authored with Heidi Harms. As well, Heidi Harms and I co-authored *In Her Own Voice: Mennonite Childbirth Stories.* My latest essay, "Threading My Way," is included in *Spider Women: A Tapestry of Creativity and Healing,* edited by Joan Turner and Carol Rose in 1999.

JAQUELINE McLEOD ROGERS
I live in Winnipeg with my husband, Warren, and our daughters Hartley Anne and Morgan Leigh. I'm an Associate Professor at The University of Winnipeg where I teach writing, with a special interest in the different (and growing) forms of narrative inquiry. I'm currently studying how students are more engaged by telling stories than making arguments about academic ideas.

LILY REDMOND
Lily Redmond isn't my real name. I wanted the one I chose, however, to have some sort of connection to me, and this name honours the women who were the mothers of my parents. Even